Ladies' Home Journal

BOOK OF INTERIOR DECORATION

Ladies' Home Journal BOOK OF INTERIOR DECORATION

By ELIZABETH T. HALSEY

With the
co-operation of Ladies' Home Journal

Former Interior Decoration Editor	Henrietta Murdock
Interior Decoration Editor	Cynthia McAdoo Wheatland
Architectural and Garden Editor	Richard Pratt
Homemaking Editor	Margaret Davidson
Contributing Editor	Gladys Taber
Designer Contributor	H. T. Williams

Published by The Curtis Publishing Company, Philadelphia
and Doubleday & Company, Inc., Garden City

This charming parlor is from the famous Rock Hall house on Long Island, a fine remaining example of a Colonial Georgian great-house.

Designed by Clifford S. Smith
Library of Congress Catalog Card Number 57-9700
Printed in the United States of America

Acknowledgments

First, the writer remembers with gratitude the teachings of Richard Townley Haines Halsey, pioneer in the field of research in the history of American social background, who devoted much of his life to give us an understanding and appreciation of our heritage.

Sincere thanks also go to Colonial Williamsburg for permission to use one of their eighteenth-century wall-paper patterns as an inspiration for the end papers of this book. This generosity typifies the American way of life, which encourages our museums, manufacturers, institutions of learning, publishers, and individuals to give unsparingly of their time and money to further education and to place a book of this kind within the reach of all of us. Gratitude goes to The Metropolitan Museum of Art, The Brooklyn Museum, Yale University, and Wesleyan University for photographs and valuable information, and to Leroy Nelson and Alfred Lowden for the sharing of their wide knowledge and experience.

I'm indebted also to Richard Pratt for the use of many fine photographs, including the one on page 2—the flying divided staircase from the 1816 Thomas Ruggles house in Maine, which so gracefully leads us step by step into the subject at hand.

A last word of warmest appreciation goes to the decorators who designed the various rooms illustrated in color and in black and white; to those who supplied hundreds of pictures of room settings and special items; to clients, friends, and family who contributed ideas and encouragement; and to all the readers of this book for their interest in Home Decoration.

E.T.H.

Pleasant and comfortable living can be achieved in any period. The bedroom is from the Colonial Georgian Rock Hall house on Long Island. Notice the authentic resist fabric and how agreeably the colors in the room blend together. The attractive, modern breezeway dining room, below, combines maximum comfort and features weather resistant furniture which can be taken outdoors.

Table of Contents

A cheerful, colorful room, designed for contemporary living.

Illustrations in Color

Many people love antique furniture in a fine old house. The use here of furniture of various periods suggests a long family tradition, but the same charming effect is often achieved by collecting old pieces one at a time. They may be the pine and maple reminiscent of Pilgrim homes, or the elegant mahogany and satinwood of a later period. Suitability and beauty are the important factors in making a choice.

WAYNE ANDREWS

An Introduction

Today, especially in our American way of life, home decoration is for everybody. Since the cavemen drew pictures on the sides of their caves some ten thousand years ago, the decoration of the home has been important to man. He has gradually developed it as an art, a mark of his civilization and culture. It was part of the civilization of the ancient Greeks, and is found in the houses at Pompeii and Herculaneum, in the palaces of the Renaissance, and at Versailles, the Tuileries, and Malmaison. Of particular importance to us are the great English houses of Sir Christopher Wren and other English architects from which many of our own decorating traditions have come.

A quick review of the great periods of decoration pictures decorating on a grand scale for kings and noblemen, wealthy patrons of the arts, and the sophisticated and cultured personages of their times. Ordinary people had roofs over their heads, too, but the development of the interiors of their homes was largely a matter of protection from the weather, available materials, and a limited tradition due to a lack of travel and communication.

Today, we are all kings and noblemen, patrons of the arts, educated and cultured personages. Anything that happens anywhere in the world is known to us in a matter of minutes. We learn the history and traditions of other peoples, ancient and modern, as well as our own, in our childhood. Magazines, books, manufacturers, advertisers, the radio, television, and movies bring new ideas, inventions, materials, and conveniences to our attention every day. The problem becomes one of making a choice among this wealth of possibilities.

Suddenly we realize that we have no more excuse for drab, uninteresting houses that just grew. We want to make our homes attractive, inviting, and pleasant. What to do? Our common sense, which is the most important ingredient of interior decorating, tells us to find out everything we can about how to improve our homes and then get to work.

This book is designed to help you do just that. It is a practical homemaker's book, not a decorator's unbridled flight of fancy. It will not teach you everything there is to know, but it can make a good interior decorator out of you. You will find information and ideas for your dreams, helpful hints to make doing things easier, and also several hundred pictures to give you good reasons for doing things the way you want to do them.

Part I is background reading, amply illustrated, to help fill out your knowledge of styles in architecture and furniture with information on color, fabrics, floor coverings, lighting, and accessories. You will know just what you are doing if you decide to put a Modern sofa in a Colonial room. It will help you decide whether to paint the woodwork in a room the same color as the walls, or in contrast. There is advice on when to use nylon, orlon, Fiberglas, silk, or cotton for your curtains and upholstery. Part I is for background and information. It might be called the answer to what to do in your decorating.

Part II is devoted to practical planning, the how to do it. With a clear idea of what you want to do, you can work out a feasible plan and determine how much your budget and time will allow, how much improvement you can make by a bit of rearranging of what you have, what is fundamental to make your home satisfying to you. You can arrange a room on paper without anyone's knowing how often you have changed your mind. An idea of fabric costs and a few tables of yardages required for slip covers, upholstery, draperies, and curtains make it possible for you to determine in advance whether you can re-cover all your furniture and have new curtains, or if you must compromise in favor of some new pieces. Some things you will want to have done for you, others you would like to do yourself. If sewing is not your forte, you may become an expert at painting or refinishing furniture. You may find other skills which will give you the fun of actually creating something for your house with your own hands. Do you know how to put fixtures for curtains, cornices, pictures, and mirrors into various types of walls so that they will not sag or fall? This kind of help is also included.

Part III provides pictures of rooms for everybody. Man or woman, married or single, old or young, each of us faces a decorating problem at some time in our lives. Consciously or unconsciously, we all have preferences, definite likes and dislikes. Here we can find the type of room which appeals to us. Maybe some of our ideas seem like whims. Do not be scornful of a whim. It is a lovely thing, especially in decorating, and may give the fillip to your room which makes it yours.

ROOM ARRANGEMENT BY DOROTHY PRATT; PHOTOGRAPH BY EZRA STOLLER

This is the downstairs drawing room in the early nineteenth-century Nathaniel Russell house in Charleston. The beautiful pair of eighteenth-century Chippendale mirrors, repeated on either side of the doorway, lead into a magnificent hallway. Staircase is a splendid example of the joiner's art.

Ladies' Home Journal BOOK OF INTERIOR DECORATION

PART ONE : BACKGROUND

In traveling through New England we see many houses of this type, one or two stories, always well groomed, neat and characteristic. You will recognize the Cape Cod house whether it has one story or two, or looks like a salt-box.

The tradition of the oversized fireplace with a tea kettle hanging from a crane is well illustrated here. Probably the plaster in this room was originally made with crushed oyster shells as a basis.

Architecture

Exterior and Interior Styles

As your own decorator, you need not be an authority on architecture, but a little knowledge of the names and characteristics of the basic styles which have been developed in this country over the last three hundred years will help you and give you something solid on which to build. As you examine the individual houses to be found around us everywhere, you will note that though they may take many forms, they are mostly variations and adaptations of a very few basic well-known styles. The story of the growth and changes in these styles is chronological and simple.

To the earliest settlers, the necessity for shelter was paramount. Gradually with more time, experience, and wealth, houses became more comfortable and more thought was put into making them beautiful. Changes were slow, and always the climate, available materials, traditions and craftsmanship of the builders had to be considered. For many generations our forefathers in many localities looked to England for inspiration and followed English styles, adapting them to their own needs and materials. In some places, where the people came from other countries, there were evidences of other influences. News of new styles and tastes traveled slowly and developed in this country under the special circumstances of each period.

XVII CENTURY

To begin at the beginning we should look at the houses built in the seventeenth century. The task of putting up any kind of dwelling when a man had to start by clearing the land, cutting trees and sawing them into beams and timbers, making mortar and plaster, pegs and nails, seems almost insurmountable to us with our steam shovels, sawmills, and machinery. The early settlers did all this by hand and did it well. By 1642, just twenty-two years after the Pilgrims landed on Plymouth Rock, we find Edward Johnson writing in his *Wonder Working Providence of Sion's Savior in New England:* "Further the Lord hath been pleased to turn all the wigwams, huts and hovels the English dwelt in at their first coming, into orderly, fair and well built houses, well furnished many of them."

The wooden houses of this time were rectangular with a chimney at one end and had but one room. Later, houses were built with a chimney at each end and the room was divided in half. By the end of the seventeenth century, a single chimney was placed in the center of the house, sometimes a second story was added and some attention was given to decorative detail.

We have existing examples of this type of house in America today. One of the earliest is the Parson Capen House at Topsfield, Massachusetts, built in 1683. The outside walls have horizontal sheathing and the second floor protrudes over the first floor in an "overhang." This overhang is decorated on the corners, on either side of the front door and at the eaves of the roof with large wooden drops characteristic of the period. Simple as it is, this was a fine house at the time of building and gives us an indication of early architectural pretense. Most of these early houses had casement windows with diamond-shaped panes such as the settlers had known at home in England. On these houses we find also the heavy nail-studded doors with iron hinges and latches. The interiors are exactly as you would expect to find them.

The rooms were small with low ceilings, and the enormous fireplace, taking nearly one entire wall, dominated each room. Often a brick oven was built into one side of the fireplace and always there was room for three separate fires. The walls were sheathed in pine boards or plastered with rough white plaster, and the corner beams and ceiling beams were usually left rough and showing. Wide boards covered the floors. Such houses have been restored for present-day living and occasionally copied, especially the exteriors, but they have not been as adaptable or popular as those of the later periods.

The Cape Cod house, which was the next development chronologically, is another story. It has been popular from the end of the seventeenth century to the present day. You will see examples from Maine to California—old ones, new ones, and adaptations similar to that on page fourteen. Some are simple rectangles, like the originals, others have ells, wings, woodsheds and today even a breezeway or a garage added. The Cape Cod house is still the prototype. Windows are small and divided into small panes with narrow mullions in a double sash. Mostly these houses are one story high, but often they were built with one and a half or two stories like the beautiful one opposite.

Although we are inclined to copy the one-floor Cape Cod house today, our ancestors expanded this simple house as they grew more affluent and included a second

Room from Hart House, built about 1640 in Ipswich, Mass.

Here is the parlor from the Hart House.

floor complete with paneling and fireplaces. In New England many of these houses were elaborate enough to have a ballroom, usually on the second floor. When the house had two stories on the front and one on the back with a slanted roof, it was called—the salt-box house. Shingles or clapboards were used to face the outside and were painted red, white, yellow or grey with contrasting trim. In some parts of the country the shingled ones were left without paint and these weathered to a beautiful soft silver grey. Today we paint houses of this type any color we like. White with a bright red front door is popular, but you will also see green or pink, blue or turquoise doors.

The interiors of the old houses of this period followed the earlier ones with sheathing and plaster, but gradually became finished and decorated. The edges of each board were bevelled and often a molding was put around the fireplace opening and the door frames. Paneling was used in various ways—sometimes on the fireplace wall only, often there, and halfway up the wall on the three other sides of the room. There are also fine examples of rooms that were entirely paneled, including the ceiling. Today, if we have such paneling most people like to leave it in the natural wood with just a touch of stain rubbed down with oil or wax. Our ancestors liked to paint their paneling whenever possible.

Another type of informal house for present-day living finds its prototype in the Pennsylvania Dutch farmhouses. The originals of these were built about half a century later than the Cape Cod houses and continued in the same tradition for nearly a century, that is, well into the nineteenth century. Many people in recent years have found great joy in acquiring one of these old farmhouses and restoring it for present-day living. We associate the name of Bucks County, Pennsylvania, with this type of architecture because so many fine examples have been found there. Pennsylvania Dutch houses come in many shapes and sizes, but all are sturdy, built wholly or partly of tailored stone with wooden cornices, and all primitive in decoration. They have a special charm which their owners love. The shape and style is not unlike the Cape Cod house, but somehow the houses are more robust inside and out. The paneling is heavier, the floors often tiled, the chimneys are broad. Quite often we find typical Pennsylvania Dutch designs of tulips, conventionalized leaves, and other plants painted on the paneling. Everything speaks of a different tradition from that of New England.

Each of these early houses has much to recommend it to our attention, and you will find many traces of their influence on the houses we build today.

So far we have been thinking about old houses, but only to discover the source of styles that are used today. These two new houses have preserved the shape and much of the flavor of the old Cape Cod houses. The central chimney has been moved over a little to provide a fireplace for the living room only. We still love a fireplace, but modern heating does not make it necessary to have one in every room. Bedrooms, bathroom, kitchen,

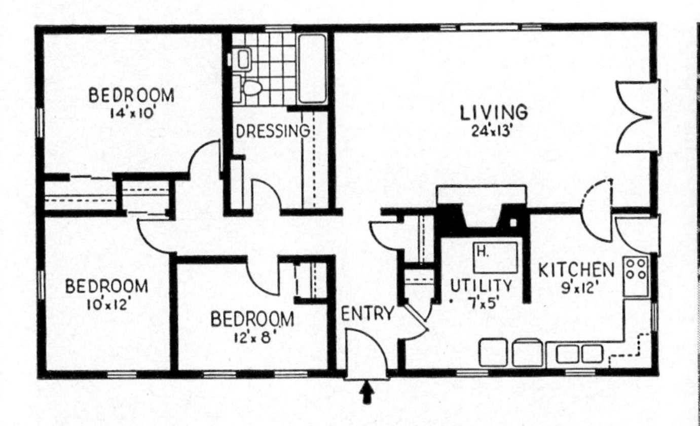

These new houses have preserved the shape and much of the flavor of the Cape Cod house. The central chimney has been moved over a little to provide a fireplace for the living room only—modern heating does not make it necessary to have one in every room. Bedrooms, bathroom, kitchen, closets are requirements today that the early settlers never heard of. The floor plan shows how well everything has been fitted into a space that accommodated only two rooms in the original houses. Both houses are very attractive and practical.

A formal Philadelphia parlor showing typical mantel and overmantel with broken pediment is characteristic of the Chippendale period.

PHILADELPHIA ROOM IN AMERICAN WING OF METROPOLITAN MUSEUM OF ART

closets are requirements today that the early settlers never heard of. Notice on the floor plan how these things have been fitted into a space that only accommodated two rooms in the original houses. Both houses are very attractive and practical.

GEORGIAN

To go on with our story, as the new country grew and prospered, people had more leisure and more money. They began to live in cities as well as in the country and in addition to farmers and clergymen, there were ship-owners, bankers, lawyers, merchants, and a class known as the "landed gentry." These people had more pretentious ideas of the kind of houses they wanted. Such ideas came from several sources. Many of the fine English architectural books in small and also elephant folios with handsome engravings of architectural drawings found their way into gentlemen's libraries. Young men were sent abroad to finish their education and described what they had seen in England and on the Continent. More and more finished craftsmen sought refuge in the New World. We get some idea of all this progress from an advertisement in the Maryland Gazette of May 22, 1751:

"John Griss—By the Subscriber (lately from Great Britain). Buildings of all Sorts and Dimensions are undertaken and performed in the neatest Manner, (and at the cheapest Rates) either of the Ancient or Modern Order of Gibb's Architect and if any Gentlemen should want plans, Bills of Scantling, or Bills of charges, for any Fabric, or Public Edifice, may have them by applying to the Subscriber at Major John Bushrod's at Westmoreland County, Va., where may be seen a great Variety and sundry Draughts of Buildings in Miniature, and some buildings near finished, after the Modern Taste."

Beautiful Troth's Fortune, with its distinctive brick, gambrel roof and shed dormers, was built in Maryland in 1676.

RICHARD PRATT

This gives us a picture of an entirely new and more sophisticated type of house which is known as "Georgian," because it grew up and flourished during the reigns of the first three King Georges of England in the eighteenth century. Many beautiful examples of this style are still standing and some are very well known, like those in the restoration at Williamsburg, Virginia, Mount Vernon, the houses in the park in Philadelphia (especially Mt. Pleasant) and the Hammond Harwood house in Annapolis, illustrated on page 23. Every old city along the eastern seaboard has fine examples, but for our purposes it is important to know how to recognize the style and what details of it are still used to enhance everyday houses.

Georgian houses are usually of stone or brick, though sometimes of wood, and much attention is paid to the exterior and interior decoration. The ceilings are high and the windows large with carved trim. A Palladian window is often used, that is, a large central window with rounded top and two smaller windows on the sides. Much attention is paid to outside doors, especially the front door which can have a simple pediment, or broken pediment with carved ornament. This is illustrated in many houses over the country. Aside from those mentioned, a fine example was the balcony door on the Thomas Hancock House in Boston, copied by the New York State Historical Society for their headquarters at Ticonderoga, New York. The name of Sir Christopher Wren is associated with this period, as he was largely responsible for the type of architecture used in the rebuilding of London after the great fire of 1666, though it seems to have taken a long time for his designs to show their influence in America. It is interesting to note that the Rebuilding Act of 1667 in England, insisted that brick and stone only should be used for the rebuilding of houses. This became so much the vogue that when a house here was built of wood it was painted and sanded to resemble stone blocks. Mt. Vernon is an example of this treatment.

The interiors of these houses were spacious with large rooms and handsome fireplaces decorated with carved overmantels like the one pictured on page 18. Paneling, rococo carving, rosettes, broken pediments on fireplace and doors, elaborate stairways with carved stair ends, inside shutters plain and carved, rococo plaster work on the ceiling, open shell cupboards, are a few of the things that characterize the interiors of this period. Everywhere you will see the influence of Thomas Chippendale, a famous cabinetmaker in England in the middle of the eighteenth

DAVISON ART CENTER, WESLEYAN UNIVERSITY

Here is a Classic Revival parlor with the familiar mythological figures and classic decoration painted on the plaster. The interior of the house also introduced the Greek fretwork, columns, and reeding on doors and fireplaces; dentils, bead and reel, gouging and pearls, and egg and dart moldings (see opposite page) wherever possible.

century. We usually associate this name with furniture, but he did have a definite influence on the architectural detail of the time and much of the ornamentation of interiors looks very much as if it had been done by cabinetmakers.

It was an age of elegance and beauty and deserves more than a few paragraphs. If you wish to pursue the architectural aspect of interior decorating further, and it is a very rewarding study, there are many fine books on the subject with very handsome illustrations of all the houses mentioned here and many others. Here we must confine ourselves merely to getting enough idea of each style to be able to recognize each when we see it and to know to what we owe that beautiful Palladian window on the stair landing of the house next door, or why we find so much Chinese influence in architecture, furniture and ceramics of this period. It was the heyday of trade with the East, both for England and America. As far as Chippendale himself was concerned, at one period he was so much influenced by Chinese taste that "Chinese Chippendale" almost became a separate style. In this country we were importing Chinese pottery, wallpaper, silks, as well as styles in architecture. This was true in the early days of this country and is true today.

THE EARLY REPUBLIC

With the impetus that an appreciation and knowledge of our own traditions has had in recent years, no one makes the mistake any more of thinking that a colonial house is one with a row of white columns across the front. To be very exact there were a few such houses built in this country while we were still colonies of England, but this classic type of architecture did not come into its own until after the American Revolution. The same men who made the young Republic took an interest in this new style, and to one of them in particular we owe much of the growth and popularity of the classic style in America. It was Thomas Jefferson, interested in architecture from his college days at William and Mary, who fostered it and developed it. We know that the Maison de Salm which he had seen in Paris made a great impression on him, for many of its features were used at Monticello, Jefferson's home in Virginia, illustrated on page 22. His designs for the capitol at Richmond, for the University of Virginia and other houses started the ball rolling. Houses in the new style were built in many different parts of the country and, though some turned to Jefferson for inspiration, builders were also guided by what was going on in England. A great number of new books of designs were imported. Robert Adam, whose name is always associated with the classic revival, had published a new book with designs and measured drawings of the Roman palace of Diocletian; Charles Morris, famous English architect, brought out a book of *Select Architecture*, and a group of Englishmen, known as the Society of Dilettanti, spent a fortune in producing a book of engravings of *The Ionian Antiquities*. These and many others suggested designs which the American architects and builders adapted and made peculiarly American. The architecture of many buildings from the end of the Revolution to the present day can be traced directly to this period.

A city post office, courthouse or bank may have an imposing colonnade with columns capped with one of the three famous Greek orders, Ionic, Doric or Corinthian. A private house may be content with simple pillars supporting the roof over the front door. Homewood, built in Baltimore by Charles Carroll, is an example of an old house of the classic revival. This brick house stands on the grounds of Johns Hopkins University and in spite of its bow to the new style of the early Republic, it retains the older Maryland tradition of grand houses with its two wings connected to the main house with "hyphens." These wings usually housed the owner's library in one and the kitchen and servants' quarters in the other.

The interiors (one of which is illustrated on page 20, now the museum and part of the art school of Wesleyan University in Middletown, Connecticut) carried out the exterior tradition in introducing Greek fretwork, columns, and reeding on doors and fireplaces; dentils, bead and reel, gouging and pearls, and egg and dart in moldings wherever possible. Robert Adam's delicate designs were modified and simplified for the decoration of fireplaces and ceilings. A truly American decoration, introduced at this same period and mixed with the classic, was the eagle, recently adopted as the symbol of the new Republic. Jefferson was the leader in Virginia. In New England the names of two men have come down to us: Charles Bulfinch of Boston, architect, and Samuel McIntire of Salem. Both men built many houses in the classic style, but McIntire in addition to being an architect was a furniture maker and carver.

It is important to emphasize that houses before the age of manufacturing were all much more custom-built than they are today. Each house, each door, each window, though it followed the general style of its period, was especially built for its owner and reflected his experience and taste. Communication was not rapid and many older styles continued long after new ideas had become well established. It is very difficult to draw absolutely clean-cut lines between each period and often it is confusing to

Egg and dart

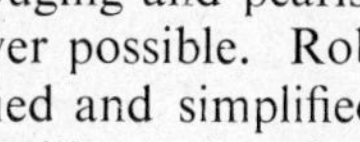

Bead and reel

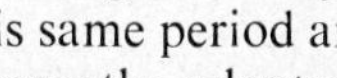

Gouging and pearls

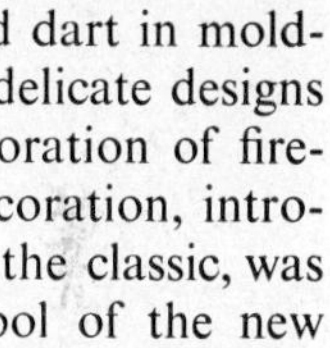

Above: Homewood, Baltimore. Classic Revival or Early Republic. *Below: Monticello, Thomas Jefferson's home. Classic Revival.*

find elements of several periods in one house. Individual owners did not hesitate to adapt a style to their own taste, as we find in a Greek revival house in Middletown, Connecticut, below.

Some of the details of this house and the fact that it was built by Richard Alsop in 1840 make us think of the words Empire or Regency to describe the style, instead of classic revival. The story goes that the Alsop family spent the winter of 1837 in Europe and were particularly interested in Potsdam in Germany. Thus it was no accident that the exterior is almost identical with the house of an architect in Potsdam, or that the unique interior decoration of painted walls resembles that of the Royal Palace in the same city. There are rectangular pillars supporting the porch roof on each end of the house, but the porch across the front of the house is supported by ironwork in which have been incorporated three arrows, another typically American design.

From the day of the classic revival, each new style developed was a revival of an older one, adapted, as always, to economic conditions and available materials. It was almost a century before we found a style that was really new.

We can hurry through these revivals, as we are all familiar with examples of them, good and bad, to be seen everywhere. After the Greek came the Victorian. This started as a revival of Gothic lines with elements of baroque. Its development knew no bounds, but many of the early Victorian houses are quite simple and charming. Some of the windows have pointed Gothic arches; often a steep gable is the feature that distinguishes the house. The use of wrought iron and later cast iron provided all sorts of new possibilities inside and out. Iron was strong, inexpensive, and could be molded into anything from a fine balustrade to a deer for the lawn. The day of the custom workshop was coming to an end, and factories were producing everything for building—stock moldings, door trim, doors, windows, mantelpieces, fretwork, ironwork, colored glass, skylights, and newel posts, to suggest a few items. The demand for houses was enormous and each owner seemed to vie with his neighbor to make his house the most ornamental. Soon new places to ornament had to be found and fretworks of grape leaves and vines began to appear along the edge of the gables and porch roofs. We call this gingerbread, but actually gingerbread is very plain by comparison. The Mansard roof, sloping upward on all four sides of a house and allowing straighter walled rooms for the top floor, was revived from the work of an Italian architect of that name who lived two centuries before this time. The bay window became popular.

The Victorian interior matched the exterior in ornate treatment. Florid wallpapers and flock which resembled cut velvet were used and picture moldings were gilded. Windows were tall with very low sills, or were cut down to the floor and the hall often boasted an elaborate stained-glass window. The dining-room chair rail was moved nearer to the ceiling to make a plate rack all the way around the room. Sometimes doors were of mahogany with silver handles, but more often oak was used, ranging from golden to dark brown, in the woodwork and doors. You will think of other things that you can see every day

Hammond Harwood House, Annapolis, Maryland. Georgian.

Davison Art Center, Connecticut. Empire or Regency.

which belonged not only to the full Victorian era (which did have a certain authentic charm) but to the nondescript period which followed. It was a period of copying anything and everything which had ever been seen before, including among others the stucco half-timbered cottages of England and the bungalow. The latter deserves special mention, not for its beauty, but because like the Cape Cod house it is to be found in every community in the land. It is difficult to trace the source of this popular American house. The shingles, rough stone, larger dormer windows suggest some of the cottages in the Alps. Low roof overhanging a wide verandah is not unlike many houses built in India for protection against intense heat. Wherever it came from, we changed it somewhat and made it our own, as we did every style that came to our shores.

MODERN

The twentieth century found us experimenting with an entirely new style, copying nothing and based on a new conception of the function of the home in a new way of life. The new emphasis was on inventions, convenience, health, travel, communication, outdoor living, efficiency, and machines. Fewer families were born, lived, and died in the same place. There were fewer servants and modern temperature controls had almost eliminated the need to consider climate in building. Compact kitchen, lavatory, and bathroom installations in the new streamline trains and ocean liners suggested that the division and use of space in the home be reconsidered. The main driving force behind the new style, however, was an entirely new point of view. Instead of building a traditional house and dividing and arranging it to suit the family's needs as far as possible, the new idea was to consider the needs first and build a house around them. Many of the first houses constructed with this idea were grotesque almost to the point of being ridiculous, but gradually the architects developed houses in the new style which were both functional and beautiful.

We call the new style modern for want of a better name. There was a time when Georgian was called modern. Understanding the principle of modern architecture is simple. It has taken many forms and will take many more, but basically the houses are horizontal in line with flat roofs, and there is great emphasis on oneness with the outdoors. Large glass windows are everywhere, sometimes making an entire wall and opening on a porch or terrace so that the living room becomes part of the outdoors. Symmetry gives way to a more asymmetrical treatment and the tradition of a room for every purpose like living, dining, cooking, sleeping, is abandoned in favor of large open areas divided by screens, bookcases or lattices or not at all. Any feasible and practical material can be combined with any other—wood, glass, concrete, brick, plastic, and stone. Lines are straight and plain and beauty is found in proportion, texture, light, and shadow. The natural terrain is used as much as possible. We should think of the modern house as walled-in space for comfort and privacy.

Modern interiors also develop the straight line and avoid moldings and any heavy decoration. There are living, working, and eating areas, rather than rooms. The large window and the view are more important than the fireplace or the placing of the front door.

The ranch house uses many features of what we know as modern, but is apt to be more conservative. It is almost always all on one floor and will have one or more picture windows. We think of it as rustic in conception and finish, but actually a ranch house today can be any house anywhere, either in a small housing development in New England, or spread all over a western prairie. In California and the Southwest a special feature of these houses, borrowed from our Mexican neighbors, definitely influences the designing of houses. This is the desire for some kind of patio or outdoor terrace usually protected on three sides by the house itself or screened in some way to provide privacy. This is another example of the modern tendency to suit our houses to our way of life instead of suiting ourselves to a traditional architecture.

We have raced through several centuries of architecture, any period of which might make a year's study, but each here is only suggested by a few words and illustrations. At least, we have learned that changes in architectural styles always, today more than ever, depend on taste and culture, economy, and leisure, and above all man's effort to make his home reflect his way of life.

Yellow paneled door, sparkling white trim, blue-painted vertical siding, provide a colorful background.

LADIES' HOME JOURNAL'S MORE IDEAS FOR THE MONEY PORTFOLIO HOUSE NO. 4

This 3-bedroom house illustrates the versatility of the modern style.

LADIES' HOME JOURNAL'S MORE HOUSE FOR THE MONEY PORTFOLIO NO. 3

Plenty of space, color, and variety is a complete departure from older architectural traditions.

Carved oak press cupboard, above, is from last half of the seventeenth century.

Seventeenth-century highboy, right, is veneered in burled walnut with cup turning. Etched escutcheons and pendant drops for drawer pulls.

Late seventeenth-century court cupboard, above, has turning and spindle decoration.

Early eighteenth-century highboy, right, features trumpet turning and contemporary-style hardware.

Furniture

Period and Contemporary Trends

Sometimes a little knowledge is a dangerous thing, but actually that is all we need to enable us to distinguish between different styles of furniture and make a fairly accurate guess at the period of their origin. We are not interested in searching through a furniture encyclopedia for an exact picture of a chair or table, because not even the best one can hope to follow and picture the great variety in each period and the special order or vagary which made one craftsman carve a heart in the back of a chair, while another making an almost identical chair left the back plain. If we know the differences in feet, legs, backs, construction, hardware, and wood, all of which have been classified, we will get the feeling of each period and assign pieces to their proper category with ease. This is quite different from being the expert who can distinguish a genuine antique from a fake, or quibble about the exact year that a piece was made. There are many transitional pieces with feet and legs of one period and the rest belonging to the preceding or following era. The examples illustrated on the next pages and the small drawings of details are fundamental. You will soon discover which go together and which you prefer. Unless collecting old pieces is your hobby, or a matter of investment, do not be concerned with the actual age of a piece: only with the style and beauty. Very often a good reproduction of a fine piece is much better than one whose only claim to beauty is its age. There are plenty of ungainly antiques and still more ungainly reproductions. A decorator's aim is to study the best of the old to appreciate good designing and good lines which may be used to produce a pleasant room. Color and finish are also important factors. Old pieces, if they have been cared for at all, will have a dull soft glow known as patine. Edges are worn through use and polishing and very few pieces will have escaped the scars of several generations of being bumped, moved, and stored away. Stains and woods fade in sunlight as much as colors. Our best manufacturers of reproductions recognize all these things and in addition to copying old pieces faithfully, without change of line or proportion, they are able to produce a good color and even an appearance of scars through a process they call "distressing." A distressed piece of furniture is not usually trying to pretend to be an antique, it is merely trying to get away from the machine-made look. For some reason, most people like automobiles, iceboxes, household appliances and such to look like machines, but they like furniture, textiles, metalwork and carving to look handmade.

To start in the beginning with furniture, as we did with architecture, we must find out what the Pilgrims had in their first "fair and well built houses." It is hard to believe that there was much room on the tiny ships for furniture, but there were plenty of memories of what they had had at home and a fair knowledge of cabinetmaking. The pieces on the opposite page, beginning with the handsome press and court cupboards, and including the two highboys, show us what sort of furniture was made for storage purposes in a day when there were no closets and few built-in cupboards. The very early cupboards are Jacobean in

These seventeenth-century chests, with some decoration, show the variations beginning with the chest itself, then the chest with one drawer, then the chest with two drawers.

Wainscot chair, far left, was typical of the Pilgrim period. Heavy pieces gave way to more practical styles as the typical slat-back, middle. Bannister back, right, was made by splitting spindles, placing them vertically in back.

Chippendale furniture is extremely versatile in design. The first two chairs, beautifully designed, have the typical cabriole leg, ball-and-claw foot of Chippendale. Notice the perfectly straight legs and openwork molded slats on the last chair, known as a ladder back.

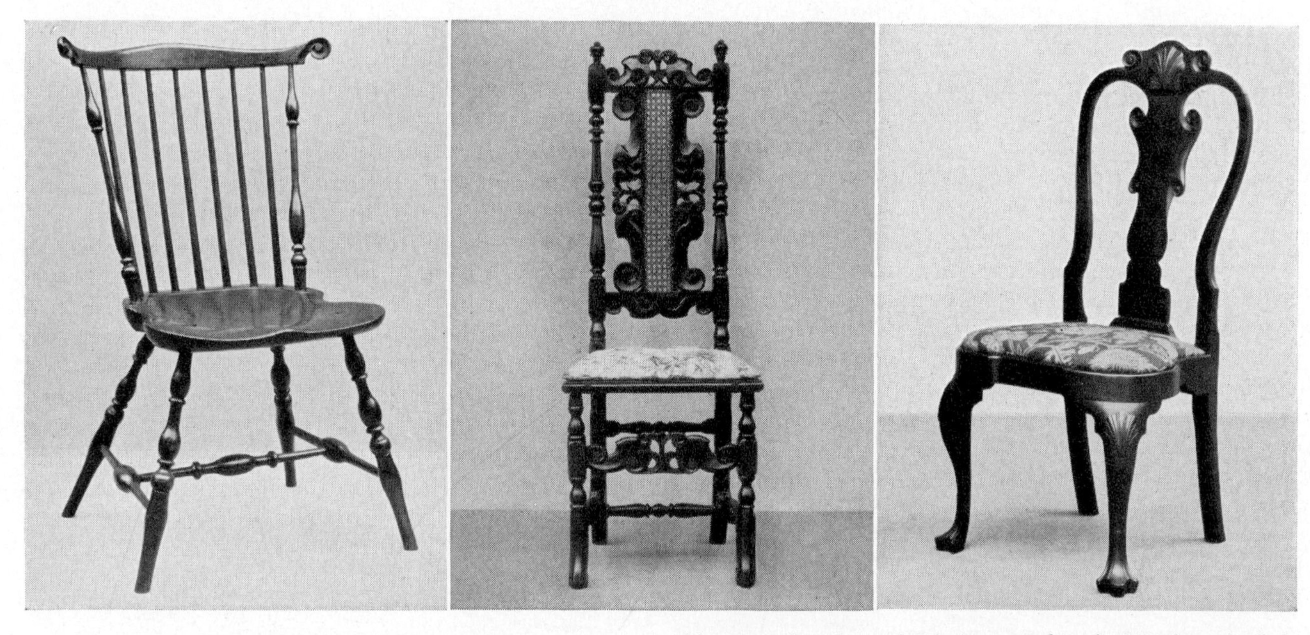

Most popular chair of Pilgrim period is the Windsor, far left, which has many variations. "Cain, black or India" chair, next, came later and was also very popular. Queen Anne, right, beautifully carved, forecasts Chippendale.

In addition to the finely carved Chippendale wood pieces, there were many excellent upholstered pieces. The arms and the back of the sofa above are typical of the period. This one belongs to the straight-legged variety, others, of course, may have the cabriole leg and ball-and-claw foot.

design and carving, made of oak, and reminiscent of the Elizabethan era. They are seldom seen nowadays and almost never copied, but are of interest to us in showing that from the earliest days the colonists had lathes. At the bottom of the page is a group of sketches of the fine turnings they produced from the beginning on these primitive lathes. You will notice these types in early furniture and different turnings in later periods.

Not every seventeenth-century house had as fine a thing as a court cupboard, but certainly each one had some form of chest. These were made in all forms, from the crudest kind of box to the beautifully decorated pieces found in all parts of the country. The chests on page 27 show some of the variations, beginning with the chest, then the chest with one drawer, chest with two drawers, and finally the highboy with a series of drawers mounted on a base with legs. The early highboys had turned legs, four or six, and were often accompanied by a similar base without the drawers, called a lowboy. These two pieces became very popular and were made from the seventeenth century until the end of the Chippendale period, about the time of the American Revolution.

To complete an early room we need only a few forms, small stools with turned legs and plain stretchers, for seats, and possibly an armchair, and an all-purpose table, large enough to serve as a dining table. That is all that a Pilgrim family would expect in addition to the many cooking pots and utensils, dough trays, Betty lamps and candlesticks. In reproducing such a room today for living purposes we would want a few upholstered pieces and more cupboard space. Most people have been unable to make the necessary compromise for comfort and are inclined to make these early rooms into dining rooms, but a careful selection of small chairs and sofas with lines similar to the early pieces can be used very well.

The cupboards and chests changed very little, were different in various localities, but remained much the same over a long period of time. What did change much more quickly and offered infinite variety throughout the Pilgrim period were the chairs. In addition to the forms, the earliest settlers made heavy oak wainscot chairs, turned and carved very much in the manner of the court cupboards, as you can see from the simple one on page 28. Many were much more elaborately carved and some were chair-tables with a tall back on a swivel, so that it could be lowered to rest on the arms and form a table.

These heavy pieces soon gave way to a lighter, more practical style which has actually been popular ever since those early days. The slat-backed chair shown is typical, but only suggests a whole series which included many variations of this one with plain and pierced slats, different sizes of knobs, with and without arms; and also the bannister back, made by splitting spindles and placing them vertically in the back. These chairs all had turned legs and rush seats. They were made of pine or maple and occasionally of fruit wood, always in a light finish. The most popular chair of all belonging to this general period is the Windsor, which also has many variations; from the one by the fireplace in the dining room on page 14, to the tall comb-backed rockers of the middle of the next century. These chairs are still standard for informal living and are made today in every size and shape.

The lathe has always been the cabinetmaker's friend. Even the earliest furniture developed beautiful turnings culminating in such as the trumpet on the left and the cup on the right. Below, the Portuguese influence is seen in the first example. Next to it is the ball with shoe.

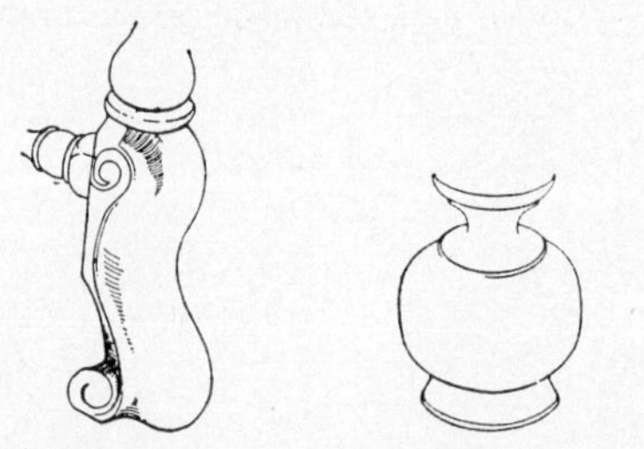

Remembering in the early days that craftsmen brought their own traditions from many countries, it is no surprise to find, below, first a Spanish, second a Dutch, and finally an English influence in chair feet.

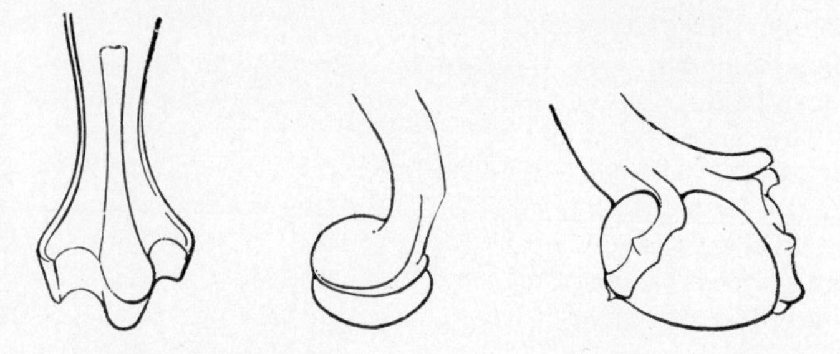

Queen Anne highboy has matching lowboy with gilded shell on the middle lower drawer.

The next early chair comes as a surprise because the style was revived at the end of the Victorian period and many copies of it are still to be seen in large houses, halls and hotel lobbies. Actually these "Cain, black or India" chairs pictured on page 29 originated toward the end of the seventeenth century. The style came to us from England, but shows marked Spanish, Portuguese and Flemish influence. It enjoyed a long life, as it was still being advertised in the colonial newspapers as late as 1750 when the styles of William and Mary, Queen Anne and Chippendale were well established.

From a decorator's point of view we can pass quickly over William and Mary styles and Queen Anne, as neither are being used or reproduced in any quantity at present. Queen Anne furniture is important, however, in showing the transition from the earlier pieces to the great Chippendale period. Also we must not forget that the use and reproduction of different periods of furniture follows a vogue too. Today Sheraton may be the rage; tomorrow the demand may be for Queen Anne, like the chair illustrated, which is of walnut and has beautifully carved volutes on the back and a shell decoration. The fine cabriole leg ends in a Spanish foot. The simpler type of cabriole leg pictured on the highboy and lowboy above, and the Dutch cushion foot sketched opposite are also characteristic of this period and were used on the chairs as well as on other pieces.

We are now well into the eighteenth century and the name in furniture style which immediately comes to mind, and rightly so, is that of Thomas Chippendale. He was an English cabinetmaker working in London and the first to bring out an illustrated book of important furniture designs. His *Gentleman and Cabinet Maker's Director*, published in 1754, became every cabinetmaker's bible, in both England and this country. Many of his designs were executed and copied, adapted and changed, but all pieces of this period bear enough resemblance to his work to be called Chippendale, no matter who made them or where they were made. In this country they were made mostly of mahogany, a beautiful new dark wood from the West Indies, which took a fine finish, could be carved with a sharp edge and was exceedingly durable.

Chippendale furniture is very versatile in design. So much so, that often we are surprised that two such different pieces could belong to the same era. The cabriole leg for chairs, highboys, tables, often handsomely carved, took on great significance. At the same time the makers of Chippendale furniture were making other pieces with perfectly straight legs and stretchers and decorating various pieces with a delicate fretwork inspired by Chinese designs. The seats of all these chairs were larger than those of their predecessors and the backs were made lighter in design by open work, carved ribbons and open volutes. There is also a Chippendale type of chair with openwork moded slats at regular intervals, known as a ladder-back. All of these pieces are beautiful in design and workmanship as you will see in the illustrations. The designs also had an influence on the less sophisticated craftsman who sometimes made chairs with the turned characteristics of the earlier chairs but a pierced vase-shaped splat in the newest mode. Another design which we identify with Chippendale is the ball-and-claw foot which he made very popular. It is difficult to say whether the fine Georgian interiors that the architects were producing inspired cabinetmakers to make suitable furniture, or whether Chippendale's designs for furniture called for more elegant interiors.

Every period has its characteristic chairs and tables, but there are also pieces of furniture which were used for a definite purpose for a while and which gave way to something quite different in appearance. In the first half of the eighteenth century, for example, a highboy and, if possible, a matching lowboy were essential. These followed the lines and treatment of their times and were important enough to merit the best skill and design of their makers. The two pieces illustrated here were probably parlor pieces, and are important in showing the degree of elegance attained, as well as the kind of drawer pulls with which they are decorated. Hardware is a study in itself, often complicated by replacements on an earlier piece of much later styles in brass. The small plate with a single drop pull as well as wooden knobs is associated with early furniture. Later these larger plates with handles were more in keeping with the lines of the furniture. You will note that, in every style, the hardware changed with the lines.

The story we have been telling, of turned members, stretchers, cabriole legs, different types of feet, and carving, holds true for the tables of each period, as you will see from those illustrated here and on the opposite page and in the various period rooms pictured. Early tables had turned legs and were strong in structure, if sometimes crude in finish. The long trestle table shown is over twelve feet long, probably similar to "1 table board and joyned frame" listed in a Plymouth inventory of 1638. The large gate-leg table also belongs to the very early period. This is another example of a style which has been popular since its inception. It has been copied and adapted in every kind of wood for every table purpose, varying in size, shape, wood and number of legs. The charming little butterfly table has also been reproduced in a variety of shapes and sizes for modern use.

As we go into the eighteenth century, we find our ancestors needing, in addition to dining tables and side tables, two new types, for tea and card playing. The rectangular tea table shown with its simple cabriole legs and slipper feet suggests Queen Anne. The tilt-top tea table is

Many early tables had turned legs and were strong in structure, if sometimes crude in finish. The charming little butterfly table, below, has been reproduced in a variety of shapes and sizes for modern use. The long trestle table shown is over twelve feet long, probably similar to "1 table board and joyned frame" listed in a Plymouth inventory of 1638. The large gate-leg table also belongs to the very early period and has been widely copied and adapted.

The early eighteenth century found our ancestors yearning for new types of tables for tea and card playing. The rectangular tea table, below, shown with its simple cabriole legs and slipper feet suggests Queen Anne. The table below it has a folding top and is lined with felt for playing cards. The tilt-top or pie-crust table, elegant and very popular, is typically Chippendale.

typically Chippendale. These were also made with a plain edge and simpler foot, but the most elegant and popular has always been of this type, known as pie-crust table. In the Chippendale era we also find a new type of table with a folding top, the inside lined with felt for playing cards. This style continued through the Victorian period with various mechanisms for turning and supporting the top. The round finished wood corners on this one were meant for candlesticks and quite often you will find a similar table with small oval bowls carved out of the top in front of each player for his loo counters. One other table which belongs to this period is the pier table, usually a long narrow table intended to be used against the wall and therefore straight on the back with elaborately carved legs and front.

The first desks in this country were simply boxes, mounted on a frame with turned legs, but at an early date these boxes were enlarged and fitted with pigeonholes and a slanted front which could be lowered to make a writing surface. This slant-top construction supported by small pulls when open, and with no shelves or cabinet above the slant, is known as a Governor Winthrop desk, after John Winthrop, a seventeenth-century governor of the Colony of Connecticut. Later the space below the slant top was filled in with drawers and the desks were finished and decorated according to the style of each period, but the name

Governor Winthrop for any slant-front desk of this type was retained.

By the middle of the eighteenth century the desk had become an important piece of furniture, and in addition to the Governor Winthrop, we find the kneehole desk and a great variety of secretary desks with shelves above the slant top and solid wooden doors. These were mounted on heavy bracket feet and surmounted with a broken pediment, allowing a place in the center for a bust or an elaborately carved finial. It is in these handsome secretaries that the cabinetmakers really showed their skill, especially in the construction of the *bombé* or kettledrum base shown and the block front.

The block front as shown in the kneehole desk on page 35 was one of the few designs which originated in this country and became typically American. It reached the height of development in the hands of John Goddard, of Newport, Rhode Island. He not only was a master of the block front, but also used on his secretary desk the two raised shells with a depressed shell in the center, the hooded top, and special urn-shaped finials. When all these characteristics appear together in the same piece its identification is unmistakable. Goddard used fine heavy mahogany, and though he undoubtedly made many other types of furniture, the name *Goddard desk* always designates one of this type.

In addition to the finely carved Chippendale wood pieces, you will want to be able to recognize the Chippendale sofa. The arms and the back of the one illustrated on page 29 are typical of the period. You are now familiar enough with Chippendale to know that this one belongs to the straight-legged variety. Others may have cabriole legs with ball-and-claw feet, or may be much smaller, but the lines will be essentially the same.

Although we seem to be discussing antique furniture in considerable detail, a decorator is really interested chiefly in learning about line, style, and proportion. Once oriented in periods, you will have no trouble in knowing how far to go in changing and adapting to meet special needs. Not many of us can have museum pieces, which most of the pieces we have been studying are, but once we have seen and get a feeling for fine originals, we are much better able to judge and choose from the hundreds of good and not so good reproductions that are available today.

As soon as the smoke of the American Revolution had blown away and the thirteen states were beginning to feel established as a new Republic, people began to turn their attention to a new style which had been known in England for some time, but neglected here during the trying years of war, the fight over the new Constitution, the lack of free trade and the consequent meager incomes. When a new house was to be built now, the designs of Robert Adam seemed more fitting for the times and the Chippendale furniture, overheavy and ornate.

Early eighteenth-century scrutoire, or desk, is familiarly known as a Governor Winthrop desk.

The delicate interior woodwork, cornices, and fireplaces of the new elegant simplicity certainly called for something of the same order in furniture. Two English cabinetmakers arose to meet this demand. Each was primarily a designer and each published a book of designs. The men were George Hepplewhite, who published *The Cabinet-Maker and Upholsterer's Guide* in 1788, and Thomas Sheraton, whose famous book was *The Cabinet Dictionary, containing an Explanation of all the Terms used in Cabinet, Chair and Upholstery branches, containing a display of useful articles of Furniture* (1802).

They both seem to have been very erratic young men and no one knows just how much actual manual cabinetmaking they did themselves. Their designs were often similar and they both made extensive use of satinwood and other exotic woods in elaborate inlays and marquetry. They were both capable of very beautiful, graceful, wellporportioned designs and also of bizarre and downright hideous ones. However, we owe to them the origin of an entirely new fine style which became popular in the early days of the young Republic and is probably copied in contemporary furniture more than those of any other period.

Like Chippendale, Sheraton and Hepplewhite have come to be the names of styles, rather than of men, and

strangely enough, though there is little basis in fact, we have come to associate certain details with Sheraton and others with Hepplewhite, though many of them were used by both. When the emphasis is on the rectangular shape and straight line the piece is usually called Sheraton; if it is on ovals and circles and curved lines, we call it Hepplewhite.

It becomes easy, then, to identify the three chairs of the top row of the next page, and take a guess at the one at top, right, on page 37. It has the rectangular back of a Sheraton chair, but the ornament on the center splat and the curved shoulders are usually associated with Hepplewhite, as was the bluebell pendant motif in his inlays and carving. The shield-backed chair, with many variations, we always call Hepplewhite, although such chairs were made by Sheraton and Adam as well.

Sheraton and Hepplewhite chairs are mostly made in mahogany with deeply incised moldings and fine carving, but during the same period a vogue sprang up for painted furniture and "fancy chairs." The contemporary newspapers were full of advertisements for this new style, such as that of William Challens, of New York, who advertised in 1797:

"Fancy Chair-maker from London, manufactures all sorts of dyed, jappanned, wangee and bamboo chairs, settees, etc. . . . after the most approved London patterns."
and another in 1802:

". . . elegant white, coquilicot, green, etc. and gilt drawing-room chairs with cane and rush seats."

The chair and the settee illustrated on page 36 are of the Sheraton type. These were the forerunners of another painted chair which became even more popular from 1818 forward and is used today in both formal and informal settings, that is, the Hitchcock chair. For these, painting was done on pine or maple chairs with no carving, relying entirely on the artist to paint in his moldings and shadows.

Another new effect was achieved by the copious use of marquetry, or inlay. In this field our cabinetmakers made their pieces peculiarly American in two ways. First, they discovered that maple took as light and beautiful a finish as satinwood and, being much more available, could be used more generously. Second, they incorporated the American eagle into the inlays of some of their most beautiful and formal pieces. This emblem became popular at the time of George Washington's first inauguration and appeared everywhere. On furniture the eagle was usually made of mahogany and maple inlays against a green field of olivewood and surmounted with a semicircle of stars. Collectors date such pieces by the number of stars, each

The Bombé or kettledrum desk, above, with broken pediment, allows a place in the center for an objet d'art.

Block-front kneehole desk by John Goddard, below, is frequently made of fine mahogany.

The rectangular Sheraton style found many variations, often typified in different localities. In Virginia they were fond of the vase-shaped splat, while New York used a simple design. General Washington had a set of the latter in his library in New York.

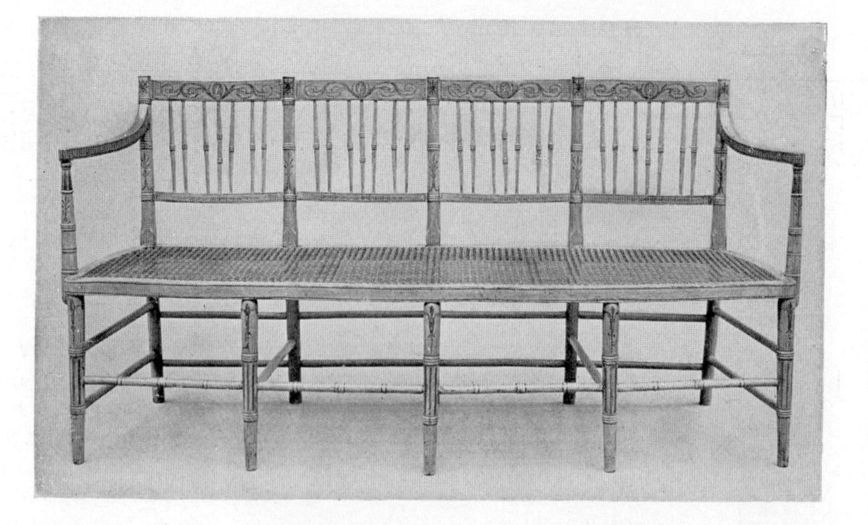

Lacquered and "fancy chairs" of the Early Republic were the forerunners of the Hitchcock chair so popular even today. Often a set of chairs had a matching settee.

The ubiquitous cane came into use quite early, here on a painted chair. The shield shape back is always identified with the name Hepplewhite though such chairs were made by Sheraton and Adam as well. Sheraton or Hepplewhite although crude in execution here makes use of the traditional Prince of Wales feathers.

The French Empire with its entirely different legs, shape, stresses and strains, is typified in this country by Duncan Phyfe, a New York cabinetmaker direct from Scotland. The two on the left illustrate the height of his art. One on the right represents the decline when the young generation took over.

Above is a fine mahogany veneered sideboard-cellarette, suggestive of Sheraton in the predominance of rectangular lines, but of Hepplewhite in the circular inlays and bluebells on the legs. Below left is a Sheraton card table with inlaid American eagle. The dining table at its right is Early Republic, made up of two half-round tables which fit together. When completely detached these half tables could also be used against the wall for consoles.

Tambour desk is inlaid with eagle, has eighteen stars.

of which was supposed to represent a state. Hence, if there are sixteen stars the piece was not made until after Vermont, Kentucky and Tennessee had been admitted to the Union, in 1796.

All the designs in the books could not deprive our cabinetmakers of their own individuality. The Gothic influence here presages the popularity it was to have in the early Victorian period. The urn-shaped finials reiterate a design which appeared everywhere in the classic period from gateposts to flower vases. The maple veneer on the entire front makes us wonder if Alexander Hamilton's recommendation, as Secretary of the Treasury, was ever adopted. Speaking of the manufacture of "cabinet-wares," Hamilton wrote: "An exemption from duty of the several kinds of wood ordinarily used in these manufactures seems to be all that is requisite by way of encouragement." A New York list of 1796 of these woods included, "Sattin and Manillia wood. . . . Sasico and Havannah. . . . King, tulip, rose, purple, snake, Zebra, Alexandria, Panella, yew. . . ." The rather heavy wooden knobs suggest that the maker was out of drawer pulls at the moment. He might have used pulls similar to those on the sideboard and tambour desk, which had come into fashion in this period. The turned legs with reeding are delicate.

The dining tables of the Early Republic were usually made up of two half-round tables which fitted together. Sometimes a rectangular drop leaf was attached to the back of each half-round and supported when open by one of the rear legs which could be pushed back under it. This made a long oval table when needed. These completely detached half tables could also be used against the wall for consoles.

A typical chest of drawers in the Early Republic period had a simple curved front. Frequently, however, the graceful serpentine front was used.

The styles of Sheraton and Hepplewhite continued well into the nineteenth century, but growing up at the same time was an entirely new style which was inspired by Napoleon's first empire. With this new style we come to the first American cabinetmaker-designer, Duncan Phyfe, whose work so far excelled that of any of his contemporaries that his name has been given to the whole style in this country. True, he was born in Scotland; but he came to America in his teens, and before his death in 1824 he had established a fine workshop and salesroom on Fulton Street, New York, employing more than a hundred men.

Phyfe's early pieces followed Sheraton lines, especially in his sofas and tables with reeded legs, but with the adoption of the Empire style, he developed characteristics of his own for which he is well known. The first of these was the use of acanthus-leaf carving which appeared not only down the front of a chair, but around an urn-shaped pedestal for a table, on the legs of tables, stiles of sideboards and bedposts. Another favorite of his was the dog's-paw leg and the lion's or dog's-paw foot for tables and sofas. He introduced the lyre back in chairs and sofa arms and also a very charming harp back, like the harp on an Irish flag. He is famous for his fine selection of mahogany and equally fine carving. His standards of workmanship were high and his supervision of his workmen must have been untiring. He had many imitators in Philadelphia and other cities, as well as New York, but none seemed to have been able to equal him in workmanship or selection of woods.

Without going into comparative statistics, we know that his furniture was of the finest and commanded excessive prices for the day. One of his bills to Charles N. Boucher, Esq., in Philadelphia, bears a sketch of the lyre-back chair pictured and the note, "Cane bottom . . . $22, Cushions . . . $3.00, Stuffed . . . $23." This would be nothing for a chair of similar quality today, which would command ten times the amount, if made by hand, but our manufacturers are turning out an assembly-line chair in the same style at about the same price.

Our attention is called, at this point, to the slip seat. Almost all of Phyfe's chairs used this new style, which consisted of a wooden frame that would slip into the chair when stuffed and covered and was attached to the chair with two large screws, front and rear. There are a few Chippendale chairs with slip seats, but they were not often made, as they required the frame of the chair seat to be finished and molded on the edge, but in this new style the slip seat becomes part of the actual construction of the chair.

The pictures on page 37 will give an idea of the style and shape of a few of Phyfe's chairs, but mention should be made of what came after, as this style slipped easily into the Victorian chair of the next era. The last chair on the right is the beginning, with the carved eagle on the center splat. This chair was not made by Phyfe and was followed by many chairs of similar design with roses, leaves, turned top rails, and also "fancy chairs" with the same general backs, but turned legs and rush seats and a painted finish.

Duncan Phyfe also had some new ideas about tables. For the first time tables are not supported by four legs, but have a center pedestal with a spread of three or four legs at the base of the pedestal. The card table shown is typical. This style was used in a much enlarged form for dining tables, library tables and large parlor tables.

He introduced several new pieces of furniture which had not been used before, such as the narrow window seat with high arms at either end, shaped like a chair back, sometimes stuffed and sometimes with the same splat or lyre of his chairs. He made many piano bases, nests of tables, flowerstands and sewing tables. He made some four-posted beds, but also popularized the vogue in the country for a bed with a head and foot board and no canopy.

Card table has clover-leaf top and acanthus-leaf leg carving by Duncan Phyfe.

The drawer pulls on Phyfe pieces, as well as others of the period were in the form of small lion's heads with a ring through the mouth to form the pull. Animal paws in brass were often put on the feet of a sofa or table and the strings of his lyres were made of brass or whalebone. There are also some pieces of this era which have strips of brass inlaid much in the manner of the light wood banding of Sheraton and Hepplewhite. Brass casters on the legs of heavy pieces came into extensive use at this time and caning in the backs and seats of chairs, sofas, and love seats was quite usual.

Duncan Phyfe was the last of the great cabinetmakers, and even his workshop finally gave way to the cheaper, more quickly produced machine-made furniture which was beginning to be made in large quantities. By 1830 there were few customers for fine handmade furniture, and all sorts of new factors made their influence felt on furniture design.

By the time Queen Victoria ascended the throne in 1837, the young Republic in America was a thriving, lusty young nation. The wealthy cultured gentry was still with us, but there was also a new middle class which was making money and wanted to spend it. Factories were springing up everywhere and the machine was the important thing. Taste gave way to speed of production, and ostentation was more important than beauty. These new purchasers were not interested in quality or workmanship. They wanted furniture that looked expensive and with which they could impress their neighbors. Lots of carving, fretwork, trimming was in demand and the newly built factories hastened to comply with this desire.

At first the designers of furniture tried variations on the Empire style, using more rosewood and crotched mahogany veneering, but they soon discovered that the Gothic and, better yet, Louis XV styles were even more elaborate and better suited to their purpose. From then on there was no limit to what the Victorian cabinetmakers or factories found to copy, adapt and improvise upon. For the next seventy years utter confusion reigned and anything went, as long as it was not simple, clear in line or classic in design. Everything was done for effect and furniture makers found they could produce fine mahogany veneering over cheaply made furniture of poor-quality wood. This was badly glued on and chipped off rather easily.

Phyfe's early pieces followed Sheraton lines. At left is a fine example of this early period. Notice the reeded legs.

With the adoption of the Empire style, Phyfe developed characteristics of his own. For example, the charming lyre design used in the arms of the sofa at left.

Hence veneering gradually became synonymous with poor quality, an idea which persists today, though that is only true when it is done in the manner of some of the hasty Victorian manufacturers. Fine veneering was painstakingly used by craftsmen of the Sheraton and Hepplewhite periods and by Duncan Phyfe, and today our manufacturers have developed a double and triple veneering which is laid with one layer cross graining another in a manner which guarantees us against chipping and warping or bulging, even with our variations in temperatures and climates. Our grandmothers were proud of their solid mahogany pieces, but this was a result of unhappy experiences with poor-quality veneering. As a matter of fact, solid mahogany is more apt to split and warp than a well-veneered piece.

If Victorian furniture is so bad, why do people still treasure some of it? Nothing is all bad. Among all the things that were turned out, there was still some demand for formality and elegance among the more sophisticated people and there were still a few designers who had had some taste and were not willing to cater to the popular fury. Then, too, it was often the incongruous mixtures of styles and ideas which gave the style a bad name.

Actually, a fine Victorian room furnished completely with Victorian furniture may have great charm, as we see from the pictures on pages 42 and 43 which represent Victorianism at its height. It is pleasant to imagine the formal, proper Victorian ladies and gentlemen moving around such a drawing room either at tea, or in full evening dress. It is fun to imagine the little girl in the picture in the hall having a house party in the bedroom upstairs with its two tremendous canopied beds.

In the drawing room you will find a gentleman's chair by the pianoforte and a ladies' chair in the curve of the piano. Both these chairs are a product of the era and usually went together. The large sofa back in the immediate foreground, like the chairs, suggests the name of John Belter, one of the few designers who stand out in the mid-Victorian period.

The sofa in the hall is almost Empire with just a trace of the more elaborate carving that characterized the new period. The curve of the arm is similar to the curve of the sleigh bed, another invention of this era.

Great restraint is shown in the drawing room here in the matter of omitting three or four footstools, a picture or two on an easel, one or more *étagères* or whatnot shelves, and some bronze statuary. We like it better the way it is, but a century ago, it would have been considered quite bare in furnishings.

All of us can add to what is here from our own knowledge and experience in Victorian furniture, but there are

Downstairs hall has curving staircase. The sofa is almost Empire with just a trace of ornate carving.

Tremendous canopied beds in double bedroom are typical of this period.

This Victorian drawing room from Belle Mead in Tennessee is a fine example of the real charm Victorian can have.

a few other pieces which we should definitely identify as belonging to this period. One of these is the rocking chair. The Victorians simply added rockers to many existing chairs, like the slat-back chair pictured on page 28 and the well-known Windsor-type chair, but they also developed several upholstered chairs with rockers and the famous Boston rocker with its high back and curved seat. These were usually painted black and gold with a stencil or picture on the top of the back similar to the Hitchcock chairs. The other type of Victorian rocking chair which you will run across constantly is the gooseneck rocker which had an upholstered high back and seat and wooden, partially upholstered arms which ended in a gooseneck similar to the blue chair in the foreground of our drawing room on page 43.

We cannot leave this period without mention of the marble tops used on tables, bureaus and washstands, and the contribution of the iron foundries in making beds, garden chairs, hatracks, lamps, stoves and grates for the parlor.

It was a wondrous period indeed, and though we are apt to poke a little fun at it and marvel at some of its grotesqueries, we cannot help feeling a little sentimental about it, just as our grandmothers did.

MODERN

By the beginning of the present century, haste and mass production had reduced the general taste in home furnishings to a very low point. The importance of charm and beauty in everyday surroundings had almost disappeared and the words *cheap* and *ugly* were practically synonymous. A few architects, designers, and artists felt that this could not go on, and put forth two new important ideas. The first was that the copies and adaptations of older designs were no longer suitable for an age of inventions and innovations. The second, though this did not bear fruit until much later, was that inexpensive and mass-produced objects could be beautiful.

The engineers and inventors had supplied a new approach to designing. There was no prototype for the telephone, the typewriter, or the automobile engine. The inventor simply decided what were the important elements to make his invention work and then how to design it to comply with human anatomy and convenience for maximum use. The designer of new furniture now turned his back on his well-known prototypes and tried to produce something entirely different which would still answer the purposes of sitting, dining, sleeping, and storing things away. It was a challenge to his ingenuity, and though some of his first attempts were grotesque and others reminiscent of older designs, he did take some first steps toward an entirely new style.

Experiments proved that wood was still the best material for furniture, but it was used more sparingly and finished in different colors. Ebony was inlaid with ivory and silver bronze, and tulipwood could be stained to a rich lilac color. Curves and carving gave way to angles and plain surfaces. Glass, aluminum, and bakelite were used, plus a metal tubing which seemed to come directly from a plumber's shop. New ideas in construction were tried out. A table could be supported on three sticks fastened together to make a tripod, and a tubing chair could do without back legs, if the front legs were bent back on the floor far enough to provide balance.

These first things were all somewhat exotic, specially designed and built at excessive costs within the reach of very few. The public in general was not receptive, partly because of the cost and partly because none of the new things could be used with what they already had. There was considerable ridicule of the more extreme pieces and cartoonists delighted in sketches showing how uncomfortable or downright dangerous the new furniture could be. It was a start, an idea, but far from a popular movement. All of this, if not forgotten, was temporarily put aside in the preoccupation with the first World War.

Above are two sets of modern chests of drawers designed by the Knoll Associates Planning Unit. Drawer fronts are sloped, thus eliminating need for drawer pulls. On the top of the page opposite is a light-colored chest, hinged to allow it to be lowered into a coffee table supported by the long-handled drawer pull at top. The fine modern wallpaper is one of Katzenbach and Warren's. At the bottom is an example of combining a light wood with an ebonized finish on the same piece, producing an effective ensemble and relieving the monotony which seems to overtake too many plain light wood surfaces in the same room.

KATZENBACH AND WARREN

DUNBAR FURNITURE CORPORATION

After the war, however, the idea of a new style sprang up again and this time it was very different. People, especially young ones, were ready for a new life, as far removed from the old as possible. Their funds were limited, but once again they sought to express this new life in their daily surroundings. Designers were quick to realize that just being different was not enough. The new furniture must be functional, inexpensive, different and really serve its owners in their new needs.

Many circumstances had contributed to change these needs. Living space was much smaller and there were few, if any, servants. Many wives were working outside the home and leisure was not to be spent doing housework, but in being out of doors as much as possible. Emphasis was on informal living and informal entertaining. The smaller quarters became even tinier, if divided up into the usual living room, dining room, bedroom. Hence the partitions were often omitted and one large room served all the same purposes, divided only by furniture grouping into areas for different uses. With all of this came new standards of cleanliness in a house which banished everything that was hard to clean or collected dust.

The new furniture designs which we call "modern," because as yet there is nothing newer, found answers to all these needs and added a few ideas of their own which have influenced the reproduction of period furniture in many instances. There are still many people who prefer the old styles, but most of these will admit that modern usages have made their old favorites more adaptable to the present-day needs.

Seeking an answer to comfort in smaller living quarters produced many pieces which served more than one purpose, like the low coffee table which could easily be turned up to make a standard-height dining table, or a card table opening to seat ten people. All sorts of divans and sofas were designed which could be made into real beds. A chest of drawers was no longer purely a bedroom bureau, but came in a variety of sizes and heights to go into any area of a modern room as a sideboard, bureau or night table.

All sorts of furniture were built in to save space and other pieces designed as units which could be combined in different ways to make furniture arrangements very flexible. A pair of night stands with drawers could also serve as the ends of a dressing table with a simple hanging shelf between them, or might be used as the pedestal ends of a desk connected by a plain top laid across them.

Sometimes a sofa was made along the new lines in one piece to seat three or four people, but more often each seat was constructed as a separate unit or chair which could be detached from the sofa. Thus two armless units could be placed between a left-arm chair and a right-arm chair to make a sofa with four seats, or one unit could be withdrawn to make a smaller sofa with a matching armless

EDWARD WORMLEY, DESIGNER DUNBAR FURNITURE CORPORATION

Above is a modern curved sectional sofa complemented by an oversize coffee table. The cane and mahogany modern sofa bed, below, combines beauty and grace with usefulness.

EDWARD WORMLEY, DESIGNER DUNBAR FURNITURE CORPORATION

A modern compliment to the Early American tradition is designed by George Nakashima for Knoll Associates, Incorporated. It recalls the Windsor type of captain's chair but clearly belongs to the present century.

A tripod table with unusual connection joint is designed by Swiss Hans Bellman for Knoll Associates, Incorporated. It has a natural birch top, ebonized legs and is a fine example of the multi-purpose modern piece.

chair in the same room. A right-arm chair and a left-arm chair could be placed together to make a love seat, or a table put between them. Add corner units and rounded-end units and you have combinations for any kind of arrangement or space.

Simplicity and informality were achieved by eliminating all carving and elaborate details. The lines of the furniture were straight and clean and light colors in woods were greatly preferred to the dark walnuts and mahoganies of the previous era. However, these woods were still superlative for the making of furniture, which led perhaps to the greatest innovation of all, the light and bleached wood finishes. Up to this time furniture woods had almost always been stained before finishing to make them darker. Now they were left in their original color, bleached nearly white before the final finish was added. Mahogany, walnut, oak, birch, pine and the fruit woods all took on new shades under this treatment and in many of them the grain and beauty of the wood itself was more apparent than it had ever been. This light finish solved another problem, that of making an old piece of furniture fit in with the new style. A blond Sheraton secretary desk or an unfinished pine cupboard suddenly looked very well with modern furniture and added a tradition and mellowness which was sometimes lost in a completely modern room. Today many manufacturers of period furniture finish them in both light and dark colors. Modern furniture makers also experimented with other finishes like pickling, frosting and lacquering, which describe themselves in their very names.

Glass became very important for table tops, especially for coffee and cocktail tables, for it was practical, as well as easy to keep clean and prevented many of the new very large tables from looking too heavy and cumbersome. Clear and smoked mirrored glass was used like veneering to face entire pieces or on screens.

When you start looking at actual pieces of modern furniture, you may be surprised to find that the prices can run the complete gamut from the very expensive to a figure within the reach of everybody. Quality and price, in this field as in most others, have a direct bearing on each other, but on the whole the less expensive modern furniture will be of better wood and better made than inexpensive furniture with machine carving and tawdry decoration. A superior modern piece will be beautifully tenoned, hand fitted and finished, while a less expensive piece is an assembly-line product, resorting to glue and screws. However, the simplicity of design and new methods of finishing give the second piece more of a chance than it used to have. The alcohol , burn- and water-proof finishes are easily applied to either class, but there is still no substitute for fine designing. The good designer envisions his work executed in small quantities with the greatest of care to an extent which is often impossible or impractical for mass production.

There are hundreds, or perhaps thousands, of good designers today of almost every nationality, working in their own countries and here. A few believe firmly in certain fundamentals and their style is almost as definite and recognizable as that of a well-known painter. Others experiment with various ideas, construction and media, seeking beauty, pure art, or an ideal. Still others serve the strictly practical-minded household. It is difficult to believe that any one or two names will finally be used to designate this furniture when it can no longer be called "modern," and fun to speculate on what it will be called. A few names are attached to our illustrations—all good designers—representatives of a profession which has reached the status of fine art. There might be a hundred others we would also like to include.

Although the modern artist is apt to put "being different" above everything else, occasionally he will try, often quite successfully, to see what would happen if he were to apply modern ideas to some of the earlier designs in furniture. The chair on page 47 is one example, but you will also see definitely modern furniture with traces of Empire, Sheraton, or Chippendale. The Chinese influence which appears in various forms in every period is also important to moderns. It is often more than an influence, for some of the most striking modern pieces are pure copies of eleventh and twelfth century Chinese prototypes. This emphasizes once more the tremendous advantage we all have in our museums, libraries, ease of transportation and communication. The opportunities for observation and inspiration today are limitless. The wonder is that a designer can ever produce something original.

If the moderns have drawn somewhat on the past, they have also contributed some very definite things to it. Their chief competitor for popularity is the reproduction of period furniture and another combination style, known as "contemporary." The latter is composed mostly of present-day designs which are not strictly modern, such as the Lawson sofa, the Cogswell chair, and the breakfront desk, but it also includes reproductions of earlier styles which have adopted some modern notions. Thus, a sectional sofa may be essentially Chippendale in design, a Phyfe base is used on an oversize coffee table with a glass top, or twin beds with a single headboard may be of mahogany, inlaid with satinwood in the manner of Hepplewhite.

Whether the discovery of the sunshine Vitamin D or a new love of informality and out-of-door living came first is hard to determine. In either case, the old splint rockers, hickory porch chairs, and sun-porch wicker seem unimaginative compared to what is now available for a maximum of charm and comfort for this kind of living.

Cast-iron and aluminum, rattan, peel, fibre, glass, redwood, pine, cedar, Formica, plastics, string and canvas are used and combined to give us a wide variety of furniture for all sorts of purposes. The designs have a definitely

This cast-iron bed with its attached night table is usable in almost any type of room, including period ones.

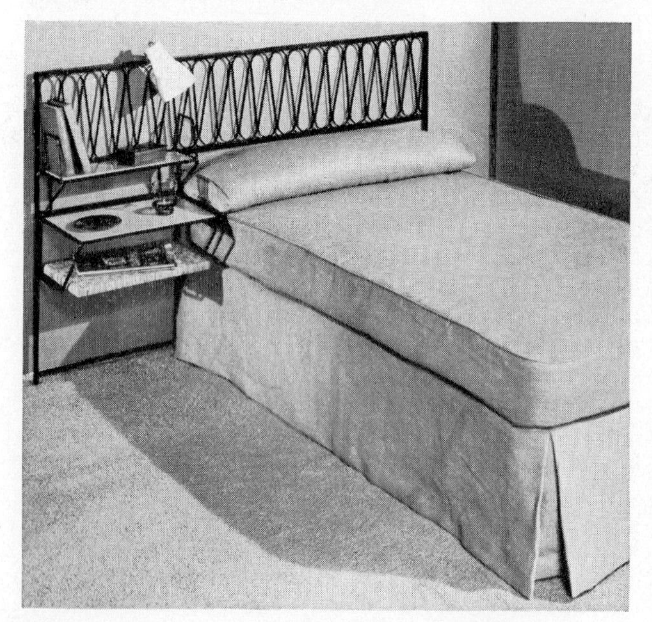

Cast-iron dining set serves equally well indoors or out. Light and graceful, it is strong and durable, too.

TEMPESTINI DESIGN—JOHN B. SALTERINI COMPANY

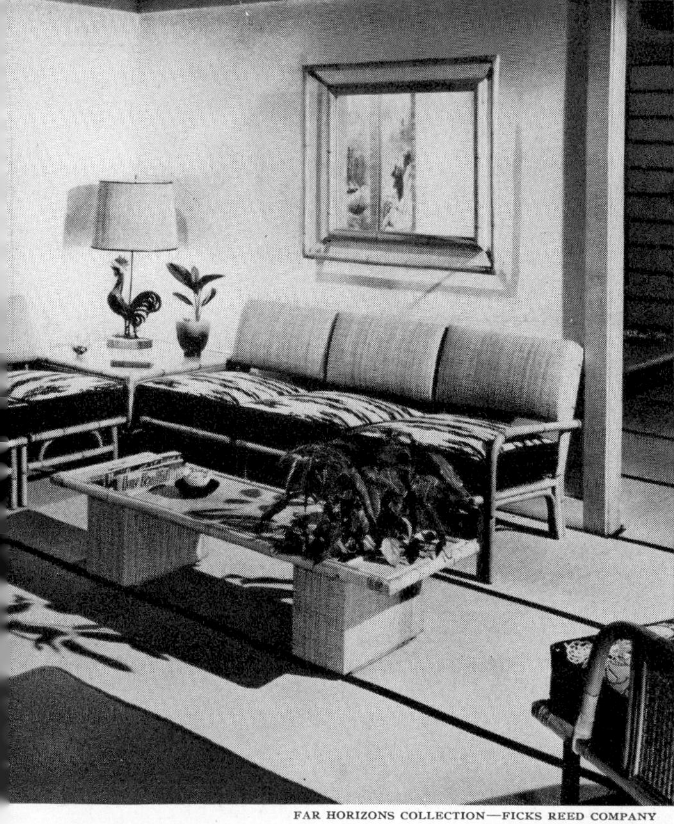

FAR HORIZONS COLLECTION—FICKS REED COMPANY

Rattan combined with woven cane is used most effectively on a sun porch or in an informal living room. The sectional pieces and corner table arrangement give maximum seating capacity in a small room.

TEMPESTINI DESIGN—JOHN B. SALTERINI COMPANY

Woven wicker and iron can be used on a covered porch or terrace successfully. These chairs are comfortable and easy to move around.

The cumbersome redwood furniture of the past has emerged with new trim lines. Here redwood is combined with iron for the uncovered terrace.

UTILITY CABINET COMPANY

For the lawn, modern methods have produced a rustproof electroplated metal group which is comfortable without cushions and can stay out the whole season.

JOHN B. SALTERINI COMPANY

modern trend, but actually have become a separate style, based on materials and practical usage.

Cast-iron pieces are used both for sun porches and terraces, but may also be smart in a bedroom or dining room. They are made in a variety of designs and available in colors from statuary bronze to flamingo or aquamist. Table tops are made of glass, chairs are cushioned. It is most practical for sun porches and covered terraces, but can be used in the open, if the cushions are covered or removed when not in use. It is particularly good for small areas, as it is not bulky and often is a happy solution to many decorating problems in providing color and variety. The bed illustrated on page 48 with its attached night table is very usable in almost any type of room, period rooms not excluded. The shelves forming the night table are detachable, providing room for a full-sized bed if preferred. The "ribbon candy" motif, which also appears in the dining set on the same page, might belong to any period, but the whole is unmistakably the product of a modern designer like Maurizio Tempestini.

Rattan furniture has gone almost completely modern with its sectional sofas, corner tables, trick dining tops, built-in planting trays and portable bars. This furniture is ideal for sun porches, cabanas, and very protected terraces, but not suitable for any but most informal indoor rooms, nor is it as flexible as the cast iron in usage. It has the advantage of being light in weight and achieves something of a built-in look around the edges of a sun porch. It can be very simple like the pieces illustrated on page 49, or quite elaborate. Many people prefer it for sun porches because the rattan or bamboo effect seems more comfortable and warmer than metal furniture.

Moving out of doors, however, to the covered terrace, there is some hazard from weather, and neither the rattan nor the cast iron with their necessary cushions is feasible without a lot of trouble. This is where a combination of iron and wicker, or electroplated metal is essential. The barbecue terrace with wicker and iron chairs, illustrated on page 49, is charming and practical, as well as comfortable. Here again are chairs which might be used elsewhere in other rooms in the informal house.

Moving out of doors to the uncovered terrace, we find that redwood, long a popular all-weather wood, has been combined with iron to give a modern effect. As shown on page 49, it looks suitable for the most formal terrace or the children's picnic lunch. Only the cushions, which are not essential, need make the householder beware of sudden rain.

There are, however, some pieces of furniture in the modern field, that are really stay-outs in all kinds of weather. First come the rough woods, unfinished or painted, which will last several seasons, but eventually will warp, rust at the nail holes, or rot. More lasting and comfortable are the painted or, better still, electroplated metals woven in a mesh which has considerable flexibility and acts like a cushion. These are surprisingly comfortable and present no housekeeping problem or worry about weather.

FOREIGN INFLUENCES

In directing our attention to making a choice in decorating, from the point of view of what is practical, available, and feasible, we have been interested chiefly in the most popular styles with emphasis on the American tradition.

There are several others which we should know about, and a few that merit at least a bowing acquaintance. The most important of these is French Provincial. You will see it in city apartments, country houses, and in some types of business offices as the perfect solution for those who want something light and informal, but definitely not modern. Most of what we see is copied or adapted by present-day manufacturers and might almost come under the heading of "contemporary," except that it has a definite period prototype and inspiration.

This came, as the name implies, from the French provinces. In the late eighteenth century, when the French court was formally devoted to the elaborate designs typical of the reigns of Louis XIV and Louis XV, this much simpler style was growing up. Marie Antoinette, with her playing at "country life," was partly responsible for its popularity, but the backbone of the movement came from the country people.

Craftsmen in the provinces took the woods at hand, mostly fruit woods and walnut, and worked out simple pieces in imitation of the fashionable rococo of the period. The cabriole leg was used universally with some scroll, carved, or molded decoration. All sorts of scalloped edges were used for shelves, and as aprons on tables and cupboards. The backs and seats of chairs were often caned, with separate, tied-on cushions. Beds were sometimes all of wood, but more often had upholstered headboards. The pieces varied greatly from the open-shelved, rather crude cupboards which the country artisan made for his own use, to the very sophisticated and decorated poudreux with a disappearing mirror, and the handsome escritoires made by an expert cabinetmaker for the nobility.

Two other styles almost contemporary with the Federal or early Republic in this country and inspired by the same classical sources are the French Empire and English Regency. Both are formal, usually of mahogany, and rely on simplicity of line and fine workmanship for their beauty. The side chairs of the French Empire are reminiscent of those of Duncan Phyfe, in our minds. Tables were often round and had a metal pierced-work gallery around the top. One particular piece of furniture which comes to us from this period is the Madame Récamier sofa

BRUNOVAN, INCORPORATED—PHOTOGRAPH BY DEMAREST

A love seat in the French-Provincial manner can be used in a formal room. The upholstery and fabric give it sophistication. The mahogany table with its brass gallery is Directoire.

which was popular in her day, but immortalized, if that is not too strong a word for a sofa, in the portrait of her by Louis David.

The English Regency seems to have been a period of exaggeration and flamboyance. You will find elements of Sheraton, classic pillars, wide inlays of satinwood or rosewood, much attention to grillework and hardware, and a combination of straight lines and curves, carved griffins and lions' heads, which foretell the Victorian furniture to follow.

We might also group together two widely different types and dates of furniture because of the similarity of the character of the people who developed them. First, the Pennsylvania Dutch, who took many of the simple country styles of all kinds of furniture, painted them in bright colors and added stencils of hearts, tulips, plants and conventionalized designs to produce a style of their own, characterizing the warmth, simplicity and cheerfulness of their way of life.

In the early nineteenth century the Germans took a look at the French Empire style and adapted some of the pieces to make a much more durable, sturdier type of furniture. Like the Pennsylvania Dutch, they were interested in depicting the simple charms of everyday life and to this end inlaid small figures of animals, garden flowers and children as their decorative motifs. This furniture, called Biedermeier, a name which personified the average kindly family man, was usually made of light woods, carefully inlaid with darker ones.

In choosing a style of furniture today, we combine most of the influences which developed different styles, except that we have much more to choose from, and we know that a judicious mixing of styles based on appreciation of line and knowledge of historical background will make for success in achieving our decorating goal.

To simplify the study of style in line, wood and treatment, our attention has been turned exclusively to uncovered furniture which emphasizes the outstanding characteristics of each period. In these we find our best clues, but we certainly cannot ignore the upholstered furniture which really plays a more prominent part in a completed room. The emphasis on these pieces is necessarily on the fabric and the lines developed by the upholsterer. On page 53 we get a quick look at typical chairs, upholstered in the simplest manner, and note how easily they make the change from one tradition to another.

BRUNOVAN, INCORPORATED—PHOTOGRAPH BY DEMAREST

This cupboard suggests the work of a provincial maker, except for the grille work. The chair with its upholstered seat and carving suggests a more skilled maker. Contemporary.

The delicate Queen Anne "occasional" chair has duck feet and goes well with even the earliest Pilgrim furniture which really gives us nothing in a comfortable chair for today's home. The two large open armchairs belong to entirely different periods. One has the straight legs and stretchers of one type of Chippendale, the other has the slim delicate lines and reeded legs which we associate with Hepplewhite. Correctly used or not, "Martha Washington" is the popular name for such tall-back chairs. The wing chair has the ball-and-claw foot and cabriole leg beloved by Chippendale, but there are as many sizes, shapes and styles of wing chairs as there are of people.

The first of the modern chairs seems to be an interpretation of period prototypes, but the second one incorporates an entirely new conception in line and technique for an upholstered chair.

As we continue with a study of fabrics, upholstery methods, room planning, we will find many variations of these chairs and several other types.

THE WEIMAN COMPANY

Wide satinwood edges, lyre-shaped pedestal, beautiful workmanship, characterize this as a Regency table.

This painted chair, with its large one arm that serves as a book rest or for writing a note, is the forerunner of the comb-back rocker of the Victorian era. It is from Malvern Hill in Kentucky.

Center fluted columns, brass gallery around each tier in this tier table are typical of French Empire workmanship.

BRUNOVAN, INCORPORATED

METROPOLITAN MUSEUM OF ART

METROPOLITAN MUSEUM OF ART

METROPOLITAN MUSEUM OF ART

A Chippendale chair that is simply upholstered, with straight legs and stretchers.

The Queen Anne "occasional" chair has duck feet and goes well with even the earliest Pilgrim furniture.

The wing chair, above right, has the ball-and-claw foot and cabriole leg beloved by Chippendale.

METROPOLITAN MUSEUM OF ART

This chair, right, has the slim delicate lines and reeded legs we associate with Hepplewhite. Correctly used or not, "Martha Washington" is the popular name for such tall-back chairs.

This Modern plastic shell represents a completely new technique in upholstered furniture.

However, this Modern suspension chair incorporates an entirely new conception in line and technique for an upholstered chair.

EERO SAARINAN, DESIGNER—KNOLL ASSOCIATES

FRANCO ALBINI, DESIGNER—KNOLL ASSOCIATES

This contemporary living room personifies a "warm" color scheme. Three quarters of the picture window is covered with a no-iron, over-all printed sheer, a cotton-and-Dacron mixture. The sofa is covered in red denim with pillow accents of gray and brilliant green. Color fan shows the inexpensive, sturdy material used in the photograph. Predominant colors are taken from David Porter's flower painting.

Textiles

Fundamentals to Decorating

The real fun in decorating begins with textiles. Here is our greatest chance to express every whim and dream and add our own touch of color and taste to our creations. All of us would like to occupy ourselves sometime with woofs and warps, aniline dyes, block printing and hand screening. We would like to know what process makes brocade different from cut velvet, but actually our first and final interest is in knowing how to make a selection for a definite purpose from the thousands of materials we find on the market today.

There is a great tendency at present to cut across traditional lines in choosing fabrics and consider them from the point of view of color and effect, rather than of period. Thus, what is getting to be a rather stuffy Victorian room may have its spirits lifted considerably by using a gay cotton taffeta plaid on the sofa or love seat. Perhaps a review of the traditions in fabric will help us to decide when to be conservative and when to take advantage of some of the newer ideas in fabrics.

For this purpose, it seems only practical to put aside at least the old names of fabrics and adapt this study to the wealth of materials available to us today, noting which are exactly like the old ones and which give a similar effect but have very dissimilar names. For example, brocade, brocatelle, velvet, damask, taffeta, chintz, gauze and linen have changed only in method of manufacture and increased color range. Fustian, paduasoy, perpetuana, sarcenet, bourette and lutestring, if not impossible to identify, are certainly not found under those names today, but antique satin, faille, cretonne, textures, organdy and matelassé are available in every good fabric house and known to everybody. We must also consider Nylon, Orlon, rayon and Fiberglas, for many of these synthetic fabrics are woven to resemble closely in appearance the old fabrics and are much more practical for our use.

Textiles can be divided into periods almost as definitely as architecture and furniture. Their use and type was determined by the same influences of economic conditions, inventions, and contemporary events, but new ones were added to the collection without being replacements for older ones. Today we can choose from the whole range of weaves and designs that have been developed for centuries, which makes our first consideration one of suitability in period and use.

As you may well imagine, the Pilgrims were more concerned with being warmly dressed than they were with decorative fabrics, though even the earliest colonial records show that they had small bits of cherished velvet and damask or turkey work. For instance, in the will of Major General Edward Gibbon, a Boston merchant, who died in 1654, we find thirty-one cushions—four damask, four velvet, two leather and one turkey work. The other cushions were probably of wool, for in the seventeenth century wool was the most popular and available material spun, woven and dyed at home. It has been the least popular with us because of the difficulty of cleaning and danger from moths. However, with new mothproofing and cleaning processes it may come back into vogue, as it hangs softly, takes beautiful colors in dyeing and seems to belong with pine and maple furniture. However, there are some rayons, nylons and textured cottons being made now which give very much the appearance of the homespun wools of our forebears.

For their fine silk fabrics and painted and printed cottons and linens, the colonists relied on Europe and the Far East. Most of the velvets and silks came from Italy and France; the cottons and linens from England and France or directly from India. The French were largely responsible for the development of printed fabrics which we have carried on and made our own today. The first painted "veils" or "palampores" from which this industry was developed came from India and were mostly made in one large sheet with a Tree of Life design covering the whole piece. These were used as wall hangings and cut up into bed and window curtains regardless of the large pattern. As early as 1683 there is an order from the East India Company to their agent for "100 suits of painted curtains and vallances ready made up of several sorts and prices, strong, but none to deare, nor any over mean in regard." Added to this order was the comment, "You know that only the poorest people in England lie without any curtains or vallances and our richest in damask."

These painted pieces were imported into Europe at the same time in large quantities and very soon the European craftsmen began to imitate them, at first by painting and later by printing from blocks. The French, in particular, quickly developed some ideas of their own and found they could produce continuous patterns with smaller repeats that could be run off in indefinite yardages, rather than being limited to one large piece. The first patterns were taken from the Far Eastern designs and included every variety of pinks, chrysanthemums, pomegranates, peonies, lilies—all done in an all-over design connected with branches and stems, as illustrated below. Pinks, and carnations, which belong to the pink family, predominated and gradually were isolated in small spotted designs or interspersed with delicate stripes. These were used through most of the eighteenth century in competition with the silks and brocades and were extremely fashionable even at Court. Another type of design was growing up at the same time, and although it was produced by many different factories in many parts of France, the master of them all was Oberkampf who had a factory just outside of Paris at Jouy. Oberkampf produced many floral prints, but the scenics, especially those designed by Jean Baptiste Huet became so famous that today the name, Toile de Jouy, is applied to most printed cottons and linens done in a scenic design. The scenes were of contemporary pastoral life and each design had a name like The Four Seasons, The Pleasures of Farming, The Four Parts of the World, or celebrated an event such as the first balloon ascension, or the Feast of the Federation. Some were made, especially in England, for the American market and lost nothing of their charm or characteristics in depicting Washington riding with Liberty in a chariot drawn by two leopards and

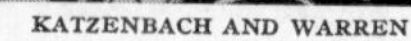

KATZENBACH AND WARREN

METROPOLITAN MUSEUM OF ART

Above is a red and white English cotton print showing George Washington and Benjamin Franklin. The typical exotic floral design at left imitates the early India painted fabrics and is a copy of an old paper used in the Williamsburg restoration. The page opposite shows the agreeable use of "Toile de Jouy" on the French Provincial chairs and cupboard doors.

escorted by Indians with trumpets. Elsewhere on the same piece is Benjamin Franklin walking with France. Each figure has hold of one end of a ribbon bearing the inscription, "Where Liberty Dwells there is my Country." There were several others, as well as some illustrating the well-known stories of Paul and Virginia, and the Miller, His Son and the Donkey.

With the invention of the copper engraved roller for printing fabrics, the pattern repeats became smaller and a new type of design appeared. The subjects were much the same, but instead of undefined groups, each scene was outlined or placed in a cartouche. The designs were much smaller and quite often placed on a latticed or diapered background. By the beginning of the nineteenth century just as architecture and furniture took a definite turn toward the classical, the fabric designers began introducing classical figures in their designs and views of cities like Rome and Paris. At this period the new patterns in both brocades and printed fabrics also turned to wreaths like those of the brocade on the sofa on page 20,

METAL BY TEMPESTINI. JOHN B. SALTERINI COMPANY

Contemporary American

A strong-patterned fabric with a definite personality will bring charm and unity to the most mixed-up collection of furniture. It can provide a color scheme and determine the predominating style. The fabric in a room carries a great part of the responsibility for success in achieving your goal in decorating. You cannot take too much care in selecting a good one.

to snowflakes, small medallions, and evenly spaced stripes of all kinds. The multiple stripe of uneven widths which is very popular at present is a comparatively recent development.

The Victorians made the rose, which had appeared in small and very restrained versions in earlier fabrics, into the most important flower of all. The curtains of the living room on pages 58-59 are a mild suggestion of the large red, pink, and yellow cabbage roses that predominated in the last century. Gradually narcissus, lilacs, lily of the valley, tiger lilies, morning-glory, and all the garden flowers were used for designs until now you can find a fabric with almost any favorite flower as well as specimens that few of us could name.

With the beginning of the eighteenth century, these fabrics continue, but the more sophisticated furniture calls for something more formal, until with the Chippendale era, silk damask in rather large designs, velvet and tooled leather become important. The printed fabrics of this period are bold in design also and tend to follow the arabesques and rococo carving of the furniture and mantelpieces of the same period. The use of Chinoiserie, or designs of Chinese influence, is particularly charming, and little pagodas, Chinese figures, and flora appear everywhere in both brocades and printed patterns. As most of the fine fabrics were imported from France, we find also pure Louis XIV and XV patterns of festoons and garlands of flowers, cupids, tiny roses and combinations of flowers and stripes.

After the American Revolution, with the rise in popularity of Sheraton and Hepplewhite furniture, elegant simplicity was sought in beautiful formal fabrics in plain colors, very narrow stripes, rosettes, medallions and urns. The scenic prints, all called Toile de Jouy now, were often used in semiformal and informal rooms to line the walls, cover the furniture and decorate the windows. In this same period small floral patterns in tight little sprigs dotted over a plain or pinpointed background and feather plumes, like the Prince of Wales feathers carved on the chairs, appeared as motifs in woven and printed fabrics.

The revival of interest in classical subjects opened a whole new field for fabrics designers, for their medium was far less limited than those of the architects and cabinetmakers. Classic ruins replaced the cottages of the earlier scenics and figures from mythology were widely used. The traditional victor's wreaths of laurel and bay appeared in designs from two inches in diameter to twice life size. All sorts of evenly spaced medallions of foliage and conventionalized designs were introduced. Wider and more definite stripes in two colors and self-woven patterns in stripes, fishnet and diamond patterns were in vogue. Satin, brocade, damask and taffeta were favored for the drawing room, but the same designs on cotton and linen were made for less formal rooms.

The Victorians loved velvet and all the pile fabrics, especially plush, corduroy and frieze. Satin was next in importance and the black, plain and figured, horsehair which we always associate with that era. In printed fabrics the

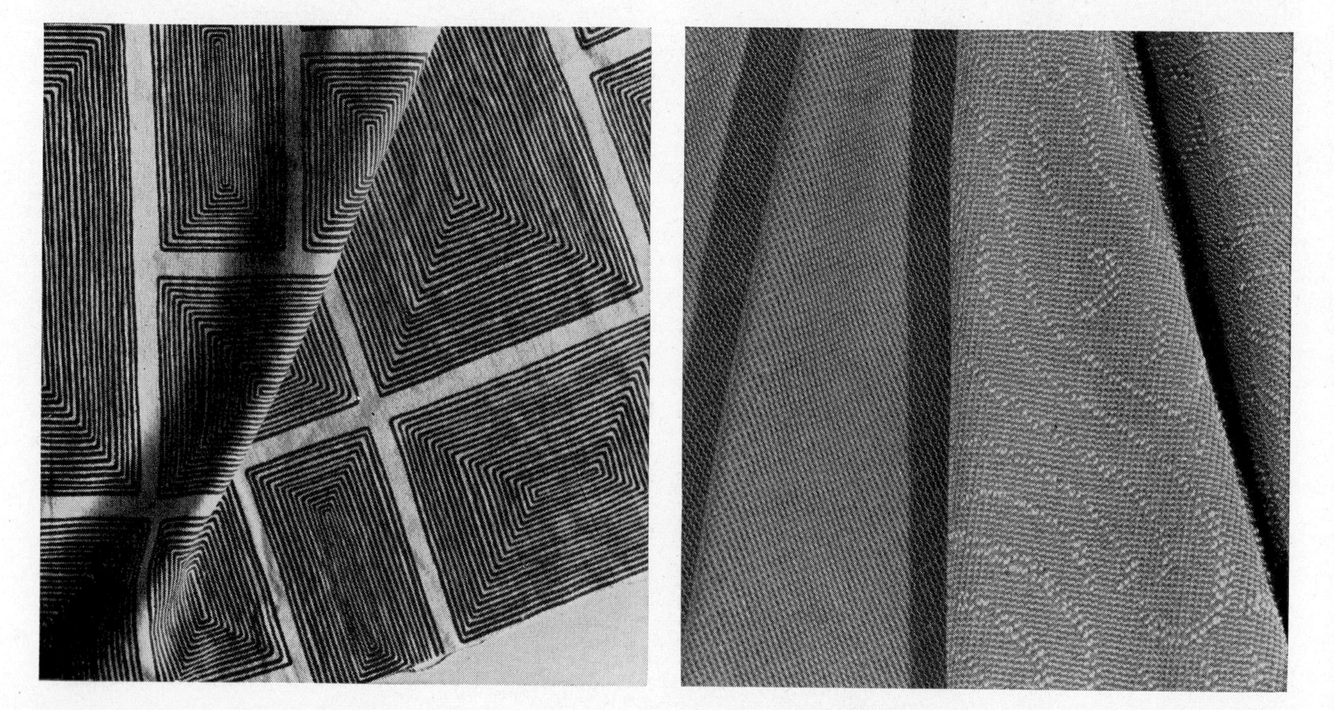

patterns were heavy, with roses and other garden flowers predominating as a matter of course.

From the time of the perfecting of the Arkwright power loom for weaving in the latter part of the eighteenth century, the growth of the textile industry in this country was phenomenal. Up to that time all textiles were woven by hand, which made them expensive and comparatively scarce. With the wide use of machinery at home and greater speed of importing European fabrics, the supply and variety increased rapidly and frequent replacements became possible.

Today our manufacturers are making almost all of the old materials in the tradition that has come down to us from earliest times, like the linens as fine as those found in the Egyptian tombs, and silks and velvets beautiful as the best from Lyons in France and Genoa in Italy. Old patterns for printed linens and cottons are being unearthed daily to be reproduced and adapted to go with old and contemporary furniture. In addition to all of these there are two entirely new groups of textiles.

The first of these are design fabrics made in weaves we have known for hundreds of years, but with subjects drawn from every phase of modern life. Ships, airplanes, horses, maps, bits of newspaper or magazines, birds, ivy, fruit and vegetables, houses and buildings, buttons, bones, carriages, cars, bottles, jelly molds, trains and elephants are but a few proper subjects for fabric design today. In addition to these, there are hundreds of geometric, asymmetrical and abstract designs to go into modern interiors of which the two illustrated are a conservative indication. The moderns have also incorporated modern designs into damasks and other materials, but have usually changed the weave a little, using a rough thread which produces a nubby effect. In plain materials and even in some of the prints this nubby effect is very popular. It belongs to a whole group of fabrics, called textures, which are almost universally used on and with modern furniture.

The textured effect varies from a short irregular tiny roughness like that in a dull antique satin or ratiné to lumps as large as garden peas in heavier materials. Some of the textures are quite smooth, but of a heavy warp and woof that resembles homespun, and others quite elegant with long loops pulled out and cut like fringe all over the fabric. Many of the textured weaves have a gold thread all through them. This tarnishproof thread made of metal foil laminated between layers of cellophane gives a bright tinsel effect which we see again in some of the bright gold paint of the printed cottons.

The second new group of fabrics is entirely new because its members are all made from threads developed in the chemical laboratory. Rayon, which came on the market as early as 1911, was the first important artificial fabric and still holds its own for many purposes on a par with cotton and silk. Each of the newer artificial materials has been designed to have certain improvements over its predecessors, or was developed for special uses, not only in decoration but also for clothing, industry and medicine. Nylon, Dacron, Dynel, and Orlon are the best known in general use today with many newer ones still in the experimental stages. Without going into charts of tensile strength, chemical properties and manufacturing methods, these materials interest us from a decorating point of view because of special advantages that they offer both in appearance and in making the care of them easier and surer. For instance, nylon, Orlon, and Dynel are unsurpassed for glass curtains of all types as they are dirt- and moisture-resistant. Their tendency to return to their original shape after washing or cleaning has almost eliminated the problem of stretching and ironing. The synthetic yarns will go a long way to reviving the vogue for fine casements, organdy, and taffeta glass curtains which add so much charm and privacy to a room, but until this new development were too much trouble when there were so many other things to do in a household.

Man-made fibers are also woven into excellent upholstery fabrics—velvets, textures, friezes, damasks, and antique satins which are dirt- and moisture-resistant. What might have been a fatal accident of spilling on natural fabrics may often be quickly sponged off a synthetic material, and moths will not harm them. However, there are many factors which influence our choice and we simply add these materials to the wealth of possibilities at our disposal.

Leather, though it is not a fabric, is used chiefly for upholstery and table tops and therefore is grouped in our minds with materials. As a matter of fact, it is probably the earliest upholstery covering known and has been used widely in both the simplest and most elegant houses since chairs had any coverings at all. Leather may be the hide of any animal which has been stripped of the fur and tanned. However, most of our leather-covered furniture is done in cowhide, which comes in three grades, made by slicing the tanned hide into three separate layers. The best is the top grain, which is quite tough and shows the tiny marks left by the hairs. This takes a hard finish and wears very well. The next layer, called the deep butt, is softer, but flexible and good when a dull chamois finish is desired. The layer nearest the flesh is called the split. It is rough and inclined to be stiff, and will not wear as well as the other two.

Leathers are purchased by the square foot, or by the hide, which will measure approximately fifty square feet. They can be dyed almost any color and finished with a high glaze, antiqued, lacquered or burnished. Almost all commercial leathers have some kind of finish which seals the pores and makes keeping them clean with a little soap and water the only care that is necessary.

Always popular for dining-room chairs and father's easy chair in the home, it now appears on the tops of many of our contemporary tables whether they are adaptations of Sheraton or Chippendale, and it is extremely popular for flat-topped desks, card tables and occasional chairs. It belongs exclusively to no period, as it was one of the products that could be grown at home and did not depend on importation.

Originally in imitation of leather, but actually a type of upholstery material in their own right, are the heavy plastics which resemble leather in outward appearance and are as easily cared for and practical in the house. They have most of the same uses as leather and for some purposes, like outdoor seat cushions, are better and much less expensive. However, each type should be tested before using it for a specific purpose. For instance, a heavy all-plastic covering will look well and give good wear on chair seats and smooth backs, but a chair which requires stitching, like a channel-back chair, will be inclined to tear along the stitching perforations. Some of the plastics are plastic on one side and woven cotton on the other, avoiding this difficulty and not tearing or cracking where there are folds or tufting in the upholstery. All these plastics, especially the last mentioned, are being developed rapidly in smooth finishes, graining to look like top-grain hide, and textured two-colored effects which resemble fabric. In fact, they deserve respect in their own right without any apology for not being leather.

All of this seems only a start in our thinking and information on textiles and materials, but a start is all we can get until we see and handle the actual fabrics. At least we have added to our fabric vocabulary, have some definite ideas of quality and content, and a working knowledge of design and period.

TRIMMINGS FOR TEXTILES

Closely allied to textiles are fringes, galloons, gimps, tassels, cords, and edgings of all types because they are made from the same basic materials and are mostly used with textiles, whether in draperies and curtains or to add decoration to upholstered pieces.

It would be as difficult to determine the date of the first use of trimming as to find out when the very first needle was made, but we have seen evidence of braids and fringe among the first pictorial representations of men. A riband of blue is mentioned in the Bible and certainly the halberds and horse armor of medieval times were accompanied by fringes and tassels with cords. All of this does not concern us from an interior-decorating point of view, except to remind us that trimmings were used from early times, because they not only enhanced the object but solved the problem of finishing the cut edge of anything, rather than leaving it to ravel or making a plain hem which did not seem enough, especially in the case of handsome fabrics.

Dating trimmings exactly for each period is mostly a matter of elegance and refinement characteristic of the furniture and carving of the time. This can be carried too far, however, as we often run across an old curtain made in the eighteenth century and find the original fringe of heavy silk on a light cotton printed fabric, or a velvet chair with an eight-inch cotton fringe around the base. Perhaps the best way to get at the subject is to consider what kinds of threads were at hand and most commonly used in each period and what was the degree of craftsmanship.

Any housewife could pull the woof or the warp threads on the edge of a piece of material to make a fringed edge, but it was soon apparent that this edge would keep raveling and must be fastened in some way. Knotting a few threads together made a tassel and from this simple beginning the whole range of elaborate tasseled fringes began. Woven tapes also made a good edging and it was immediately apparent that a fringe added to this tape and sewed on provided many more possibilities in the way of looped fringes, cut fringes, and heavy corded fringes. Also the weight could be varied, and a contrast in color and thread was possible. Once this experimentation started there was no end to what could be done. Simple fringes were homemade, especially in the early days in this country, but this was not always true, as we know from the advertisements in the Maryland Gazette toward the end of the eighteenth century, offering "Edging" and "Curtain fringes, lines and tassels." By the early days of the New Republic, wooden round and trumpet-shaped beads covered with silk became very popular and the Victorians found in fringes the perfect answer to their taste for embellishment on curtains, furniture, lambrequins, table covers and lampshades.

Contemporaneously, we have learned to use trimmings with taste and judgment in the style and mood of our decoration. A plain tailored curtain may be untrimmed, or acquire considerable sophistication with a contrasting galloon applied to the front edge and across the bottom. A fine damask curtain seems unfinished without an equally fine fringe, and a simple chintz or other printed cotton curtain takes on charm and importance when a well-chosen cotton fringe is added in contrast or to emphasize a predominant color in a room. Sometimes a fringe is used merely to soften the framing outline that curtains make to the outside view and again to add interest to a room that is a little dull or severe. Present-day manufacturers are producing all the fringes that have ever been used, developing new ones of the new threads, and offering hundreds of new ideas for improving your decorating by the judicious use of trimming.

An interesting use of textile is shown in the room above, with its gay, washable, flower-patterned chintz shades.

These plates issued by La Mesangère in Paris in the nineteenth century were for the use of designers. Festoons of these curtains were usually of colored silk with a two-colored silk fringe. Side curtains were white with white fringe.

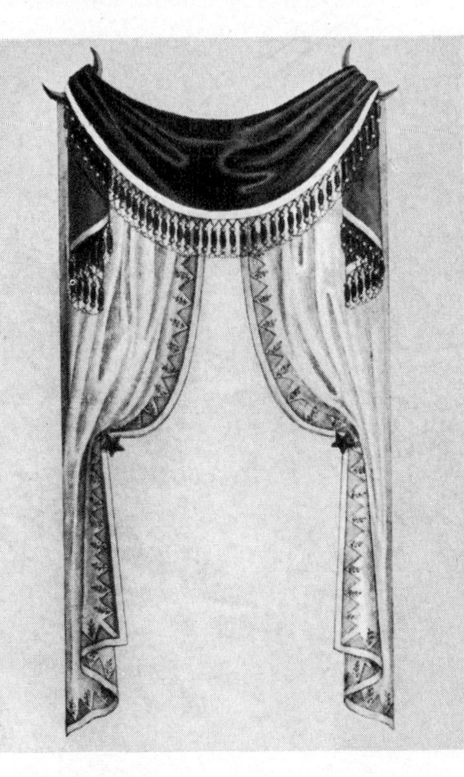

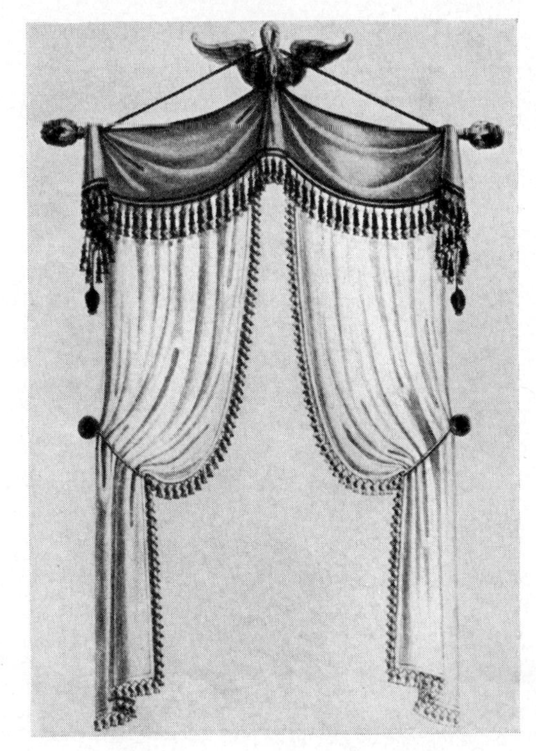

This colorful and dramatic wallpaper adds height to the room, forms an effective background for the fireplace arrangement, and shows what can be done with the adroit use of stripes on a wall surface. The use of so startling a wallpaper is not recommended for all four walls.

Charming louvered wallpaper, which camouflages a doorway, incidentally, is imaginatively used at the top of a stairway and adds unusual interest to an unexciting area.

DR. JOHN B. GOLDSBOROUGH

Wallpaper

Periods, Designs and Textures

In January, 1738, Thomas Hancock, uncle of John, the signer of the Declaration of Independence, was building his home. He wrote to his stationer in London, "Sir, Inclosed you have the dimensions of a Room for a Shaded Hanging to be Done after the Same Pattorn I have sent per Capt. Tanner who will deliver it to you. It's for my own House & Intreat the favour of you to Get it Done for me, to Come Early in the Spring or as Soon as the nature of the Thing will admitt. The pattorn is all was left of a Room Lately Come over here & it takes much in ye Town & will be the only paper-hanging for Sale here which am of Opinion may Answer well. Therefore desire you by all means to Get mine well Done & as Cheap as Possible, & if they can make it more Beautiful by adding more Birds flying here & there, with Some Landskip at the Bottom should Like it well.......In the other parts of these Hangings are Great Variety of Different Sorts of Birds, Peacocks, Macoys, Squirril, Monkys, Fruit, Flowers, etc......... I design if this pleases me to have two Rooms more done for myself. I Think they are handsomeer & Better than Painted hangings Done in Oyle, so I beg your particular Care in procuring this for me, & that the pattorns may be Taken Care off & Return'd with my Goods."

And so the story of wallpaper in America begins, as early as 1738, A Tree of Life design, similar to the one illustrated, brilliant in color and recalling the designs of the Indian veils on page 56.

A second great source of wallpapers in the eighteenth century was China, where the craftsmen were very fond of depicting scenes of Chinese life—the complete story of rice growing, or silk making, but sometimes, as in our illustration on page 66, content with typical Chinese scenery—red-roofed pagodas and the flowers and animals they knew so well.

By the end of the eighteenth century and even prior to the American Revolution we were making wallpapers in this country, as we see from an advertisement in the Pennsylvania Chronicle of 1768:

"To be sold by Plunket Fleeson, Upholsterer, at the corner of Fourth-street, in Chestnut-street, AMERICAN PAPER HANGINGS, Manufactured in Philadelphia, of all kinds and colours, not Inferior to those generally imported, and as low in price.....And as there is a considerable duty imposed on paper hangings imported here, it cannot be doubted, but that everyone among us, who wishes prosperity to America, will give preference to our own manufacture, especially on the above proposition, *of equally good and cheap.*"

These were undoubtedly as described in the advertisement of "all kinds and colours," following closely in each period the patterns of the textiles. We find bits of old wallpaper lining trunks and hatboxes, some still visible in old houses where they were hung originally, and still others come to light in restoration work, under one or more coats of paper of a later vintage. The patterns are simple, naïve, sophisticated or elegant, depending on the period in which they were made and the type of house in which they were used. Our manufacturers have taken full advantage of the hundreds of designs which have been authenticated as old, and have copied, reproduced and made many of them in a full range of colors. Papers of this type are called, like copies of old fabrics, "documents," a name that you will hear frequently in selecting wallpapers. Many documents have names—Hampton, Haverhill, Devonshire, Whistler—and others go by a descriptive title such as acorn

Modern designers have fashioned papers suitable for every room in the home from nursery to dining room. Typical Chinese wallpaper, above, used here in the middle of the eighteenth century, is appropriate in a period room both earlier and later in date. Left, a panel of English wallpaper of second quarter of the eighteenth century. Birds are cut out, pasted onto background of Tree of Life.

and oak leaf, shell, or ivy. There are flock papers made by putting glue on part of the design and sprinkling the paper with fine particles which adhere to the gluey parts of the pattern. This was a fairly early technique, but became exceedingly popular in the Victorian era. The various motifs that we found in the period textiles appeared on contemporary wallpapers, so that it becomes difficult to decide from a picture of a design whether it is a fabric or a wallpaper.

France was another great source of wallpapers in the eighteenth and nineteenth centuries and many of its papers have been found in this country from Boston to Virginia. The hunt-scene paper illustrated here was made by Jacquemart and Bénard in France and is easily dated by the early-nineteenth-century style of dress of the men and women. This is often a good clue in determining dates of old papers, as people appear much more often in wallpaper than they do on fabrics. However, lacking costumes for this purpose, you will have no trouble with Chinese flowers, pinks and carnations, cupids and wreaths, stripes and arrows, cabbage roses and lilacs. Each seems to fall into place naturally with the style of architecture and furniture to which it belongs.

New processes and ideas have brought us a wealth of new papers which are extremely versatile in creating special effects, and we have learned many new ways of using wallpaper in addition to simply choosing a paper we like and putting it on the four walls of a room. The first of these are papers which look like wood, and in many cases are made from wood patterns by a photographic process. Others suggest the charm of wood, but are intended only as a suggestion of a very pleasant texture, rather than an attempt to make a wall appear to be of sheathing. Other papers simulate the most beautiful of marbles and are used very successfully in many places. There is another paper which looks like a whitewashed brick wall and may be combined with rolls of the same paper with espaliered lemons or tomatoes.

Early-nineteenth-century hunt-scene paper made in France.

HAVERHILL PARLOR, METROPOLITAN MUSEUM OF ART

The modern designers have been very busy making textured papers which may have a depth of as much as an eighth of an inch and resemble grooved wood, matting, or rope squares. They have been occupied, too, with making designs to go with modern furniture and interiors, and like the fabric designers have introduced many new subjects and motifs into wallpapers to give us every kind of paper suitable for a nursery or kitchen, dining room or living room.

Often in period houses the walls of a room were covered with the same fabric that was used in the draperies. Now several firms have produced wallpaper and fabrics of the same design and color which create the same effect without the complication of the special frames for the wall hangings.

Chinese designs are still popular with almost any period and particularly with modern furniture. The paper illustrated on page 66 is an old one, but has many modern copies and adaptations.

Here we have a few suggestions of the types of papers available to us. Multiply those shown by a thousand and you will have an approximate idea of what you have to choose from in selecting wallpapers.

Wallpaper presents an endless variety of color, texture, style. Here you can have whitewashed brick, geometrics, freely flowing flower patterns, simulated reed or rattan. These are but a few of the thousands of ideas which have been expressed in the medium.

Cool

HAROLD FOWLER

Color effectively establishes mood, atmosphere. Notice the delightfully "cool" feeling achieved by the blue room; the "warm," friendly feeling embodied in the red-pink one.

Warm

HAROLD FOWLER. PORTRAIT BY CHARLES BASKERVILLE, COURTESY OF PORTRAITS, INC.

Color

Accent to Decoration

The soft blues and bright accent color have taken their cue from the beautifully framed Renoir print on the wall.

All the time we have been considering periods, styles and forms of architecture and furniture, and thinking about textiles, we have purposely avoided any discussion of color, even though we were entirely conscious that color was going to be a very important factor in every phase of decorating. The very first impression of a room is largely based on its colors and we realize immediately that colors are responsible for the personality and create the mood of the room, as well as telling us much about the designer.

Most of us love color just for itself and can get real enjoyment in just looking at colors we like without any consideration of how we could use them. In decorating, however, we find these colors, in addition to being beautiful, can magically change the very appearance of a room. For instance, a little observation will show that cool colors, that is, all those which are close to the blues on our color cone on page 72, seem to move away from us or recede. Thus we have a kind of paradox, in that a small room will look larger in a cool color, as the walls seem to recede from us; but a too large piece of furniture will look smaller when covered in a similar color, as it gets smaller when it appears farther away. The warm colors are red and yellow and carry their orange mixtures with them in warmth. These colors advance toward us. They will make a large room more intimate in bringing the walls in closer and will make a small piece of furniture seem larger and more important. The greens and purples, containing both cool and warm colors, are more or less neutral in changing the size of anything, except that as either approach their warm or cool component, they tend to take on some of its powers.

In addition to changing the appearance of the size, different colors can change the climate of a room. Yellows will brighten a dark room that has little light, yellows and reds and the colors between will make a north room warmer, a dull room gayer. Blues and all the variations of grey will make a warm room cooler, absorb some of the light in a very sunny room, and make a lively room calmer.

All of this applies to individual colors. When it comes to colors schemes, there is still more magic in color in the use of the complementary colors which are opposite each other on the circle of the color solid—red and green, blue and yellow, orange and purple, both at their full strength and again in proportion, as the various shades reach toward lighter and darker shades, or move toward black and white. The complementary colors, such as red and green, used in a room, will tend to intensify each other and increase the original brilliance of the pure color. Two strongly contrasting colors, such as yellow and red, will do the same thing, making for gaiety and liveliness. Shades of the same color will cut down the intensity of each. This accounts for our tendency to prefer neutral backgrounds, selected from an area close to the grey center of our color solid, with accents in complementary and contrasting hues. Color, then, like music, can be worked out logically within a definite framework, but the beauty comes from combinations inspired by taste and experience.

Some excerpts from advertisements that appeared in colonial newspapers just prior to the American Revolution indicate that the paints available were very like what we have today. "Fine Vermillion, French verdigrease, superfine ultra-marine, blue, white and red lead, yellow and red ochre, umber, and lamp black" appear over and over again. Until quite recently our own method was to start with a pail of white paint and add a bit of one color or another until we had the exact shade desired. Often, however, this was very frustrating as it was often difficult to determine what to add and suddenly the whole thing turned into a muddy unpleasant color. Now paint manufacturers are offering more and more ready-mixed colors so that we have to cope with this problem only if we enjoy working it out.

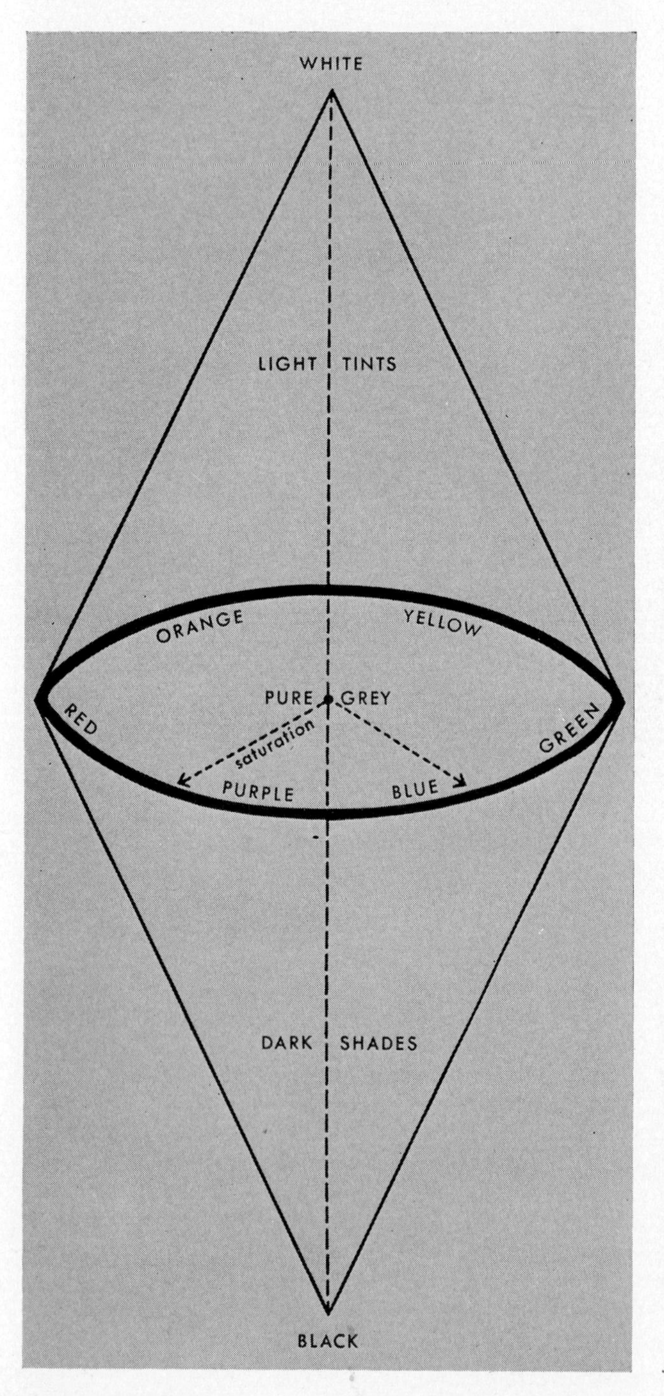

Always and *never* are words we cannot use in connection with color, as the sources were so varied, but in general there are some things that are quite certain and some trends in different periods which were quite consistent. Various shades of red, green, dull yellows, black, and the tans, blues and greys we associate with stone colors were used from the first settling in this country until the days just prior to the American Revolution. We have no difficulty in concurring with these authentic colors, as they still look so right with the maple and pine furniture of the same era. These colors continue through the Queen Anne and Chippendale eras, the reds becoming clearer and stronger and the yellows less muddy with beautiful soft shades of green and old gold.

After the Revolution with the daintier, more delicate styles of Sheraton and Hepplewhite, pastel shades gain in popularity and there is much more use of ivory, pearl grey, rose, light blue and green with the occasional appearance of a bright color or black as an accent. In the days of the young Republic with Duncan Phyfe, Empire and Regency furniture the pastels continue, but we find in addition a bright grass green, purples, deep blues and bluer reds which are still important in the Victorian period. On the whole, however, the latter, despite the flamboyance of their decoration, preferred browns and henna with muddy greens and yellows, mauve and purplish reds which we would scorn today.

Color Solid

A glance at the Color Solid, left, tells the whole story. It gives us the three primary colors: red, blue and yellow around the rim of the circle, and shows that red and blue will make purple, blue and yellow make green, and yellow and red make orange. We can also imagine the orange nearest the yellow on the curve will be lighter and yellower than the orange near the red, which will be more influenced by the red. This follows in the same degree with the greens moving toward yellow or blue and the purples going toward blue or red. Exactly on the circle edge are all the true hues of each color. As we move toward the center of the solid the colors are tempered with grey and as we move upward all colors become lighter and more brilliant. The opposite is true as we move toward the bottom black point where the shades become darker and have less brilliance. On a large enough color solid you could place, either on the surface or inside of it, every color and shade that your eye can see or your mind imagine, from turquoise to café au lait.

HAROLD FOWLER

Inspiration here comes from beautiful blues, greens, violets on white background of delphinium-print chintz. Color fan shows fabrics and colors for other room furnishings.

HAROLD FOWLER

This attractive rug is machine-made, braided, reversible.

HAROLD FOWLER

Floor Covering

Underlying All Decorating Plans

Strangely enough, though we go back to the cavemen for our first records of wall decoration, to thousands of years before the Christian Era for the first known use of dyes, and to the Egyptians and pre-Biblical days for weaving, the general use and comfort of floor coverings, especially in the Western world, are believed by experts to have been almost unknown before the sixteenth century. A few earlier examples have been found, but there is no doubt that there was no great demand until the greatly increased trade with the East developed a taste for this luxury, both in Europe and this country.

Certainly a Pilgrim housewife might put a piece of fabric on the floor, or even weave a rush or straw mat, but real rugs and carpets in this period all came from the Orient and were rare and expensive. Until the time of the American Revolution only the most elegant houses had rugs, and more often than not, they were used on tables and as wall hangings, if we are to judge by the contemporary paintings.

The finest handmade rugs and carpets, called Orientals, have always come from Asia Minor, Persia, India and China, and each is known by the name of the exact locality where it was made. A glance at a map of this part of the world shows these places and brings reality to what seemed always to be a confusion of romantic luxurious names. Kirman, Hamadan, Sarouk, Kashan and Shiraz in Persia; Bukhara and Samarkand in Turkistan; Agra and Kulah in India; and Ushak in Turkey are all perfectly familiar names, but to distinguish the special type of knots and designs, colors and materials used in each place and be able to recognize a rug of each name, is a matter for experts.

In general the finest Oriental rugs were made in Persia with India and China running strong competition, but the best known to us is probably the blue and red Ushak of Turkey.

Even the novice in the matter of Oriental, or in fact any type of carpeting, will find a few obvious factors by which he can determine quality. The first of these is the number of tufts or knots to the square inch which may vary from nine to four hundred. Few people would want to count the tufts on the back of a carpet especially when they run into the hundreds, but even a superficial glance would give an idea of the fineness of the weave. The average European- or American-made Oriental-type rug will not run more than sixteen to thirty tufts to the square inch. Observe also the length of the pile, the finish of the edges and ends and the amount of gloss, especially in a wool carpet. Wool itself has no gloss when dyed, but can be made to shine with glycerin and ironing. This will not harm the rug if carefully done, but it is usually done in conjunction with the use of acids to fade the colors into a semblance of age. The latter process unquestionably shortens the average life expectancy of an Oriental rug.

These Eastern floor coverings were made in both smooth and pile weaves, each tuft being knotted in by hand which together with the interlacing of the threads through the heavy web accounts for their great durability. Although the pile rugs have always been the most popular, it was the smooth or tapestry type which was most copied in Europe in the beginning. The French in particular took up this weave and developed the famous carpets of Aubusson, Gobelin and Beauvais. These soon became typically French in color and design, and patterns followed the styles of each period as it developed.

Handmade carpeting was and is still a luxury with the special charm of slight irregularities in weave and color which give it a special flavor, but with the impetus of carpetmaking machines, floor coverings have become a necessary comfort and are used with much more versatility.

Almost every day we hear the name of a new carpet and there have been many innovations in the last ten years, but the first of the machine-made carpets are still being made and serve as a starting point for all modern carpeting. The very first was Brussels carpet, made of wool-loop piles on a foundation of linen, jute, and cotton, reinforced with the extra wool of the pile not used in the pattern. The loops form a ribbed effect quite different from Wilton carpet which was made at about the same time, but became more

Light neutral floor covering, above, is used successfully in almost any kind of room. Royal Corday® carpet, left, adds charm to a room in the Colonial tradition. Below, this carved all-over leaf design blends beautifully with the Victorian era.

PHOTOS BY COURTESY OF BIGELOW RUGS AND CARPETS

popular because the loops were cut, giving a soft plushy finish with a pile about 3/16ths of an inch deep. In machine-made carpet the knots become points, but quality is still judged by the number of points to the square inch. A good Brussels carpet will have about 90 points to the square inch, and the first-grade Wilton between 95 and 128 points. Both of these types were comparatively expensive to make and much of the wool thread was buried in the weaving and did not show, which is uneconomic from the point of view of excessive use of yarn.

The latter drawback was overcome in the Axminster carpets, which more nearly approached the method of Oriental rugmaking, except that the tufts were drawn through, but not knotted. The number of tufts in a good Axminster should be about 45 to the square inch, but cheaper and better grades were made and in the very best the tufts were tied down at the base by an extra weft shot. The three aforementioned carpets were limited to the size of the loom in the width in which they could be produced, but a new type of Axminster called Chenille was soon developed which could be made in any width up to thirty-three feet. This carpeting is woven of chenille fur made by cutting a prepared woolen cloth into strips of from ½ to 1 inch wide, depending on the height of the pile desired. Thus it is usually chenille carpet that calls forth the description, "up to one's ankles in carpeting."

Occasionally you may run across Kidderminster or ingrain carpet, but these are seldom used or made today. In fact the first term that we hear the most often is broadloom, which means any kind of carpet that is woven on a loom larger than the 27 inches of the earlier periods. Today the standard carpet widths are 9, 12, and 18 feet, which avoids the many seams formerly necessary.

Fundamentally, most of our fine woven carpets are based on one or more of the old methods with variations in the twist of the yarn, the addition of rayon, cotton, and nylon as basic materials, and the introduction of modern designs. They go under a legion of trade names suggesting the style and pattern and use, and sometimes the quality and price. Mostly they are sold by the square yard, cut and bound to your room size or purpose, but there are also a number of custom-made carpets. These are dyed to match a color scheme.

Another material which is becoming increasingly popular and versatile for floor coverings is cotton. We are familiar with the rag rugs and braided mats of cotton, but today cotton has taken on considerable style. The long looped twisted cottons in a rainbow of color have found their way into living rooms, bedrooms and nurseries, but retain a certain informality. Now cotton is being used throughout the house even where formality is required, in a weave not unlike the best chenille with a thick cut pile. It is also used in a woven tweedy effect and in a hooked style of rug similar to the old hooked rugs of the previous century.

The story of carpeting today is actually endless, and only starts the whole subject of floor covering. For instance, what do we use on the floor of sun porches, terraces, informal modern rooms and for coolness in hot weather? The first thing that occurs to us, after cotton rugs, is the great variety of fiber and straw carpets and mats. From Japan we get rice-straw matting which is fairly thin and comes in a light natural color and also a heavier rush oval rug which is slightly more greenish in color and comes in sizes up to nine by twelve. Slightly more expensive, but more durable than either of these, are the one-foot squares of sisal fiber which come in many colors and can be sewn together in almost any checkerboard type of pattern though many prefer the coolness and calmness of using all the same color squares. There is also a variety of fiber rugs, most of which, like the straw and sisal ones, are reversible, and many of which make an adequate substitute for wool carpeting at comparatively small expense.

We still must cover our kitchen, bathroom, and vestibule floors. Here again is a wealth of material at our disposal and through it an opportunity to add beauty to rooms which are chiefly utilitarian, or were until the many new ideas and devices were brought out to change them into some of the pleasantest rooms in the house. Our first thought is of linoleum which is being made more practical and in better colors than ever with the added fillip of the possibility of a contrasting border or a design in the center. It wears almost too well, if you like a frequent change and the new finishes and waxes make it very easy to keep clean. However, to be right up to date, before purchasing linoleum, it may be well to look at asphalt and rubber tile squares, Linotile and cork tile. Not all of these can be installed under every condition of floor, but certainly among them you will find one you can use that will completely satisfy your desire to have something you will enjoy and at the same time meet your budget and structural conditions. Quality is important in selecting a kitchen floor covering, as it is basic, and becomes the actual floor of the room, getting a maximum of wear and cleaning.

Finally, on our background on floor coverings, we should consider that they not only lie under our feet, but are underlying in color, texture, quality, and durability in our decorating. With a few obvious exceptions our floor coverings represent our largest outlay in money and we live with them longer than anything except our best furniture. Whether they should be rug size, or wall to wall, what to put under them and how to care for them is a matter of practical planning which is the entire subject of the next section. Here we are thinking about what we would like to have on our floors.

Lighting

Essential in Decorating

The candle has provided light in American homes from the time of the first settlers to the present day and in spite of whale oil, kerosene, illuminating gas, and electricity, there probably never was and never will be a home without some candles in it, and consequently candleholders in styles to match every period and design from the plain wrought-iron spike to the most modern asymmetrical branched candlestick. No dissertation is needed on why we want artificial light or what it is made of, but it has two important aspects from a decorative point of view. Taking the candle for granted, even the most meticulous antiquarian is going to insist on electricity for most of his lighting needs. His problem and ours is how to adapt this essential to various periods and make our lighting a dramatic part of our decorating.

Since everyone has and uses candles somewhere in the house, and candlesticks are often used to make lamps and other electric fixtures, a little knowledge of period candlesticks should start us off. Not counting the candles that were wedged into bottles or set up on a saucer, there are as many styles and materials used for candlesticks as there are periods.

In almost every period wrought iron, brass, pewter, silver, pottery, glass and also wood were used with a few special media like ormolu, silver gilt, china and alabaster in special periods.

In an early American room with pine or maple furniture, the candlesticks and stands could be of black wrought iron, bright brass or pewter. Each would be simple and have the appearance of being handmade, with the function of holding the candle and catching the dripping tallow or wax being more important than the shape and turnings. There might also have been a few Betty lamps of iron, which consisted of a small black ladle-shaped bowl with a closed top, hung on the end of a jointed primitive handle. These usually contained a wick and burned oil of some kind. Firelight was probably the brightest and best light of the early days.

From Edward Winslow and Paul Revere to Tiffany and Georg Jensen, our American silversmiths have made beautiful silver candlesticks, both single and branched. The early ones had simple moldings and turnings like the early furniture. In the pre-Revolutionary period they became more elaborate and the classic designers of the late eighteenth century and early nineteenth found the fluted columns ending in a small urn to hold the candle or *repoussé* acanthus leaves, all well adapted to the silver candlestick. The Victorians went in for *repoussé* silver in an all-over pattern of roses, and again with a border or garland of roses on a simpler column and stand. Modern silver designers emphasize proportions and form with simple lines and little decoration.

Glass candlesticks appeared early in the eighteenth century, but probably reached their greatest vogue in the white and vaseline glass we call Sandwich. Of these perhaps the most charming were the sticks in which a grace-

Chelsea candlestick made in England just prior to the American Revolution.

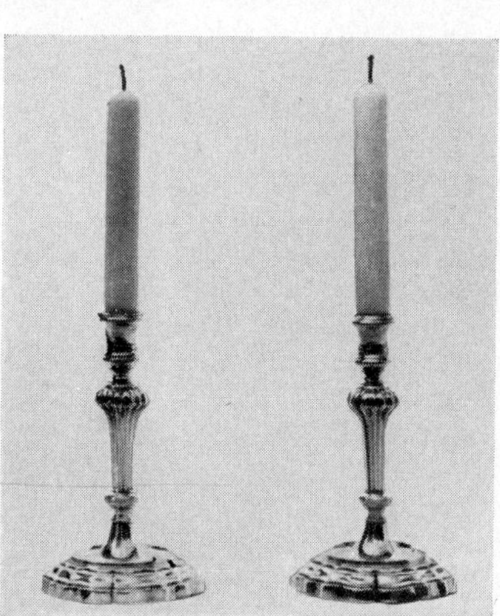

METROPOLITAN MUSEUM OF ART

Fine pair of silver candlesticks made by a famous American silversmith, Jacob Hurd, about 1740.

ful dolphin formed the column. The second important era in glass candlesticks was in crystal and cut glass which abounded in the last century. The bobêche, drip plate at the base of each candle, on the top of the stick, was usually decorated with hanging drops or prisms of glass, similar to those of the chandeliers.

Sheet iron and other metals were also used to make candlesticks which were painted or lacquered and decorated with designs, usually in gilt. These are the tolewares which we are more familiar with in trays and tea caddies, and are very popular today in making lamps and lamp shades.

The pottery, porcelain and china makers of almost every period included candleholders in their manufactures, and today we make good use of their products as well as others which were not primarily intended for lighting purposes. To choose well in the ceramic field is not difficult, because our choice depends more on color, size and suitability than it does on a careful study for historical accuracy. This is true partly because color, size, and degree of formality conform so well in each period, and partly because the various styles were repeated for long periods and the objects handed down from one generation to another.

The Chinese and Japanese have always been famous for their ceramics, and their wares were used in every period, no matter when they were made. This is as true of the time of Chippendale as it is of the most modern style of today. Staffordshire, Chelsea, Derby, Worcester, Spode, Wedgwood, Coalport, Bow, Sèvres, Limoges, Meissen are among the best-known names of European tablewares, but these factories also crowded the market with vases, statuettes, bowls, and boxes of every description all during the eighteenth century and continuing to the present day. Our most famous contribution to this type of fine ware is Lenox, though we also make many imitations of the famous old chinawares. Denmark, Italy, Spain, Czechoslovakia, Persia—in fact, almost every country in the world has been or is now famous for a particular style of ceramic. Primitive, informal, or highly decorative—there can be no difficulty in finding exactly what we want for perfection to dramatize or minimize a candlestick or lamp, if something from the field of ceramics seems indicated.

Another charming use of candles which persists today is in brackets attached to a mirror. The earliest example of this use of a reflector to multiply the light of a candle is in the small brackets attached to a shiny metal reflector, sometimes a simple piece of tin or sheet iron. However, the mirror made a much better reflector and candle brackets were attached to them quite often through the Queen Anne, Chippendale and Sheraton-Hepplewhite eras. However, this practice reached its height and was

METROPOLITAN MUSEUM OF ART

Above is an American-made girandole of gilt on pine with candle brackets and hurricane shades.

The hanging lantern, at top of the page opposite, is of amethyst-colored glass on bronze mount, made in America about 1810.

And directly below it is a bronze and cut-glass chandelier with Argand lamps used in this country circa 1815.

An old silver urn holds a colorful flower arrangement beside a matching silver lamp.

much more usual with the days of the early Republic, the Adam and bull's-eye round mirrors. Add a few hanging lusters or cut beads, as they often did, to reflect even more light, and a room "brilliantly illuminated with seven candles" as described by a colonial gentleman in Virginia, becomes more plausible to our eyes which have quite different standards of brilliance in the matter of light.

Except for their decorative quality, candlesticks are not really as important as this time and space would seem to indicate, except for the fact that with the invention and adaptation of electricity for lighting, we find standing and table lamps, wall brackets, and chandeliers, constantly using this form to carry wires, sockets, and bulbs. This is one of the answers to lighting a period room with electricity.

The overhead light was also important in the days of candles and we find the chandeliers following the styles and materials of the candlesticks in each period, but on a grander scale. The hanging lantern used in hallways and stair wells might carry from one to three candles and had to be protected with a windshield of some kind. The early ones were usually made of metal frames with small panes of glass forming boxes of various shapes, or quite often a tube of sheet iron was perforated in a design and used as a candle-flame protector, making little dancing points of light on the ceiling and walls. Another type of hanging lantern was developed in the eighteenth century which consisted of a base supporting a vase-shaped glass bowl which could be left clear or etched in the decorative designs of the period. The one illustrated at the top of this page is of amethyst-colored glass, others were etched with pastoral scenes, arabesques and, with the introduction of the star as a decorative motif after the Revolution, we find many etched all over with tiny stars. This same style of glass protection for the candle flame was used for wall brackets and sometimes on candlesticks—called hurricane shades, like the tall glass cylinders open at both ends which were used over a standing candlestick.

The first important chandeliers used in colonial times were of brass and carried from three to seven branches from a central stem. These were followed by glass and crystal and later by bronze with prisms. All of these varied considerably in size and quality—some having two tiers of arms with fine-cut lusters and chains of glass beads connecting the arms and forming an intricate pattern. There is a beautiful example of one of these in the colored illustration on page 43. These chandeliers, like the candlesticks, continued in use and were adapted to the degree of formality of each period. In the early days they were always hung quite low to give more light and facilitate the changing of candles. There are a number of incidents on record when ladies' headdresses caught fire from the lights in the chandelier.

We still use most of the old types, but wire them for electricity and use small flame-shaped bulbs with a hollow cardboard cylinder representing the candle. This simulation of a candle persisted among lighting fixtures through the period when oils were widely used, with illuminating gas, and is still common practice.

The term oil lamp brings to mind chiefly the old-fashioned kerosene glass and metal lamps complete with wick and glass chimney that are still to be found in daily use in many farmhouses. Actually the use of oil in lamps is as old as history, and many of our present-day lighting fixtures retain the oil reservoir as a matter of design, though it has no function whatever. In American decoration we have the early use of small metal Betty lamps which burned whale oil. The eighteenth century was almost entirely candlelit, but a new type of oil-burning light for lamps, chandeliers, and mantel lights called Argand lamps appeared at the turn of the nineteenth century. These lights had an urn-shaped container of glass or metal which held the oil which flowed down to wicks in the brackets. The chandelier illustrated on page 81 is a typical example with its added lusters and astral chimneys. Below are examples of the same type of lamp with two arms and a Wedgwood base. Others were entirely of metal and came in pairs for the mantelpiece, with the oil reservoir balancing a single arm.

From this period until the advent of gaslight we get a variety of lamps burning oil. One of the most popular types, which is to be found everywhere, is the all-glass small lamp, pressed, etched, clear, and in color, and ranging from the very heavy robust type to an extremely formal delicate style. Another quite formal type has a silver or metal column topped with a glass font for the oil and an astral shade. Finally in the full Victorian era

Argand lamps with cut-glass reservoirs, Wedgwood bases, and white-metal mounts, made in England early in the nineteenth century.

METROPOLITAN MUSEUM OF ART

This group of contemporary lamps offers great versatility. From left to right—strictly modern, modern walnut and brass, functional, bent glass for modern formality, informal with oil font, Provincial and colorful, and modern informal. Shades are always designed to go with the lamp on which they are to be used in the matter of style, color, texture, and material. Unlike flower arrangements, there is no rule as to the proportion of shade to height of lamp as you will note in the illustrations. In the case of a beautiful lamp important to your scheme, an opaque shade will emphasize the lamp, throwing light down upon it.

we come to the kerosene lamps of painted china with base and round ball-shaped globe to match over a glass chimney, and the well-known nickel or brass lamps with the green or white glass shades by which our grandparents did their homework.

There is not much to say about gaslight fixtures, except that they were mostly of metal with decorative shades of glass or china. The Welsbach mantle brings back quaint memories, but almost none of the fixtures and forms of the gas era are still in use with electricity and therefore they are only of academic interest to us in planning our lighting.

The development for practical household use of a new source of illumination seldom produced new vehicles for it at once. Older styles were changed and adapted to it, but gradually new designs were created, as new as the new illuminant. Fortunately the technical requirements for the use of electricity were easily adaptable to older styles of lighting fixtures and we can achieve the benefits of good lighting without sacrificing our period atmosphere. Actually many of the older styles designed for candles and oil are appropriate for all but the most modern settings and are still being made in large quantities. We have recognized contemporary furniture as a style which tends to recall various periods, but does not hesitate to adapt and change it in the light of more convenience, and new ideas. This is equally true of lighting, especially of lamps which can be and are made of practically anything from a piece of driftwood or a flower vase to a statuette or an old riding boot. The saying goes, "If you can't eat it or sit on it, you can make it into a lamp," but except for a whim or a temporary installation, most of us are happier with a certain amount of beauty and dignity in anything as permanent and important as our lighting fixtures.

With the advent of electricity fashions in lighting have followed very definite trends and offered infinite possibilities. For a number of years rooms were lit by a central ceiling light and permanent side brackets at strategic intervals around the walls. Later the side lights were eliminated in favor of more lamps which could be moved around the room and gave more direct light for reading, as well as being decorative. Soon the overhead center light was omitted entirely and lamps supplied the only light in many rooms, except for an occasional *torchère* which threw the light toward the ceiling.

Today lighting, more than almost anything else in the decorating field, has been subjected to a thorough scrutiny and consequent revision. We retain our lamps, but insist on directing their light upward, downward, out-

YOUNG MODERN GROUP, LIGHTOLIER, INCORPORATED

LIGHTOLIER, INCORPORATED

These modern lamps are supremely adjustable—they can be raised, lowered, moved from side to side, or remain put.

ward, or all three at once, depending on the need and effect desired. We are conscious of the relation of artificial light to eyesight and demand the maximum of comfort, convenience, and effectiveness.

Ideally we would like to have the same light in a room at night that we have in the daytime—not too much and not too little. To do this the light should be diffused where it is concentrated or the source hidden entirely. The first problem can be solved by the new plastic diffusers placed below the light bulbs and the perforated baffles which can be inserted above the bulb. There is no further need to be blinded physically or aesthetically by the glare of a naked light bulb.

The theater has taught us the value of concealed lighting which may be installed in a natural or false cove near the ceiling or be built into the curtain cornices. Either will give some general light in the room and contribute to a dramatic effect. From the same source we learn also the value of spot lighting, especially on a picture which need no longer be distorted by an inadequate bulb at the base, throwing a feeble light over the lower portion. A good spotlight is made as inconspicuous as possible with the light directed to bring out a definite point in the room without shining in the eyes.

Electricity can no longer be called a modern invention, but great strides have been made in recent years in improving our use of electric light. Modern lamps and fixtures, however, do not seem to draw their inspiration entirely from modern design, nor are they limited to use in modern interiors. There are many examples of heavy and light, formal and informal, sophisticated and countrified decorative effects. The effect is the final criterion in choosing our lighting fixtures, plus their capabilities to give us the light that is essential.

Attractive hanging light over table focuses light just where it is needed. Color ties in with the chairs.

This old Victorian tureen can double as a punch bowl. The repoussé box is silver on copper with some copper showing.

Accessories

Having Fun in Decorating

A colorful fruit bowl, a copper dish, a china horse, or an inlaid box are not essential to our living, but such things can provide true joy and give personality to our surroundings which the most carefully selected furniture, fine fabrics, and an excellent color scheme will never provide. These things are among our accessories and we choose them because we love them for themselves, or have a special association with them. Here is our chance to express our appreciation of great art in a tiny museum piece, or perhaps merely have fun in owning a simple ash tray of a favorite color or an unusual shape.

Whether we are indulging in a whim or solving a problem with our accessories there are a few points that should be considered. Like everything else in home decoration they fall into degrees of formality and informality, period and style, and the fashions in their use change rapidly. The Victorians had so many *bibelots* they had to provide special shelves for them. The present-day trend is toward an uncluttered look which has its influence on the selection and arrangement of all rooms of any period. This is sometimes achieved by a very few large objects, or a close grouping of smaller objects to form a single unit. This idea is carried out with pictures, too—grouping small pictures together instead of one on each wall like single postage stamps.

Certain accessories, such as fireplace equipment, mirrors, and ash trays, might be called necessary, but it would be a bare room indeed which did not boast a single unnecessary flower vase, statuette, or picture Statuettes in particular have lent their charm to every period of art and have been produced in every possible material including clay, pottery, glass, china, bronze, wood, marble, alabaster, and cast iron. Although examples of various degrees of artistic merit of all these are not uncommon, it was the great potters of the eighteenth century who made the greatest contribution toward this type of decoration for the home. In England figurines of famous people were made in a pottery called "black basalt" by Wedgwood, and by the factories at Staffordshire and Chelsea, using beautiful colors and glazes. The latter place, however, is more famous for its groups of birds and flowers, and later for the large English pug dogs we associate with the Victorian parlor. Delft cows, Sèvres shepherds and shepherdesses, Chinese figures of all sorts, whole orchestras of monkey musicians, busts of authors and philosophers—all were being made in this period and many of them are still being copied. Add to these the work of contemporary artists and that of modern designers and it becomes apparent that if your heart is set on an ornament of this type, you will have little difficulty in finding exactly the right one. In choosing consider the quality of workmanship and the general effect of crudeness or sophistication, color, line and above all your reason for wanting to have it.

Glass is another medium which has furnished us with many accessories and is particularly practical for ash trays and vases, as well as being very beautiful in itself. Museum pieces might include an ancient Egyptian blown-

A Ralph Wood 18th-century earthenware ram with lead glaze.

METROPOLITAN MUSEUM OF ART

Vases and candlestick from Meissen, Germany, about 1740.

Early glazed pottery shows a variety of shapes and colorings. The green jug used as a lamp is a rare Pennsylvania piece, initialed and dated 1808.

FROM THE COLLECTION OF GEORGE S. MC KEARIN. PHOTOGRAPH BY HAROLD FOWLER

glass bottle or a delicate vase of Venetian spun glass. We have heard of English and Irish glass and know that some of the best comes from Czechoslovakia and Sweden. The collectors of Early American glass—blown, moulded and pressed—are still numerous and we are all familiar with the shades of amethyst, amber, vaseline and blue in old pitchers, bottles, lamps, and bowls. Glass can be broken, but it never shows wear or age as furniture and even decorated china does. Hence the modern manufacturers have been able to copy nearly every fine period of glassware, actually no different from the old, except in tradition. The names we are most apt to encounter in glass are Waterford—an Irish cut glass used mainly in chandeliers; Lalique—named for a French designer, famous for his enamels and double layers of glass; Stiegel—various types of Early American glass of fine quality made at the factory of Henry William Stiegel in Manheim, Pennsylvania, in the eighteenth century; Sandwich—a pressed glass, popularized in the nineteenth century and still widely copied; Steuben—one of the finest of our modern glassmakers, examples of which are illustrated on page 90. There are many other old names and hundreds of modern factories making all kinds of glass to meet the increasing appreciation of its decorative possibilities in reflecting light and color, as well as the intrinsic beauty of the various objects, and the fact that glass is a highly practical and suitable material for many necessary objects.

Traditionally a fireplace has been the center of interest in every room of the house for many generations, but gradually, modern heating and building methods have pushed it into the place of a luxury for pure delight, reserved mostly for the living room, sitting room or den. Without the possibility of a fireplace, we have found many new ways of creating a center of interest, even resorting occasionally to a false fireplace where there is no chimney, but the special romance and warmth of an open fire with its accompanying iron firedogs or bright brass andirons is usually a part of everyone's dreams.

Fireplaces in the first American homes were necessary to family existence for heat, light and cooking and were often large enough, even in a tiny room, to burn most of a large tree trunk at one time. Actually it was more practical to build two or three smaller fires on the same hearth and consequently we find few giant-size firedogs and many smaller ones. In colonial days the natural place to turn for these was to the blacksmith shop, where any size, shape or decoration could be ordered. Iron is still in high favor for andirons—alone, combined with brass, and almost always used for the actual brackets that support the burning logs, no matter of what the rest of the andiron is made. The small pair of firedogs at bottom left on page 91 suggests an early handmade type appropriate for informal and simple rooms whether they have an early American atmosphere or are quite modern.

Historical pre-Revolutionary Chelsea statuette of William Pitt reveals the fine workmanship of the period.

This fifteenth or sixteenth century Tibetan mythological animal, horse or deer, is excellent for colonial or modern room.

English Whieldon-ware model of water buffalo from a Chinese original was made about 1750.

Chelsea group of birds and flowers, made in England about the middle of the eighteenth century, is equally appropriate in Chippendale setting or a contemporary living room.

Through the eighteenth century, brass andirons became more and more popular because they lent themselves to the more formal and sophisticated styles of decoration through the Queen Anne, Chippendale, Hepplewhite and Sheraton periods. There were all sorts of turned pedestals or uprights, reminiscent of the turning on the legs of the furniture, tiny ball-and-claw feet, vase-shaped members, turned posts with a simple brass ball on the top. With the interest in classic decoration after the Revolution and in the days of the early Republic, both andirons and matching shovel, poker and brush handles ended in an urn shape, or the entire firedog was shaped in a large urn with a flame ornament or small finial on the top. The legs are a good clue to each period as we find rococo scrolls, cyma curves, and simple posts with a spade foot. Here again the collectors and experts on fireplace equipment can date to a day or a decade the period of a certain type of foot or post, but in general, once we have the feeling of each period in mind and the atmosphere of a room, the selection of andirons is comparatively easy.

People who play with open fires have always realized the dangers involved, as well as a need for some handy equipment. Among the latter were sets of implements for poking up the fire, moving ashes, brushing the hearth, and picking up embers. In the early days of this country, these stood around the fireplace opening at random or were hung on nails driven into the great beams across the top or sides of the fireplace. Later, with the more finished drawing-room fireplaces, brass or iron stands were built with a dustpan at the bottom. One of these with urn finials is illustrated on page 92, as well as a modern contribution to the solution of this problem. The latter is a brass rack attached to the wall near the fireplace, which has the advantage of taking care of the tools without cluttering up the area surrounding the fire.

Another *must* for the fireplace is a fire screen. In the eighteenth century this article was not intended to do anything but act as a shield against too much heat for those sitting around the fire, and was a highly decorative accessory. It usually consisted of a wooden stand with a short pole on which was mounted a sliding painted or embroidered shield. Today the fire screen serves the same purpose, but is primarily designed to keep the fire inside the fireplace and as a protection for the carpet or room, especially when the fire is unattended. For many years people have been content to use a heavy mesh screening mounted on a frame, either perfectly flat or bulged out like a bustle. Sometimes these have been decorated with brass wire and handles, and sometimes hinged and folding. Cut to the size of the fireplace opening, such screens

STEUBEN GLASS

Accessories are our chance to express personality, provide gaiety. These charming glass objects can do both.

have served their purpose, but the problem of what to do with the awkward sooty thing when you do not want it in front of the fire has always been difficult. Modern manufacturers have done much to improve the appearance of the old-fashioned fire screen, but have also brought out a few new devices which are much cleaner and add considerable charm to the fire when in use. One is a draw curtain of metal links which pulls across the opening in the exact same way as a window curtain that draws, see page 93. A second is a metal flexible shade on a roller, attached inside the opening and drawn down to the floor like a window shade. In both cases the andirons are set outside the screen and the part of them which supports the burning logs is separated from the decorative front and placed behind the screen. These screens are also excellent with the basket-type plain grates for burning coal, which are in greater use than the more decorative type illustrated.

One other charming fireplace accessory is the brass fan on page 92, the leaves of which can be folded and entirely hidden behind the centerpiece.

Inasmuch as a mirror is usually hung on a wall to help complete a room, we may call it an accessory. However, there have always been other important reasons for using mirrors, and certainly in period rooms the beauty of the frames was the most important element. In recent years,

In every period firedogs are obviously made of metal, cast iron and brass predominating. Periods are easily recognized.

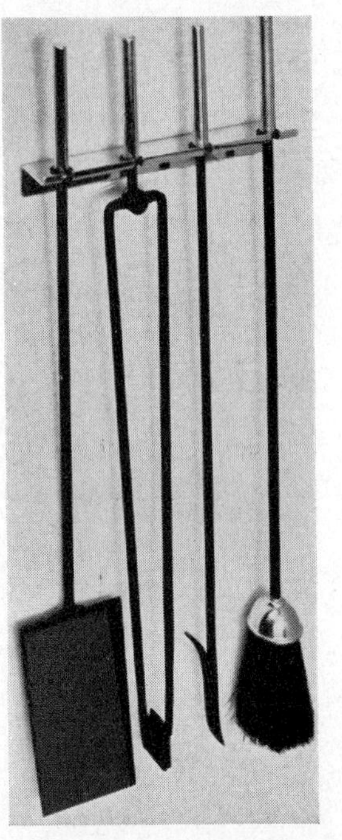

Modern brass rack attached to wall neatly takes care of tools.

FIREPLACE AND EQUIPMENT BY WM. H. JACKSON COMPANY

A handsome Early Republic brass stand has urn finials and dustpan at bottom.

the emphasis has been on the reflections of the glass itself, which becomes part of the basic plan of the room. Since this aspect belongs properly to practical planning, here we only will take note of the function of mirrors in creating an illusion in a room, and turn our attention to the styles in frames which appeared in the various periods.

Of course, before there could be any mirrors large enough to hang on a wall, a fairly good-sized sheet of glass was necessary—not as large as our plate-glass shop windows, but much larger than the tiny diamond-shaped windowpanes of the Pilgrim houses, or even small panes of the Cape Cod house. There were a few glass furnaces in this country in the first century of its settlement and some small sheets of glass were being made abroad, but it was not until the time of Queen Anne furniture, well into the eighteenth century, that suitable mirror glass was produced, and framed mirrors became an important decoration in the home. The frames, like the furniture of this time, were made of walnut with a simple scalloped top, rectangular bottom, and quite wide molding around the glass which was often in two sections with the upper section decorated.

The next important change in style came just prior to the American Revolution with the handsome Chippendale mirrors. These were made of fine mahogany and in addition to being carved and scalloped were decorated with gilded moldings and composition or wood gilded ornaments of leaves and flowers. Most of these adopted the broken pediment of the fireplaces and doorways of the time and were surmounted with a pheasant or sheaf of flowers and wheat, wired like a florist's arrangement. These mirrors were masterpieces of craftsmanship and design and varied considerably in quality of workmanship. The one illustrated on page 94 is a fine example. Others were less compact in their ornamentation and less sophisticated. Another type which appeared at about the same time was the extremely elaborate all gold on carved wood

The leaves of this charming brass fan can be folded and entirely hidden behind the centerpiece.

FIREPLACE AND EQUIPMENT BY WM. H. JACKSON COMPANY

The fire grate becomes formal and handsome when trimmed with brass finials.

mirror. The carving is quite delicate in series of scrolls and swags with flowers and often shows a marked Chinese influence with suggestions of small pagodas and some Chinese figures introduced into the carving. Some were the size of the Chippendale on page 94, but more often these mirrors were much larger and made in three sections to stretch the full length of a mantel or sideboard. This type of mirror is still very popular and copied frequently to be used whenever great elegance is required.

A draw curtain of metal links pulls across the opening in the same way as a window curtain that draws.

The general shape of the first type of Chippendale mirror continued after the Revolution, but gradually the gilt composition ornaments on the sides were dropped and the eagle took the place of the pheasant at the top or was inlaid. By the turn of the nineteenth century new types of mirrors, all of them finished in gold, were in vogue. The Adam style, illustrated on page 95, was delicate and lent itself to oval and round glasses with great ease. The round bull's-eye mirror used a convex glass for the first time which did remarkable things in multiplying and distorting reflections, but it was not an unpleasant distortion and suggests an illustration for a contemporary diary of a Miss Quincy of Boston, who wrote in 1825: The room . . . "was hung with light blue silk and furnished with sofas and curtains of the same hue. It also contained an immense mirror, placed so as to reflect the rest of the rooms." The third type of mirror, illustrated on page 95, has classic columns on the sides, a painted scene on glass at the top, and a straight cornice with gold balls and is to be found in a hundred variations. Quite often the scenes were of historical events or allegorical subjects, sometimes of a simple cottage quite primitively executed. Quite often mahogany was used or some native wood with no gilt. Here was a mirror which could be made by a great artist, and copied by a village carpenter.

It was the Victorians who first attached their mirrors to bureaus and stands so that they could be tilted, though they were also fond of mirrors of all sizes in heavy curved moldings of mahogany and tall pier glasses framed in a narrower band of gilt.

Today mirrored glass may cover a wall, make a large standing screen, face a piece of furniture like veneering, or be used as facing around a fireplace. If hung on or attached to the wall, a mirror may have almost invisible clips and no framing. If framed, the lines will be straight and simple, of any available wood or material or framed with mirrored glass mounted on wood.

These then are some of the important accessories that give charm and personality to our decorating. There are many others which we seek ourselves, or which come to us from all over the world. This has been true from the days of our earliest settlers, first through necessity, but even after our industries were well established, it has been our custom to enjoy and seek imported articles, especially in the matter of accessories. If we think this is strictly a development of our modern age, we might consider an advertisement from a Maryland newspaper, dated June 17, 1783:

"Just imported from France and Portugal by the brig, Marquis de la Lafayette . . . China ware, assortment of looking glasses with gilt frames and acajou . . . assortment of candlesticks and sconces plated with gold and silver, assortment of tongs and shovels, likewise plated, Quadrille boxes, curtain rings and printed paper for tapestry."

These hanging shelves hold a variety of Bennington ware. Both decorative and utilitarian pieces—creamers, flasks, figurines, etc., show the development of the pottery craft. The big pitcher and the stag are Rockingham.

FROM THE COLLECTION OF GEORGE S. MCKEARIN

METROPOLITAN MUSEUM OF ART

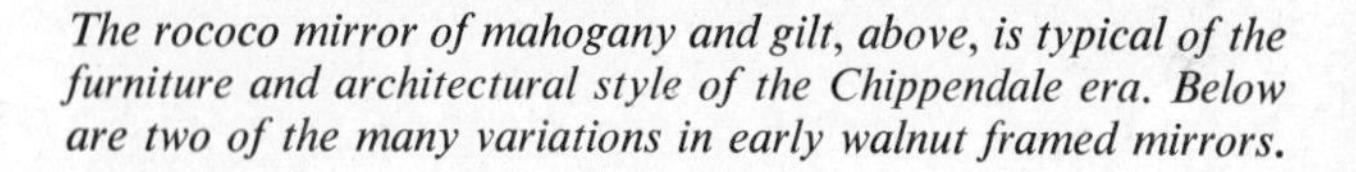

The rococo mirror of mahogany and gilt, above, is typical of the furniture and architectural style of the Chippendale era. Below are two of the many variations in early walnut framed mirrors.

DONALD STUART

The two mirrors above are early American, the first a rare piece from Rock Hall house. Pictures on the kitchen wall, center, add gaiety and interest to an important room.

Below are three different styles of mirrors—all were popular in the days of the Early Republic. From left to right: Adam, Bull's-Eye, and Classic.

HAROLD FOWLER

Here is one answer to the critics who claim that "Modern" is cold, stiff and uninviting. It radiates friendliness and charm to guests and at the same time suggests perfect ease and informality for an evening at home alone. It is as easy on the budget as it is on the eyes and should help you decide if you've been hesitating about Modern.

Ladies' Home Journal

BOOK OF INTERIOR DECORATION

PART TWO: PRACTICAL PLANNING

LADIES' HOME JOURNAL'S MORE HOUSE FOR THE MONEY PORTFOLIO NO. 5. ANTIQUE BRONZE ACCESSORIES FROM YAMANAKA

This room is colorful, informal, and livable. Tea-and-game table with its opaque glass top in deep blue is eminently practical. Rush and pine chairs, cushioned in gold silk, show Scandinavian influence in the clean simple line.

Decoration

Styled to Taste and Period

A review of our knowledge about styles and periods, fabrics, floor coverings, color, lighting and accessories gives us confidence to go ahead with some practical planning. We realize at once that this must fall into two categories—long-range planning to achieve our ultimate ideal and temporary plans to meet immediate necessities within the limits of available funds.

Flexibility is very important to us today, and we would shudder at the prospect of being born, living, and dying in the same house, as so many of our ancestors did. Our emphasis is on convenience, comfort and health, and the minute our living conditions do not provide these fundamentals, we seek a change. Often fundamental changes, such as moving to the country or suburbs for more out-of-door life or a garden, or moving to the city to be nearer a place of business, the theaters and museums, are long foreseen. Whatever the individual circumstances may be, it is given to few to be able to completely furnish and decorate their homes more than once in a lifetime. Hence a good basic plan with an eye to durability, quality and flexibility is important. Add to this the patine of personality that only long associations can give to a piece of furniture and you know that houses are turned into homes by such things as a bride and groom's first dining table in a small apartment becoming a sofa or hall table in a larger house, and Mother and Dad enjoying their breakfast at a small Pembroke end table which they have had all their lives.

In addition to being concerned with possible changes in our way of life, size of the family, degrees of formality, long-range planning should include a definite attempt to eliminate an appearance of transitoriness while striving toward the perfection of having everything in your home exactly as you have always wanted it. Success in this objective depends on how drastic the changes to be made are, and how much you can conveniently do at one time.

Ideally the average American family spends thirty per cent of its annual income for housing which must include the equivalent of rent, and also repairs, improvements and interior decoration. The initial large expenses of the last two items must come usually from special funds, earmarked for that purpose, but your ultimate satisfaction in your surroundings will be achieved by gradual improvements based on a long-range plan.

Having given some thought to probabilities and intangibles, our first actual step in practical planning is to choose a style of decoration which is most suitable to all our predetermined specifications. Here we start with the house or building and its location. In a city apartment, large or small, the outside of the building will be of little importance and you may indulge in almost any style of decoration from Mexican primitive to Louis XIV or Modern in its most abstract form. Inside, some regard for the type of woodwork, windows, and general layout of rooms will be unavoidable. The number and size of rooms will not be important, especially if they are not connected with open doorways or arches which require a correlation of decoration between two or more areas. The height of the ceilings, however, will be important in considering the general scale of various types of furniture in proportion to various backgrounds.

The outside of a suburban apartment building will have more influence on selecting suitable interior decoration, as such buildings, even though quite large, are more apt to be adaptations of a definite period style of architecture, and stand out as a unit, rather than being lost architecturally in a city block. There is still great latitude in the styles which may be suitable, but unless you love the surprise element of complete incongruity, it would be folly to choose the gloomy formality of medieval-Italian furniture for a pink brick building with the small windows and white trim of the modern adaptation of the American Georgian architecture. Here anything in the American tradition, including Modern, would be more suitable.

Houses, both in the city and country, are much more definite in their demands. This seldom becomes a problem, however, as in choosing a house, or even a few rooms in a house, the exterior becomes part of the whole plan. We build, buy or rent a modern house because we like modern styles. We move into a Cape Cod house, a Georgian mansion, or a brownstone because we have or like the furnishings that go with each of them.

Keep in mind that few of the rules of interior decoration are immutable, that you may wish to create varying degrees of formality, and above all that your final aim is to express the essence of your taste and personality and that of your family. The chart on the following pages will serve as a guide and help only in choosing your style of decoration.

Suggestions for choosing a style of Decoration

A Guide for a Good Start in Planning. Many things can be moved from one box to another and you will want to add others. Degrees of formality are volatile, but certainly the glass ash tray in your casual room will be quite different from the one in your formal one.

	Location	Furniture	Textiles	Wall Covering
Rustic	Camp Mountain cottage Ranch Log cabin Boy's room	Pine—knotty, built-in Hickory, oak Primitive Early American Modern Contemporary Simple straight lines	Textured wools and cottons Serge, flannel, blanketing Denim, duck, sailcloth Crash, monk's cloth Leather, plastics	Rough timber Sheathing Sand or rough plaster Stone, brick
Casual	Shore cottage Country studio Summer dwelling Farm Ranch house Sun porch Girl's room	Pine Redwood Maple Iron Fruitwood Painted Oak Reed Early American Pennsylvania Dutch Contemporary Modern Unsophisticated, easy lines in all sorts of country types	All kinds of textures Bold prints, stripes or plain cottons and linens Unbleached muslin Sailcloth Monk's cloth Plastics	Unpainted or painted plaster Sheathing Simple paneling Textured or plain wallpapers Wallpapers with designs simulating wood
Informal	Country house Farm house City apartment Suburban apartment Ranch house Bungalow Cape Cod and Early Georgian houses Modern Any type of room	Oak Maple Pine Fruitwoods Walnut Mahogany Iron Reed Early 18th Century American Provincial Victorian Contemporary Modern French Provincial Pennsylvania Dutch	Textured cottons and rayons Dull antique satin Silk and cotton plaids and stripes Printed cotton and linen Mohair Dull casements Organdy, broadcloth, muslin	Painted plaster, rough or smooth Paneling Simple patterned or plain wallpapers
Semiformal	Suburban apartment or house City apartment or house Country house or estate Any type of room	Walnut Cherry Mahogany Queen Anne Simple Chippendale Contemporary Victorian Modern	Antique satin Brocatelle Matelassé Velvet Textures Cotton and linen prints Fibreglas prints Mohair Gauze Bouclé	Painted plaster Paneling Printed and plain wallpapers Scenic wallpapers Stretched fabrics Limited amount of smoked or clear mirror Plastics
Formal	City apartment or house Suburban apartment or house Country estate Any room, especially drawing rooms, dining rooms, libraries, master bedrooms	Walnut Mahogany Satinwood Rosewood Ebony, tulip, or other exotic, highly polished woods Chippendale, Sheraton Hepplewhite, Louis XIV, XV, XVI, Empire, Federal, Victorian Modern	Damask Linen Brocade Brocatelle Satin Silk gauze Velvet Mohair Matelassé Bouclé Moire Taffeta Faille Tapestry	Painted plaster or wood Paneling Wallpapers in scenic and formal designs Mirrors Formal fabrics Leather or plastics

Colors	Floor Covering	Lighting Fixtures	Accessories	
Wood shades of green, autumn leaves, barks, and stone; water and sky tints and bright and deep shades of red	Fiber, grass, matting, sisal, cotton and wool textured and woven rugs, fur and Navaho rugs	Lamps and candlesticks of wrought iron, brass, tin, pewter, glass, wood, unpolished steel, primitive pottery	Primitive figures of men and animals Jars, jugs, bowls and ash trays in same materials as lamps Iron firedogs or grate basket Robust and strong pictures	**Rustic**
True, clear colors, striking contrasts Emphasis on primary colors and the simple combinations making orange, green and purple	Fiber, sisal, cotton and wool shag and twist rugs, rag and braided rugs, plain carpeting	Pressed glass Pottery Brass Pewter Twisted wire Tôle	Colored glass and pottery ash trays Metal and wooden bowls, trays, etc. Pottery and china figures and animals Iron, brass, or iron and brass andirons	**Casual**
Clear definite shades of all primary colors and mixtures Bright accents	Wool and cotton twist Hooked Oriental *Gros point* Rough and smooth pile carpeting Cut-pile carpet	Brass, copper, bronze, wire, tôle, glass, pottery, china, plaster	Same materials for ash trays, boxes, flower vases, and other knickknacks as are used in lamps and lighting fixtures	**Informal**
Grey, beige, white, ivory, and other soft tones Subtle contrasts and some accents in darker or stronger colors	Oriental Cut and uncut pile Carved and plain carpeting twists *Gros point* Wilton, Axminster	Glass—plain, pressed, blown and also cut Brass, bronze, ormolu, silver, silver-gilt Simple lusters in clear and colored glass China and porcelain	Glass, enamel on metal, cloisonné Papier-mâché, lacquer Silver, bronze, silver-gilt Pottery, china, porcelain Brass andirons, fenders and fireplace equipment	**Semiformal**
Wide range of grey and beige colors Pastels of all colors Brilliant sharp shades of red and green Strong pinks, blues and allied colors Black and white	Oriental Chenille Velvet Wall-to-wall carpeting of close weaves Carved carpeting	Glass, crystal, lusters Silver, bronze, ormolu, silver-gilt, brass China, porcelain Alabaster, marble	Figurines and candlesticks of fine china Venetian glass or other fine or delicate glass Marble, alabaster Silver and gold	**Formal**

This excellent example of before and after demonstrates what can be done by rearrangement of furniture, careful selection of colors, slip covers, and a new window treatment. For a more masculine effect try using turquoise and cocoa instead of pink and grey.

Floor Planning

Practical Room Arrangements

The practical approach to the art of interior decorating makes it more fun from beginning to end, because it transforms vague dreams and ideas into something tangible with a reasonable promise of fulfillment. Choosing a style of decoration is one step in this kind of planning; making definite floor plans is another and it is difficult to decide which is more important, or which comes first, as the two are completely interdependent. The former involves reading, illustrations, and seeing various kinds of furniture and backgrounds elsewhere. The latter is your own plan, done at home with paper and pencil, and though it may be concerned with a new room, or planning all the rooms in a new house, it is worth doing even if there is nothing more involved than the rearrangement of what you have. It gives an opportunity to experiment with different kinds of arrangements with a sure knowledge of whether the pieces will fit into a given space without the embarrassment of getting everything moved around, only to find that the new idea will not work, or you do not like it after all.

Floor-planning procedure is indicated in the directions with the sample ruled sheet and the furniture patterns for standard pieces furnished on the following pages. It is as simple and easy as it looks, with but a few suggestions here to save time and errors. The first is careful measuring, as a quarter of an inch on the ruled plan will equal one foot of actual space, and make a great difference in close places. Second, many sofas and large chairs have slanting backs, so that the actual measurement does not indicate how much floor space is taken up by the piece. In measuring, drop a string or make an imaginary line from the top of the back to the floor, and measure from the spot at which this line touches the floor to the front of the piece to find the required space. Third, take note of the amount of floor various people require for their feet when sitting on a chair or sofa and be careful not to crowd them too much for comfort. This applies also to allowing space for dining-room chairs to be pushed back when people are being seated and in the case of revolving television or desk chairs floor space must be clear on all sides. Fourth, do not overlook lighting fixtures, pipes and such, which may project at different heights and influence the placing of tall pieces of furniture.

With the mechanics of floor planning in hand and your furniture in mind, you are ready to consider the aspects of beauty, use and comfort which are your main objectives. Furniture arrangement is important in all three, and often even small changes can make a large contribution toward a better room.

For beauty we look for balance, centers of interest, repose, and an inviting air, and in achieving the first two, will find we have the other two. For balance, place a large or tall piece of furniture on the wall opposite the fireplace or a group of windows, if possible. Otherwise, balance it with doors, a tall screen, or pictures above a smaller piece of furniture across the room. A pair of chairs on either side of a sofa or facing it, a pair of end tables with matching lamps, a pair of love seats will all contribute to balance, but one or two pairs are enough. A room filled with twins is very dull and unimaginative. Similar-size chairs in different coverings, or different chairs covered alike will relieve the monotony and even end tables do not have to match. Also for balance in placing pieces which are not parallel to the walls, draw lines from the corners of the room to the opposite corners, and place cater-cornered pieces parallel to these diagonals.

Centers of interest may be provided by a fireplace, which is the natural place to group a love seat or sofa, chairs, and a coffee table. A large window may serve the same purpose, but lacking either in a room, a center of interest may be made by grouping seating furniture around the most important piece of furniture, such as a large coffee table, or drum table, or a bookcase or secretary placed on one wall. If the room is large, or used by a number of people, two or more centers of interest may be needed. The important aspect is to make your center inviting and a natural place for easy conversation.

In an area which is designed for various purposes, less moving and rearrangement is involved for each use if the areas are divided into space allotted for each purpose. However, this is often quite impossible, in which case the most important use takes precedence in beauty, use and comfort over the other purposes. It is in this type of room that some of the ingenious convertible pieces of furniture on the market come to the rescue. The sofa which can be turned into a bed has been available for many years, but is now much improved, as are the dining extension tables which may be closed to a quarter of their full size and pushed aside between meals, leaving the center of the room free for other activities.

Under use, we must observe also our own habits and those of the family, some of which can be encouraged or discouraged by the mere arrangement of furniture. A boy's or girl's room with a bed in the center, a dresser on one wall with a mirror over it, one or two straight chairs and a small table can be made attractive and comfortable for sleeping and dressing. However, if it is to be a gathering place for friends and also a place to study, it will answer these purposes better if it is arranged like a sitting room or den with the bed placed lengthwise against the wall, a large low table in front of it with possibly a magazine shelf below, an easy chair with some kind of footrest or a large ottoman, a desk or worktable with good light by day and by dark.

Often the breadwinner in a family likes to lie on the sofa and read the evening paper or take a nap until dinner is ready. It is up to you to decide whether you wish to encourage or discourage this habit by the size, shape, or location of the sofa. A soft well-cushioned sofa with a good reading light, not plainly visible from the doorway, is a strong invitation to this kind of relaxation. A curved sofa necessitating a semicircular position in reclining, with a light casting its glow too low for reading, and the sofa placed to preclude privacy will naturally have the opposite effect. These are the extreme examples. You will think of many ways in various rooms to apply this general idea.

Comfort is closely allied to use, but there are a few fundamentals to watch for in your arrangements which will contribute to the comfort and popularity of a room. Easy and adequate walking space from one part of a room to another without obstacles makes everyone happier. Lack of clutter, especially around doorways to make an easy entrance or exit possible, is desirable. Accessible storage space for books, games, records, hobbies, sewing, or anything not in constant use helps both the users and the housekeeper.

In discussing furniture arrangement in terms of beauty, use and comfort, the tendency is to start with the living room and other rooms used by all members of the family. The same general principles, however, apply to every room in the house. It is surprising what improvements can be made with a new point of view and taking another look at the surroundings we have become so accustomed to that we really do not see them.

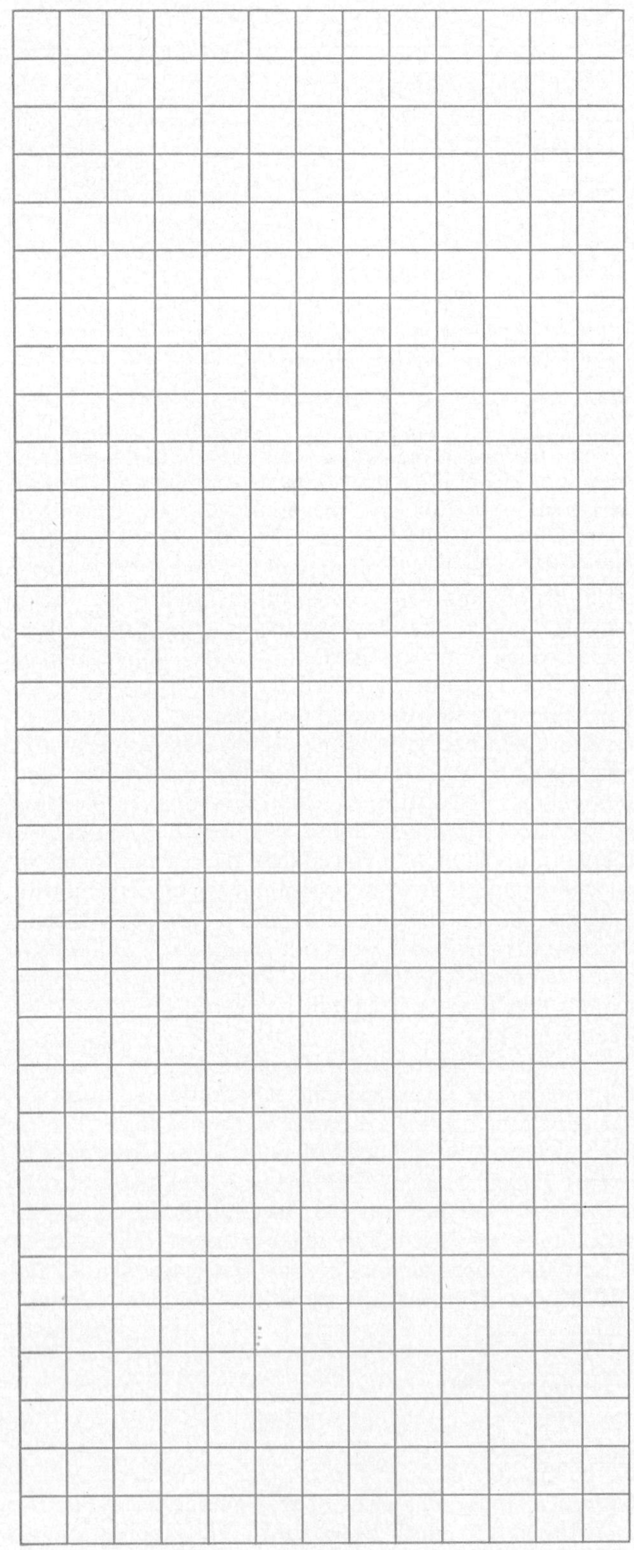

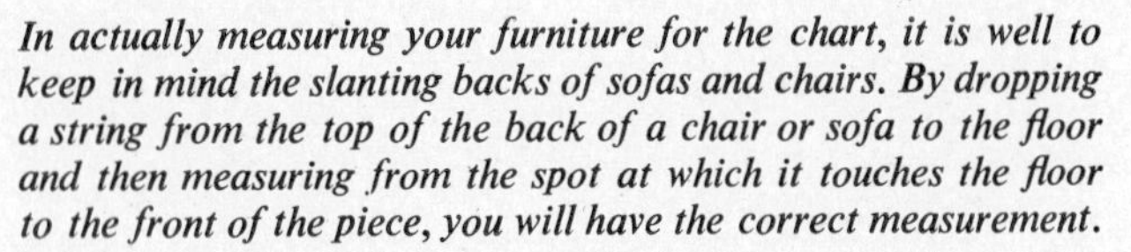

In actually measuring your furniture for the chart, it is well to keep in mind the slanting backs of sofas and chairs. By dropping a string from the top of the back of a chair or sofa to the floor and then measuring from the spot at which it touches the floor to the front of the piece, you will have the correct measurement.

Scale Guide for Planning Furniture Arrangement and Furniture Patterns

Using a scale of ¼ inch or ½ inch to a foot, draw your room on a piece of cross-ruled paper (see page opposite), measuring each space carefully. Mark windows, doors, radiators, fireplaces, built-in cupboards and stationary equipment. Measure each piece of furniture you are planning to use, width and length only. Using the patterns below as a guide, make your own patterns, drawing them to the same scale as your room pattern, adding such pieces or special shapes as you need them. Mark each with the name of the object and length, width and height measurement. If you have a colored pencil handy, color the upholstered pieces for quick identification. Any color will do and it is surprising how much this little "extra" helps in visualizing the finished room. You're then ready to try them in different positions on your room plan.

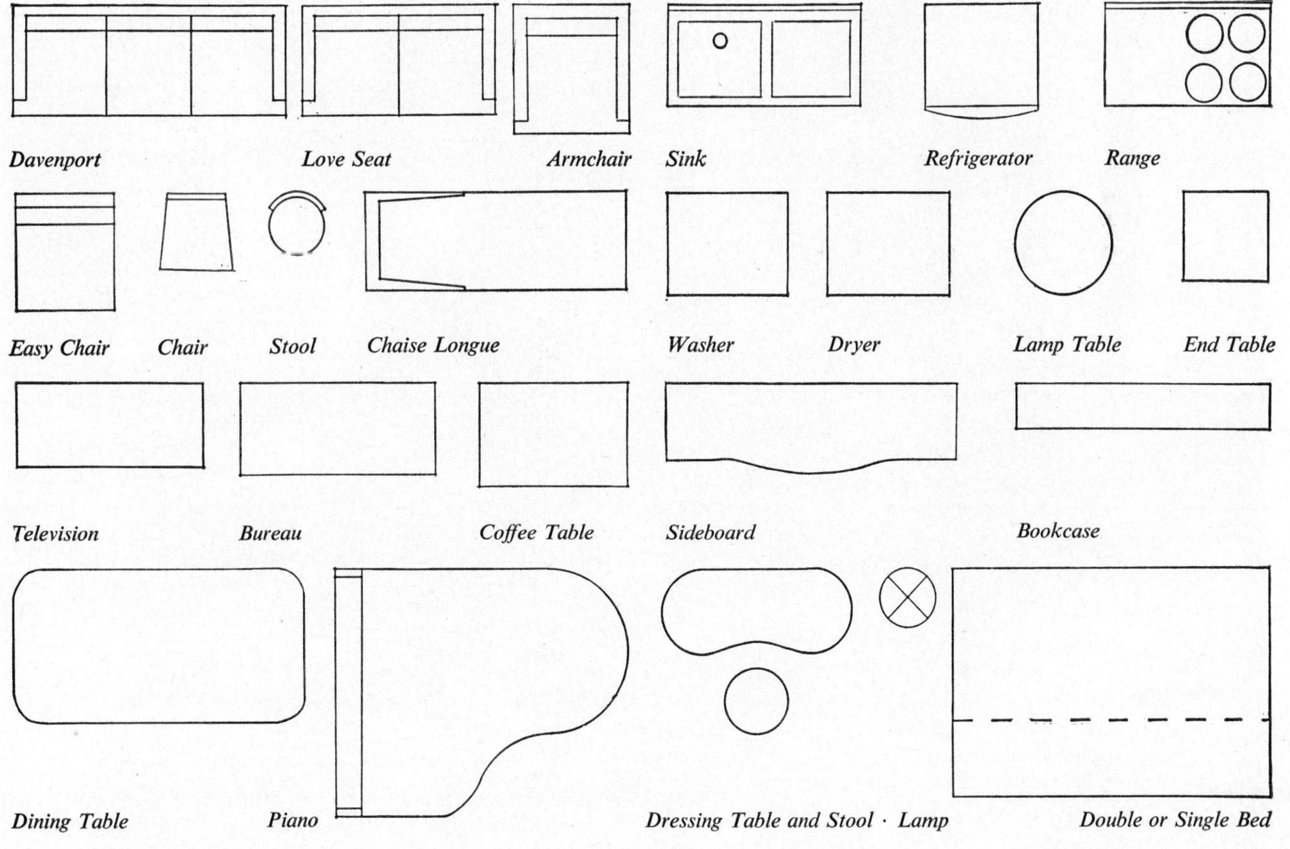

HAROLD FOWLER

Window treatment here gives this charming Victorian bedroom drama and emphasis.

Windows

Treatment, Methods, and Materials

Almost every generation has had different ideas about window treatments with only one strong conviction in common: the agreement that a house was more comfortable and livable if the windows were not left completely bare. Sometimes the sole objective was covering all, or part, of the windows to add actual warmth or the appearance of it to a room. Again privacy seemed of paramount importance, but in either case, it soon became evident also that the window draperies or curtains provided the happiest means of extending the decoration of a room.

Today our insistence, in the daytime, of all the light possible from our windows; our desire after dark for privacy and to shut out the cold stare of black meaningless windowpanes; our disregard of the function of draperies in making any appreciable difference in the temperature of a room; and our discovery of the complete transformation possible with drapery treatments make us more or less impervious to a museum accuracy in carrying out the details of curtain design for period rooms. However, in order to preserve something of the atmosphere we are striving to create, a brief review of the methods and tastes of previous generations is a good guide to our own compromises.

In re-creating the atmosphere of an early-American home, from the early Pilgrim days through the first quarter of the eighteenth century, simplicity is the keynote, in keeping with the fabrics available and the homemakers' skill and taste. Couple with this the realization that ready-made fixtures were unknown and had to be improvised by each individual to answer each particular purpose. Tapes and casings served as curtain rings and any kind of rod might be used for a pole. Such curtains were seldom drawn across the windows at nightfall, for fabrics were narrow in width and fairly scarce.

Specifications for such curtains then would call for: pairs of curtains to hang straight on either side of the window from fixtures attached to the window frame; width—one width of fabric to each half curtain; length—to the sill or wooden apron just below the sill; curtains to be shirred on the rod, or with loops; small hem top and bottom.

As the windows became slightly larger in the Cape Cod type houses and through the next period up to the Chippendale era, curtains became more decorative and a trifle more formal. A simple soft scalloped or straight valance across the top of the window might be added and the side curtains were extended to the floor for greater formality. The greater use of printed cottons and linens made linings more necessary and occasionally an old curtain of this period appears with a narrow braid or tape edging of a contrasting color.

Such styles continued in use in simple houses throughout the eighteenth and nineteenth centuries just as they do today, but with the fine city houses of the Chippendale era, formal window treatments reached a high degree of elegance and intricate detail. A study of portraits and pictures of the time, our best source of accurate information, shows the great popularity of a single wide drapery in a fine fabric, hung across the top of the window and extending to the floor, tied back with elaborate cords and tassels from one corner of the top of the window and again at the sill, making a double heavily draped festoon arrangement. Draperies of this type were often used on a pair of windows, tied back on the left on one window and the right on the other to suggest a pair of facing curtains. The sketch on page 108, left, serves as a prototype for an even more popular window treatment of this period. (The illustration of the Victorian bedroom on the page opposite shows a similar treatment.) The draped scallop across the top is called "the festoon" and the end pieces attached to it, "swags." The whole is called "the valance." This was usually attached to a concealed cornice board and the side curtains hung on a separate rod beneath. The whole was attached to the window frame, often concealing beautiful carved architectural details.

The swags of the valances in this festoon type of treatment were sometimes made long enough to reach the window sill of a small or medium size window and the side curtains were omitted entirely, as in the illustration on page 110. This still served to soften the severe lines of the window frame, but was lighter, less formal, and more suitable to some of the less pretentious rooms of the period.

Also less formal, but suitable for use on any size of window at this period, were the simple tied-back side curtains with a scalloped or shaped valance across the top. The sketch on page 108, center, serves as a model, although it shows the side curtains hanging straight. Sometimes the lower edge of the valance followed the shape of the decorative aprons on the bases of chests and desks of the time, but more often it was cut in simple

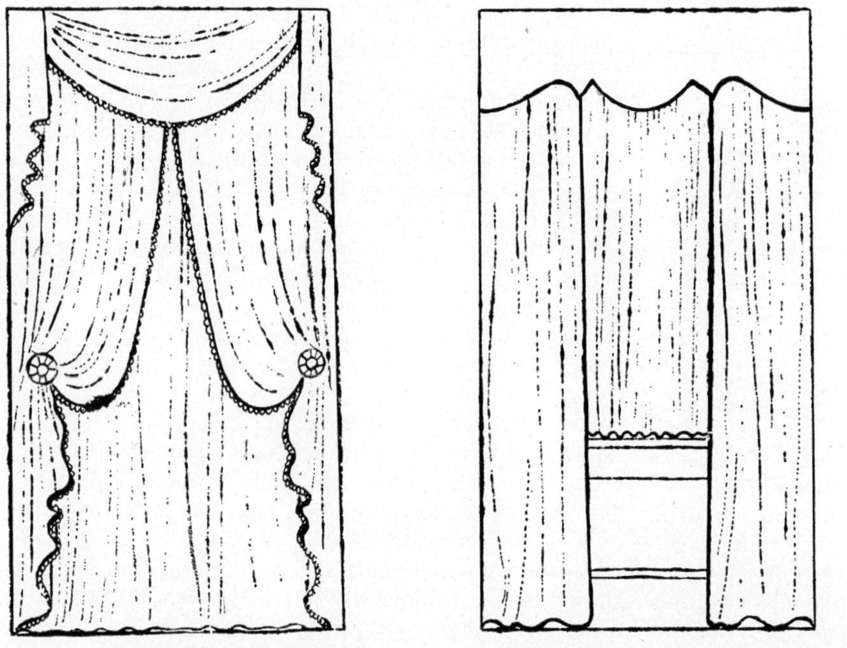

ANDREW WARHOL

Left is a formal festoon and swag window treatment, a theme capable of many variations. A basic design for window treatment, center, has a shaped valance. The elasticized kitchen curtain at right is popular and practical.

even half circles with a quarter circle on each end. Such valances were lined to help hold them in shape, but stiffening or mounting on a shaped board is entirely a modern adaptation. It has always been a very popular design, because it was easy to make, allowed an infinite variety of adaptations, and required less fabric than the festoon type of drapery.

Throughout the elegant Chippendale, Hepplewhite, and Sheraton periods we find the variations on these two styles. Such draperies were always hung on the window frame and covered much of the glass. With the new small delicate lighter furniture of the early nineteenth century, window treatments took on new forms, at once lighter and more delicately elegant. The spirit of this change is typified in the illustrations on page 63, showing silk fringed valances and transparent lighter-weight side curtains. We noted, under textiles, that the fabrics and fringes were lighter in this period, carrying out the more delicate appearance of the less heavily but not less intricately designed festoons and swags.

To these days of the Early Republic, the Empire, and extending into the greater flamboyance of the Regency, the important innovation was in the elaborate curtain fixtures, both across the top of the window and in special knobs and holders to tie back the side curtains. Painted cornices like those illustrated on page 110 were popular, as well as gilded poles with ornamental finials. Pineapples, balls, and knobs were traditional, but sometimes a carved ram's head was put on one end of the pole with the tail on the other end, and again a long gilded arrow with dart and feathers was used. For the first time designers did not confine the draperies to the window frame and often added height to windows by using a central ornament, such as an eagle or wreath, above the frame carrying either a draped part of the valance or a decorative cord.

Gradually the draped valances became more and more elaborate until we find our Victorian forebears, not unexpectedly, using every style that had gone before, but making it their own by swathing their windows in voluminous heavy fringed and tasseled draperies to which were added sets of lace, net, or marquisette curtains against the glass. Such heavy elegance was for the drawing room, dining room and other formal rooms in the house. The less formal windows in the bedroom and kitchen made use of ruffled-organdy curtains—still dear to the hearts of most women, because of their crisp freshness—tailored scrim and dimity and other less formal styles. Beginning in this period, especially in kitchens, but very usable elsewhere, were the Dutch curtains with two pairs of short curtains on each window, in the manner of the modern café type.

Today in designing curtains we seek ideas among the period styles, but our interest in them is mostly concerned with degrees of formality, elegance, or simplicity. In planning our own window treatments, we expect them to do much more for our decoration than our ancestors ever considered, in giving the windows more importance as to amount of drapery and at the same time leaving as much glass exposed as possible for greater daylight indoors. This is easily done by extending the curtain rod four to six inches beyond the window frame on each side, raising the valance above the window, and hanging both parts of the drapery to merely cover the framing of the glass. Thus, much of the fabric hangs on the wall instead of the window frame and changes in size and importance of windows are attained. A covered plywood valance board is one of the simplest solutions in meeting this desirable modern trend. However, if your design calls for a festooned valance, the window may be enlarged with a narrow concealed valance board projecting on each side and placed above the window frame in the same manner. Either board must have a return at each end, causing the front to clear the window frame by several inches. This is called *vestibuling* and is used to make the drapery hang straight over the window to the sill or floor and allow space underneath for one or more rods to carry the side curtains and glass curtains.

Another opportunity for original design is presented with adjacent windows which may be treated separately or as one large window with a single valance running across the top of the entire group. When two or three windows have a very narrow space between them and the effect of one large window is desirable, it is possible to paint the space between the windows the same color as the window frames and ignore the space in making one large pair of curtains for the group. If the space is too wide for this treatment, the wall may be mirrored between the windows from the top of the sill to the top of the window frame and be treated as one window.

Valances help to conceal rods and false height, but you can still give the importance of more width to a window without a valance, both in draperies hung *for decoration only*, as the technical term goes, and in drawn or *traverse* curtains. In the first instance the longer rods stop at the edge of the glass and are concealed by the drapery. A traverse rod must extend across the top of the window, but if painted the color of the woodwork it becomes inconspicuous by day and invisible by night.

Quite often the windows in a room are so arranged that a picture window or a group of windows takes up most of one wall with very little wall space between the outer edge of the window frame and the corner of the room. Also in many modern rooms the whole wall is taken up with windows which not only extend from corner to corner, but also from floor to ceiling. In both cases a drapery treatment from floor to ceiling and covering the entire wall when pulled together will be pleasant in the daytime and transform the room by night. The mechanics of accomplishing such an arrangement consist of either a long traverse rod placed close to the ceiling or a ceiling track and sufficient width of fabric to hang loosely when pulled. However, when such draperies are pushed back in the daytime, they require considerable space and before embarking on such a plan, it is well to estimate how much of the wall or glass will be covered at each end when the curtains are opened to the maximum measurement. This, of course, will vary with the weight of the fabric and the length of wall to be covered, but it is well to figure on one hundred per cent fullness in the drapery which means that a fifteen-foot wall would require five yards of width to each half curtain. This pushed back as far as possible would take about two feet on a traverse rod and a little less on a plain rod with rings and cord. In some cases this would be highly desirable and in others might cut off the light where you need it most.

Another problem which often arises is that of radiators under windows where a drapery to the floor seems desirable. Such a treatment is not impossible, especially if the radiator does not run the full width of the window, or if there is sufficient wall space on each side to hang part of the fabric on the wall as in widening the appearance of the window. However, if you wish the curtain to be long and traverse as well, the best solution is to make the cornice or rod project far enough from the window at the top to allow the drapery to hang straight over the radiator at night. The main objection to this solution is that the closed drapery will undoubtedly cut off some of the heat from the radiator and it would be a meticulous housekeeper indeed who could prevent the lining of the drapery and perhaps the fabric itself from becoming heat soiled. The effect may be worth it anyway. Many decorators have thought so. One other aspect of this problem is the possibility of stopping the curtains at the top of the radiator on one or two windows and making others in the same room go to the floor. This is especially true if the windows with different length curtains are not on the same wall.

Tiny windows high on the wall on either side of the fireplace or, in fact, any windows which do not fit into the major drapery plan for a room should be simply treated either with a simple casement attached with rods top and bottom over the glass only, or hanging loose to draw—also over the glass only. Deeply recessed windows, French doors, or casement windows that open inward may be treated the same way, although sometimes a full set of side curtains and valances may be used on the wall without any interference with the swing of the windows.

Many of the modern houses and apartments have corner windows in which the glass forms the corner of the room. These may be treated as one window with a half curtain at each side, drawing to the corner of the room, or, if the window is large, each wall of glass may be treated as a separate window with side curtains hanging in the glass corner. The first treatment is more in keeping with the object of the window and modern decoration; the second will soften the effect and cut down some of the glare if the exposure is too sunny.

The foregoing illustrations are but a few of the many types of windows. They are discussed to demonstrate some fundamental principles and suggest possibilities for making your own improvements in window treatments. The most important thing is to take a good look at your windows and a good look at your room. Then proceed with a well-worked-out plan. Who would dream of doing anything else? You would not have much trouble naming three people you know who might, and three more who wish they had given their window treatments a little more thought before spending their money.

Once you have worked out in your mind the style of window treatment you would like to use and have an idea of the type of fabric that you need, you are ready to translate these ideas into something tangible. There are several ways of doing this, sometimes depending on the budget, the locality in which you live, or perhaps on your desire to make the designing and execution of draperies your hobby. There are three main possibilities, one of which will match your requirements.

You may order your draperies made in a first-rate drapery workroom or upholsterer's shop. He will measure your windows, estimate the amount and cost of fabric, lining, fixtures and give you a price on the complete installation. In a good shop the draperies will be beautifully made and hung, but naturally your bill will include the time taken to measure, maker's wages by the hour, overhead, and travel time. This you should expect and it is not out of proportion to the work involved. It might be compared to having a gown made for you by one of the well-known dressmakers.

You may buy your draperies and curtains ready-made. There are many available, not only in glass curtains of silks, cottons, and man-made fibers, but also in formal full-length side curtains. The selection is more limited than in the case of custom-made curtains, but rayons, silks, cotton textures and printed fabrics are to be found in this class. You assume the responsibility of measuring the windows, choosing and installing the fixtures and making alterations, if standard lengths do not agree with the sizes you require. There are also a few ready-made valances on the market. The cost will vary, just as it does in ready-made clothes to which this method might be compared.

KATZENBACH AND WARREN

Above are dotted-swiss curtains over venetian blinds in a dining room reminiscent of the Early Republic. Below, only a modest amount of material is needed for the short, formal curtain.

You may decide to make your own draperies and curtains to get the exact material that you want and have them hung exactly as you want them. Your first attempts can be quite professional if you proceed in the same manner as the professional upholsterer does.

The steps are simple and if followed with reasonable care will produce very satisfactory results.

I. FIXTURES

Decide exactly what type of fixtures you are going to use and where they are to be placed—on the window frame, above the window, to extend beyond the window on each side, or to conform to some special need of your own. You may find it necessary to look at the various types available before you come to a decision on this matter. Good fixtures are important as they will outlast many pairs of draperies and will be largely responsible for the way in which any curtains hang. If the draperies are to be heavy or stand the strain of constant drawing back and forth, be sure that the anchorage for the fixtures is firm and adequate. If the screws are to go into the window frame, there is usually no problem, but if they go into the plaster, toggle bolts may be used or a small rough block of wood may be applied to the wall first to hold the screws firmly. Such devices are hidden by the drapery.

II. MEASURING

Measure *the area* to be curtained accurately, from the point where the rod is or will be, to the desired length and from one end of the rod to the other and around the return at each end on rods or cornices which do not lie flat against the window. Measure each window and write down the figures. In old houses the windows may vary considerably because of sagging or unskilled building. In modern houses and apartments, windows are often designed in different sizes on different walls.

Draperies may go to the floor, stop one or two inches above it, or lie in a pool, like a bride's train, on it. The most practical length for long draperies is about one inch above the floor. If you are planning wall-to-wall carpeting which has not yet been installed, allow an inch for the pad and carpet, depending on the thickness you have in mind.

The two other lengths in fashion for draperies are to the sill, which means actually brushing the sill lightly, and to the bottom of the apron which is the piece of wood across the average window just below the sill.

III. YARDAGE REQUIREMENTS FOR FABRIC

LENGTH—When you have measured your curtain area, you will know the desired finished length from top to bottom of each curtain. To this figure add 9 to 16 inches for hems and headings. Try for a 4-inch hem with an extra inch to turn under and allow 4 to 11 inches for the heading, depending on whether it is visible or not. A heading with pinch pleats which extends partly above the rod must be wider than one that goes under a valance or cornice and merely has to be wide enough to slip easily on the rod or provide place for sewed or pinned-on hooks.

The first exception to this general rule for hems and headings is in the use of transparent materials. These should have completely double hems with no ugly line of a short turn-in showing. It is often well to do the same in the heading to permit lengthening, unless the material is absolutely guaranteed not to shrink.

The second exception is in the use of patterned fabrics, which in some cases may work out better both in the fall of the design and in the yardage required, if the widths of hems and headings are slightly altered.

With plain, vertical striped, or tiny-figured materials, you simply measure the length now required and multiply by the number of widths necessary. With definitely patterned fabrics, some attention must be paid to the design, so that it will come in the same place on each length of curtain on the same window and around the room. You may take a look at the design and buy an extra yard or so to allow for matching. However, if you wish to be more accurate and not take a chance on a really expensive bad guess you can easily determine the exact amount needed of any pattern for any length of window. Measure the size of the design and divide the curtain length by this size. This will show how many times the pattern will be repeated in each length. If it comes out in a fraction or part of one whole design, take the next higher whole. Thus 4½ patterns will require 5 whole patterns to match correctly. Now simply multiply the number of "repeats" by the size of the pattern to get the required length of each "drop," or width of fabric used.

For example:

The measurement of your curtain finished is 108 inches. Add 9 inches for hem and heading. The pattern measures 21 inches. 108 inches plus 9 inches makes 117 inches, total required length. Pattern repeat of 21 inches goes into 117 inches 5 times, plus 12 inches, so you will need 6 repeats for each length. 6 times 21 inches equals 126 inches, or 3½ yds.

If you purchased only 117 inches or 3¼ yards, you would not be able to match your pattern. If you guessed at an extra half yard for each curtain, you would be really wasting material. In this example the waste is about 9 inches for each length, but some of this may be used for tiebacks. Often the pattern repeat and the required length will come out with much less difference. In most cases, however, except when you are very lucky, the larger the size of the pattern, the greater amount of waste in matching. This, of course, does not apply to panels of fabric that make one complete design in each panel.

HAROLD FOWLER

WIDTH—For draperies which are to draw across the window, allow twice the width of the curtain area, or one hundred per cent fullness. This may be shaded a trifle, but to look well draperies should hang full, even when closed. In transparent fabrics, especially if you want privacy, you may wish to use three or four times the width of the window for your material.

If the width of your area is 48 inches, one width of 50-inch fabric on one side, making 100 inches unhemmed, will be adequate. A 36-inch fabric on the same window will require 1½ widths to each side. A full wall may require as much as 3 or 4 widths to each side. When you have determined the number of widths, or "drops" necessary for the room, multiply the length to find total yardage for the side curtains.

For example: If the same room that required 3½ yards for each length has three windows of the same size, 45 inches wide, each window will require 2 drops, 6 in all, or 20 yards of 50-inch fabric. If your fabric is 34 inches wide each window will need 3 drops, or 9 in all, making 30 yards of fabric. In planning to do large windows with 36-inch fabric, it is well to consider this additional yardage, especially in comparing prices quoted by the yard.

CORNICES AND VALANCES—Unless there is some special reason for a variation, the valance at its widest point should be one eighth of the distance from the top of the drapery treatment to the floor. Sometimes this will not cover the window frame to the edge of the glass at the top of tall windows heightened by placing the valance well above the actual frame. A few inches may be added, but do not strain the depth too much, as it may throw the whole design out of proportion. It would be better to lower the valance a little from the top.

For calculating the yardage requirements on straight or shirred valances, add 2 inches to the depth of the valance for turn-in, and multiply by the number of widths required. A valance 14 inches deep and 45 inches from end to end around the corners will require ½ yard of 50-inch fabric, or 1 yard of 36-inch fabric. When festoons, swags or special draping is used, work out the required yardage from the depth of the curves of the festoon and length of swags. In using a patterned fabric the placing of the design or dominant motif should be considered in figuring fabric requirement.

FRINGE—Most curtains when trimmed with fringe call for one length of fringe down the inside edge and across the bottom. This may be set on the edge or back from the edge, but in either case the length plus the width of each half curtain will give you yardage requirement, not forgetting to add fringe for the cornice or valance. More elaborate fringe treatments must be measured out.

In the attractive room at the left, a valance board is covered with the heavy white cotton of the curtains.

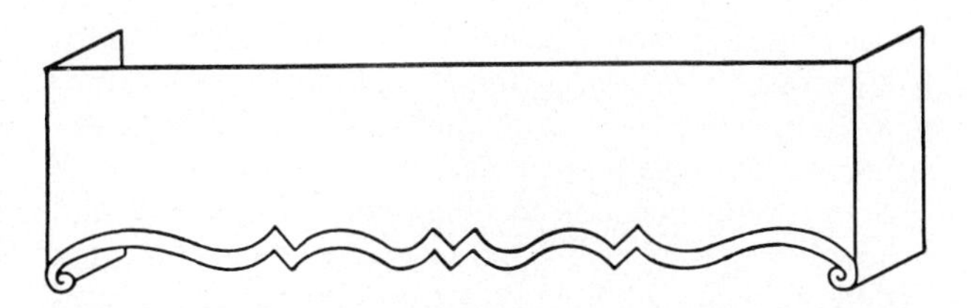

Wood valance, finished with molding—can be painted or treated in natural wood like furniture or woodwork.

Valance board in classic design is made of wood and painted, or mirrored under Greek key design.

Narrow Victorian pressed-metal valance is usually finished in bright brass.

Simple vestibule is used under festoon or shaped valance to bring it out from window frame. Width 4 inches.

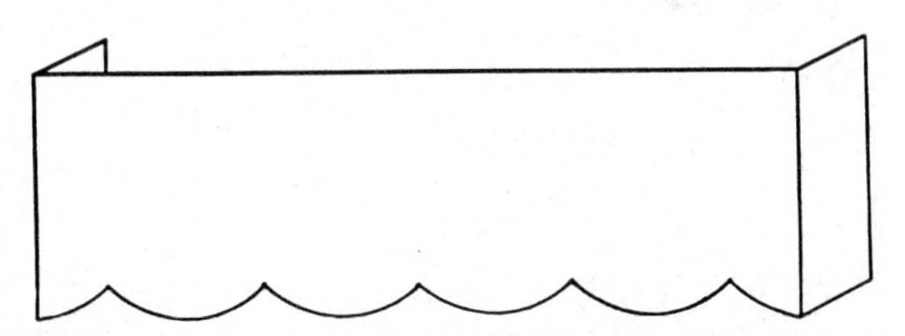

Scalloped valance of plywood can be covered with fabric or used as pattern for soft valance stiffened with buckram.

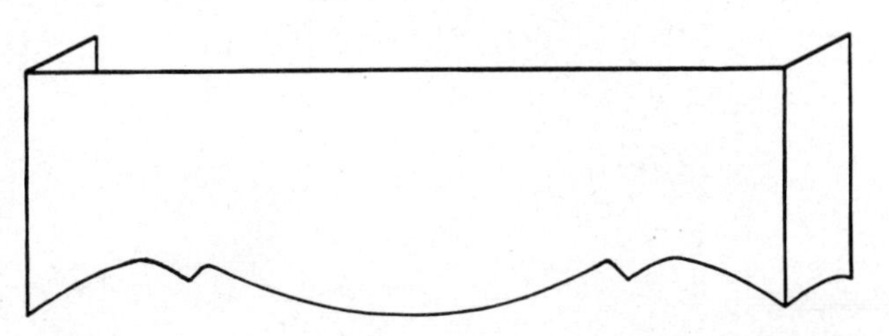

Shaped valance of plywood can be covered with fabric or used as pattern for soft valance stiffened with buckram.

LINING—Except for casement and glass curtains, all heavier materials should be lined. This gives weight to the curtains for better hanging, increases their life expectancy by protecting the fabric from the sun and light, gives a uniform appearance to the windows from the outside of the house, and increases the impression of quality and privacy. Linings are usually made of sateen in cream, tan or white, depending on the background of the fabric used and the outside of the house. There can be many exceptions to this rule, however, in the desire to use the lining as trimming or part of the color scheme. Small-patterned glazed chintzes are often used on cotton curtains, and satin or taffeta for great elegance on silks. This is particularly effective for lining swags which drape to show much of the lining.

Interlining of outing flannel had a tremendous vogue for fine draperies for many years, but it made them very heavy, and today an aluminum-coated sateen is available which answers the same purpose and is more widely used. The principal reason for such lining is to shut out heat in the summertime and keep it in during the winter.

The lining yardage requirement in almost all draperies is exactly the same as the fabric requirement in a plain or striped fabric, as no allowance is necessary for pattern matching.

FINDINGS—Stiffening for headings, or valances, sewed- or pinned-on hooks, rings, weights, rods, cup hooks and ornamental fixtures come under this heading and will vary for different window treatments. You may find it necessary to look over these items in one of the department stores or in a shop which specializes in this type of merchandise before you decide what you need or can use.

There are several kinds of *stiffening* in different widths, perforated at intervals to make pinch pleating at the top of a curtain very easy and regular. Others have a drawstring in them, but do not hesitate to buy plain buckram in the width that you need for stiffening. With a little experimenting you will find you can adapt it to your own specifications.

Heavy long draperies require the large long *hooks* sewed on in several places on the hook. Lighter curtains are better with ordinary small sewed-on hooks. *Pin-on hooks* may be used for a temporary or "hurry up" job, but the draperies will not hang as permanently or as straight when the hooks are merely pinned into the headings. This type of hook is quite useless where there is any strain on the curtain as in the draw or traverse style. With any kind of *hooks*, too many are far better than too few.

Curtain rings are used most often for hand-pulled draw draperies and on the ends of tiebacks. Very fine draperies have a ring sewed on about an inch from the outside edge and six inches above the hem, which is hooked over a small cup hook placed in the window frame or wall to hold down the back edge of the drapery in a straight line.

Lead weights may be sewn between the fabric and the lining on the lining side at the bottom corners of each cur-

A shutter arrangement can be quite effective as a window treatment.

tain to keep it from fluttering and promote straight hanging of loose ends. For glass curtains a string of lead beads connected and covered with tape may be purchased by the yard and run into the bottom edge of the hem for weight.

Curtain rods should be substantial. The traverse rods, ceiling tracks, and plain brass rods cut to measure with strong brackets are the most satisfactory. If you must use lightweight or extension rods, be sure they are firmly anchored and supported at whatever intervals are necessary to keep them from sagging. The swing rods, which are made on a hinge to move back and forth like shutters, have more than a tendency to sag downward at the inside ends, making an ugly line at the top of the window and preventing even the most beautifully made curtains from hanging well.

Cup hooks are used to hold the tiebacks, to hold the back edge straight, and sometimes at the top of the window to anchor the outer edge and prevent it from moving when the curtains are being drawn.

There are many types of wooden poles with brackets and finials, narrow, painted or gilded cornices and other ornamental fixtures. If you do not find what you want, you may have fun designing your own.

If you are planning to have your curtains made, these first planning steps in determining yardage requirements and findings will give you an idea of how much is involved in your window treatments and a fairly accurate idea of costs. The expense of labor for making will be different in different localities and for different types of work. Strangely enough, however, if you let someone else take over the complete responsibility of making, furnishing the lining and installing your draperies, the making cost, except in special cases, will almost always be within a few dollars of the cost of your fabric. If you decide to make your own draperies, you can evaluate your time from one to three dollars an hour, depending upon whether you are an apprentice or an expert. You may easily start in the first class and become an expert quickly, because making curtains is one of the easiest forms of sewing and the satisfaction in accomplishing something really important to your home is out of all proportion to the amount of skill required.

MAKING YOUR OWN CURTAINS AND DRAPERIES

1. CUTTING—For plain and vertically striped fabrics, measure off your required lengths—length of finished curtain, plus hem and heading allowance—and cut straight across along a thread.

For patterned or horizontally striped fabrics the full design or width of stripe should appear at the bottom of each piece *above the hem allowance*. Therefore, begin measuring from the bottom and let any fraction of a design you may have, come out at the top. When you have worked this out on the first length, cut it off and place it on the uncut fabric, matching the pattern exactly. *No matter how carefully you have figured, do not cut anything until you are sure that you have enough fabric to make all the lengths you need.* You may be able to raise or lower the pattern location on each piece or change your hem or heading allowance, but once the cutting is done a shortage on the last length could make you very unhappy, especially if you had to buy another complete length and the fabric was "out of stock."

Cut off the selvage or woven edge on both sides of the fabric. This edge tends to pull and cause your finished curtains to pucker at the edges.

Next, stretch out your lining material right side up and place your length of curtain material on it, right side down. Trim the lining material on one edge from one to two inches narrower than the curtain fabric and remove selvage from other edge of lining. This will make the curtain fabric turn back an inch or two on the wrong side of the curtain, giving a better line and preventing the lining from showing at the edge of the right side. On the next length of fabric cut back the lining on the opposite side to give you a left and right curtain for each pair. *Do not trim lining if you are planning to use a fringe on the inside edge of your curtain.* Now cut lining with each length of curtain fabric and fold or pin each right and left curtain, making a pair together.

Cut pieces for valances or cornices and tiebacks.

2. SEWING—Before the days of the sewing machine, all curtains were made entirely by hand. Today the finest custom-made curtains are still made by hand with the exception of the outside edge seam and the hem of the lining. The inside edge and the hem of the curtain fabric are done by hand, as well as the heading, pleating, and application of trimming. This insures good draping and

From top to bottom, a gold-plated pole with pineapple ends, used with wooden gold-painted rings; gold-painted pole with conventionalized flower ends; gold arrow used for drapery pole, design taken from a ladies' magazine published in 1806; simple gold balls of various sizes form the finials for many drapery poles.

soft hanging, no visible stitching lines and an exquisitely finished product. However, most of us do not consider this perfection of sufficient importance to warrant the time, patience and effort involved. For something only a little less perfect and entirely adequate, we are willing to see all seams done on a sewing machine, except for the hem of the outside curtain. This, like a dress hem, should be blind-stitched by hand.

Whatever the method, the next step is to sew the lining to the fabric at both edges, leaving the top and bottom open. Turn the curtain right side out and press, being sure that the turnover of the curtain fabric caused by trimming the lining comes on the right and the left of alternate lengths to make pairs of curtains.

Now finish the top of each side curtain. If the top goes under a cornice or valance you will whip or stitch the top edge of the lining to the top of the curtain fabric, turning in each piece about an inch. A casing of lining or wide tape may be sewed at the top, and left open at each end to insert the rod; or a row of stitching is made about an inch and a half below the finished top and the ends opened between this stitching and the top to make a place for the rod. Be sure that the rod carrier is ample to take the rod you are planning to use. Do not guess, but try it out before sewing to avoid broken fingernails in trying to make a too-tight casing slide.

If you are planning pinch pleats with a heading above the rod, or a simple shirred top, you will need stiffening in the heading. Cut your stiffening fabric into the lengths required to go across the top of the curtain and insert it and tack it between the lining and curtain fabric before closing the top of the curtain. Pinch pleats are usually made in groups of 3 with an interval of 6 to 10 inches between each group. Plain pleats may be any desired width and are stitched from the top of the curtain to the line at the lower edge of the rod. Making plain pleats into box pleats is a matter of pressing them flat. In planning the pleating for draw draperies, remember that when completely pleated the curtain must be wide enough to cover the window at the top. On page 117 are standard treatments for headings. There are many other possibilities and you may enjoy designing something entirely new for yourself.

The last step in finishing the heading is the sewing on of hooks or rings at regular intervals. Before you purchased the fabric you decided where you wanted the rod to come at the top of the curtain. Check your nearly completed side curtain with your measurements and decide how much is to go into the hem and how much above the hooks at the top.

Now double over each half curtain lengthwise, measure length and mark both edges at the bottom of the hem with pins or tailor's chalk. Turn up hem of lining about two inches shorter than hem of outside curtain to guard against any possibility of the lining sagging and showing at the bottom. This hem may be machine-stitched. Turn up hem of curtain and blind-stitch. The bottom of the curtain is left open like a pillow case. Press hems. Sew in weights.

Festoon valances with swags. Here you are largely on your own, depending upon your festoon design of one, two, three or more festoons on each window, overlapping, made from one piece, shorter on one side than the other. You can experiment with unbleached muslin or lining material until you get the effect you want. If possible mount a rod of the required length on a piece of beaver board, and try out folds, gathers, and shirring, remembering that the valance should be about one eighth of the total height of your window from floor to top of finished drapery treatment. Swags may be triangular pieces folded to drape in a cascade, or diamond-shaped, draped like a jabot for the center of a festoon treatment.

Valance boards—These are usually made of plywood and can be painted or covered with fabric. They are available ready-made in standard sizes in a variety of widths and designs. If you require a special size, width, or design, a carpenter can make them, or if you have any flare

Venetian blind with strips of fabric tacked on the regular tapes and contrasting slats used at intervals.

for working in wood yourself, you can make your own. In covering wooden valance boards it gives them a better appearance to use outing flannel or some soft material against the wood first as a slight padding. Cover the outside with your curtain fabric tacked firmly in place on the wrong side and back the board with lining material turned in against the curtain fabric on the back for a neat finish. In piecing fabrics that are not wide enough for the board, use one width of fabric in the center and split the other piece and sew it to either end of the middle width. This avoids a seam down the middle of the board.

Unlined glass curtains and casements—Cut off selvages to avoid puckering and turn in double hem on both sides. Top pleats are made like those in lined curtains with or without stiffening. A crisp organdy will not require it, but a texture or bouclé which tends to droop in the heading will look better with stiffening. Hems at the bottom should be double if the material is transparent, and tailored types should have weights. Ruffles should be four to six inches deep. If fringe is used the hem at the inside window edge should be no wider than the tape or heading of the fringe.

Our first concern in window treatments has been with adding beauty and charm to our interior decoration. Attaining privacy by day and night light has been a secondary consideration, but none the less important. In our times the roller shade on the window has been the practical answer to this problem. However, in spite of light and dark shades, chintz and stripes, French gathered and fringed, nobody has come to love a roller shade for its beauty and in recent years it is used as little as possible. The present-day tendency is to go back to the methods of our ancestors, using very full glass curtains over the glass, draw draperies at night, and venetian blinds or jalousies on many windows. Not new in the world, but very modern in their present-day use, are the experiments with fine split bamboo, hung both horizontally on rollers and vertically from hooks and capable of being pulled across a window. These can be used in their natural color, or painted for more formal use. They provide interesting light patterns in a room, but should be tested against a light, if privacy at night is your main objective in using them.

The top or heading of curtains varies with the material and visibility. Stiffening is added to almost all types except shirred sheers.

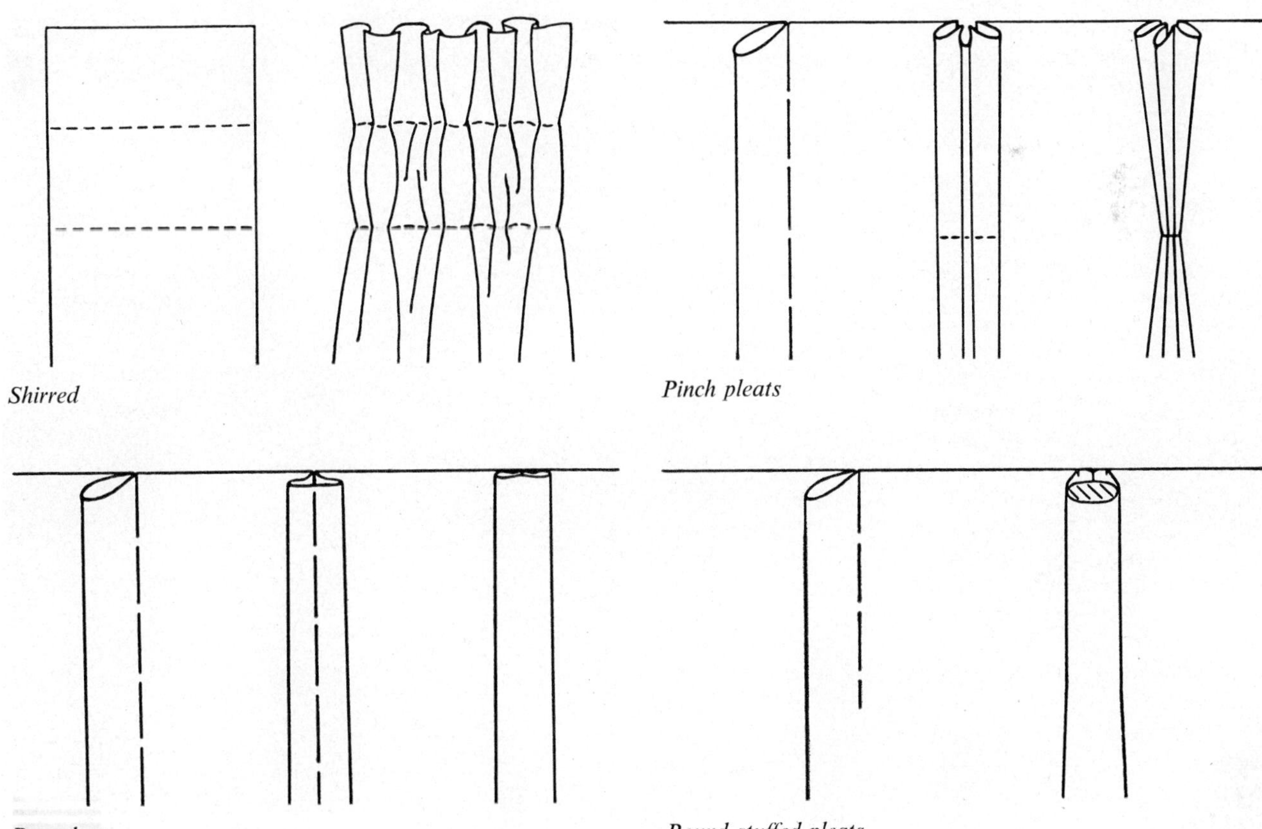

Flooring

Practical Selection and Care

In considering the floors of our home, the color, weave and size of our final floor covering is what we visualize; but actually we know what goes under that covering in the way of flooring, padding or mats is of equal importance and makes a definite contribution to the beauty and degree of formality of any room.

WOOD FLOORS. In practical planning, the wood in the floor, its color and condition, is a definite factor. In most cases the floors of our home came with it, and we accept them as we find them. However, in building a new house, or replacing or reconditioning an old floor, as well as in appraising the quality of a house we are planning to buy or rent, a little knowledge about flooring is helpful.

Although pine, maple, beech, birch, and even walnut, teakwood, mahogany and other woods have been used in flooring in different periods and to achieve definite effects, about eighty per cent of home flooring is of red or white oak. Hence we can use oak flooring as an example, though the same specifications will apply to most other woods, except in the matter of actual grade names.

Oak is put down in one of three general styles—strip, plank, or parquet. All three are available in a wide price range, depending upon the grade of the wood, whether it is plain-sawed or quartersawed, and whether it is prefinished or unfinished. The most expensive will be parquet of the first grade, clear red or white oak. The most economical will be strip flooring of the fifth grade—Victory oak. Either should give a serviceable floor, as may be seen from the Official Grading Rules for Oak.

Strip flooring of quartersawed oak is unstained but thoroughly waxed to produce a fine polished floor.

OAK QUARTERSAWED

CLEAR—The face shall be practically free of defects except ⅜ inch of bright sap. The question of color shall not be considered. Average length, 4½ feet.

SAP-CLEAR—The face shall be practically free from defects, but will admit unlimited bright sap. The question of color shall not be considered. Average length, 4½ feet.

SELECT—The face may contain sap, and will admit wormholes, streaks, slight imperfections in working or a small tight knot, not to exceed one to every 3 feet in length. Average length 4 feet.

OAK PLAIN-SAWED

CLEAR—Same as quartersawed.

SELECT—Same as quartersawed.

NO. 1 COMMON—Shall be of such nature as will make and lay a sound floor without cutting. Average length 3 feet.

NO. 2 COMMON—May contain defects of all characters, but will lay a serviceable floor. Average length 2½ feet.

VICTORY—Shall be machine-run, consisting of all official grades developed in a normal run of average grade lumber with all grades bundled together. The lowest piece admitted shall not be less than No. 2 Common and lay a serviceable floor without cutting.

Oak is a very hard durable wood, and with average household use and care will last as long as the house itself. General practice is to reserve the first grades for living-room and dining-room floors with the lower grades used in less important rooms and the lowest under tiles and linoleums, but actually oak is oak and the grades are more a matter of appearance than wearing quality. The first grades are free from knots and streaks and the less expensive grades may have both.

STYLE—that is, *strip*, *plank* or *parquet*—is largely a matter of formality and elegance and important for floors which are to be entirely exposed, or only partly covered with room-size or scatter rugs. The *strip* style is most widely used because it is most economical in initial cost and adaptable to almost any architectural style of room. It consists of flooring pieces cut in narrow strips and laid in random lengths. Uniform widths produce an even, formal floor—random widths give a more informal effect. *Plank* flooring of wider width boards laid at random is popular and informal for ranch houses, restorations of old houses and elsewhere when the accent is on casual living, or rustic and handmade appearance. *Parquet*, which consists of short lengths of individual pieces of wood laid in a definite pattern of squares, diamonds, or herringbone, was the most elegant type of flooring for formal use in the last century and is again becoming popular for both formal and informal rooms.

FLOOR FINISHING

Whether you are laying new floors, or doing over old ones, the finishing process is about the same. The most important aspect of this is the sanding or surfacing. This is usually done with an electric sanding machine, but corners, areas near the wall, and small spaces must be done by hand. Especially fine floors should be done by hand throughout. The average floor should be covered four times—first crosswise; then lengthwise three times, using a finer sandpaper with each succeeding treatment; and then finally cleaning or buffing the floor with a very fine sandpaper or steel wool, unless paste wood filler is to be used, when steel wool should not be used.

Your next step is finding the final color desired. Some like to leave the natural wood color, others prefer dark or bright colored floors, or wish to cover the streakings or stains which may be present. In any case, it is important that stain or wood filler or the first coat of any finish be applied the same day as the final sanding and buffing. After sanding and buffing, the grain of the wood has a tendency to rise slightly and make the final finished floor rough unless the first staying coat of finish is applied immediately.

Whether you plan to use wood filler or not, the next step is staining, if you wish to change the color of the floor or even it up. Using a 3- or 4-inch-wide varnish brush, begin in the corner of the room farthest from the entrance and work lengthwise of the wood, applying stain to a width of a yard or so. Apply as evenly as possible and wipe off excess with a soft cloth before it has time to set.

Wood filler is a sort of paste preparation which serves to fill in cracks and crevices. It also helps give a high sheen and luster to the floor and comes in dark and light colors to match staining. Some finishes have wood filler in them which may make it unnecessary to use it in a separate coat, except when floors are in poor shape. It should be allowed to dry 24 hours before the next coat of finish is applied. You may brush in the filler across the grain of the wood

Plank flooring is used in an informal setting with braided rug on a highly polished floor.

Parquet flooring in modern informal room makes for special interest in polished floor.

first and then with the grain, but be sure to rub off all excess filler with burlap or excelsior to insure a surface that is uniformly even.

Stain and wood filler are optional, depending upon the condition of the floor and your ultimate desire in color; the finish is what will provide durability, ease of maintenance, capacity for being retouched in worn spots without looking patched up, and the final luster and sheen. The newest finish is *floor seal* which penetrates the wood fibers and wears only as the wood wears. It does not chip or scratch and is practically immune to stains and spots. It acts as a final finish, but is duller, often a distinct advantage where a shiny floor would be out of place. The floor should be buffed with steel wool after each coat of floor seal. One coat is often sufficient, but new floors or resanded floors may require two.

Varnish will give your floors a higher shine and dry more quickly, but you will need two or three coats. It is quite durable, fairly resistant to stains and spots, but scratches easily unless the floor is kept thoroughly waxed. Be sure to use a floor varnish and be careful that floor and brush are clean and free from particles for a smooth finish. The use of shellac owes its popularity to its quick drying action, allowing a second coat to be applied almost immediately. Also it will not darken with age as quickly as varnish, but spots readily if any liquid is allowed to stand on it for any length of time. With the use of shellac there are a few small precautions which will help toward success, if you are warned in advance. First, do not use shellac which has stood around in a metal container as it accumulates salts of iron which discolor your floor. Use a wide brush and make the strokes long and even with laps joined smoothly. Use three coats, rubbing down each one with steel wool or fine sandpaper and sweeping the floor thoroughly between each coat.

WAX—Two or three coats of paste or liquid wax thoroughly rubbed down with an electric polisher or just cheesecloth and elbow grease will be the final finish on your floor, protect the floor seal, varnish or shellac and prevent dirt from getting ground into the floor. When it becomes soiled, it is easily removed and clean wax applied.

If your floor problem is not one of new flooring, but discouraging because the floors have had very hard wear and it has seemed impossible to keep them up, consider doing them over gradually—one room at a time. It really is not as complicated as it sounds, and you can do it yourself with the help of a rented sanding machine. Restoring a badly worn floor is in many ways more satisfying than new wallpaper or curtains, especially to the men of the family.

Linoleum, still in great general use, has been with us for many years for kitchens, bathrooms, playrooms and the like, but today is moving into other parts of the house along with the many new materials and new versions of old ones which we find on the market today. Certainly there are many places or reasons why we might find something other than wood more practical, solving a problem,

Koroseal tile can be elegant and effective as well as practical.

Clay tile dramatically used for dining room in a country house.

or even handsomer for certain floors. Our minds jump immediately to rubber, asphalt, and plastic tiles which are easy to put down and provide infinite variety in style and color. Cork squares, clay tiles, brick, and slate have special appeals and qualifications. However, here is a place where each one needs expert advice, for not all of these materials can be used under any conditions and it is well to find out which will best answer your particular problem. Fundamentally almost every type requires a smooth sound floor for a basis and will not look or wear well over a warped or rough floor, much as we would like to use them for a quick easy solution to that difficulty.

Again starting with a smooth floor, though the color of the wood and the breadth of the boards do not matter, a very pleasing informal floor is attained by painting. Here again the possibilities in choice of color are unlimited. Battleship gray, walnut brown, black are the usual colors, but a pink and gray bedroom might take on new interest with a painted pink floor under a gray rug. The spatter floors we associate with early-American houses have a special charm with their many bright colors against a neutral background. It is true, a painted floor will show wear quickly, but it is one of the quickest and easiest to touch up or repaint.

For an unusual floor of surprisingly good wearing quality and at a very low cost, you might try using wallpaper. It can be made very durable, resistant to dust and grease, and is easy to clean. Here is how you do it.

Select an appropriate design of paper, suggesting tiles, or having a geometric figure, or possibly a paper that is textured or ribbed. Clean and size the floor with regular sizing, filling dents and holes with plastic wood first. Apply wallpaper, as for a wall, matching pattern and

Light braided rugs are a pleasant contrast to the warm flooring in this bedroom from The Denison Homestead, Conn.

EZRA STOLLER

smoothing out carefully. Now 3 coats of waterproof lacquer, and 6 coats of colorless heavy plastic varnish, allowing 24 hours between each application for thorough drying and hardening. After a month, if the floor shows any signs of wear, another coat of varnish will keep it in fine shape.

CARPETS AND RUGS

The luxury of wall-to-wall carpeting, the richness of Orientals, the practical aspect of a large carpet which can be turned around and shows a little floor at the edges, scatter rugs are the final decoration of our floors. Color, degrees of formality, durability, care, cost must also be part of our thinking on this subject. There are devotees of each type of floor covering, and they will make many sacrifices to gratify a dream of long standing, or to be up-to-date with the latest style, but when we are given a free choice, we know that our floor covering can help immeasurably in solving decorating problems and we will be chiefly guided in our aspirations by this consideration.

Since floor covering is one of the largest items in our budget, we consider it thoroughly in long-range planning. In making a choice for the living room, would it be wise to select one that could be used in another room at a later date or better to get an inexpensive covering that can be replaced, if necessary? Would a cotton wall-to-wall carpeting do more for a given room than a smaller more expensive quality? In making these decisions, we are guided by the desired effect and which type of floor covering will give it.

For instance, wall-to-wall carpeting, whether it be cotton, twist, or chenille, will help tie unrelated areas together and increase the size of one room and the sweep

Wall-to-wall carpeting adds spaciousness and gives a unity to the modern room that rugs could not accomplish.

of a series of rooms opening into each other. It will promote the feeling of luxury and formality as well as serenity and quiet. All of these things may be important to you, or your living conditions such that the greater difficulty in cleaning and the constant wear on parts of it are negligible considerations.

Orientals, of course, are famous for wearing quality, conceal spots in the pattern, and impart color and elegance to a room. They are most successful with plain walls and upholstery fabrics, in fact, tend to control the colors and decoration of the room they adorn. It is well, if possible, to try for a size which leaves from 6 inches to 12 inches of floor on all four sides of the room. Too often much of their beauty is lost in being too short or too narrow for a room. This may be somewhat compensated by the addition of a similarly patterned scatter rug or runner where too much floor is showing.

To the practical-minded, the ideal floor covering is a plain-colored or self-patterned rug, cut and bound to fit the room, leaving as much floor as you like on all four sides, or even having it almost touch the wall. This carpet may be turned around from time to time to permit even wear, is easily turned over to be cleaned on both sides or removed for hot-weather coolness.

Almost every home will have some scatter rugs, either on top of large carpeted areas, or in hallways, vestibules, bedrooms and sometimes in a living room.

Carpeting the stairs in one way or another has become almost universal in the American home, both for style and finish, and to cut down on the noise made by passing feet. Stair carpeting should be considered in conjunction with the downstairs hall and living room. If these are entirely carpeted, the stairs will look better if carpeted right out to the edge, as in the illustration on page 123. However, if your preference in the hall has been for a runner or rug on a polished floor, you may well decide to use the regular twenty-seven-inch stair carpeting made for this purpose. In choosing a carpeting for the stairs, it is well to remember that it will get more wear than the rest of your floor coverings. It can be moved from time to time. That is, with a few feet of extra length folded under the last stair rise at the bottom of the stairs, or concealed at the top stair, when worn spots begin to show on the edge of the tread, the carpeting may be moved down to make what was the front edge fall into the base of each stair rise and a new surface appear on the front edge. However, in your long-range plan, if you can possibly manage it, it would be well to buy enough extra carpeting to replace the stair carpet, should it wear out completely while the matching floor carpet is still in good condition. This, again, depends on the size of your family and the kind of use you can expect them to give the stairs.

You are not through with the consideration of your floors until you decide what is to go under the carpet to increase its thickness and consequent luxury and comfort, to make it wear longer, and in the case of scatter rugs to insure anchorage and safety. Some of the new carpetings today are painted with rubber or plastic on the back which prevents them from slipping, and there are thin rubber mats for small rugs under which a heavy pad would be awkward. Under larger rugs and carpets of all types, a heavy pad of felt or foam rubber will earn many times its cost in prolonging the life of the floor covering. Nowadays the pads can be permanently mothproofed, and the foam-rubber manufacturers have eliminated the odor which was apparent, especially in warm weather, in the first attempts to substitute this material for felt.

Finally, when everything is decided, bought and paid for, and you have stretched your budget to provide good floor coverings, there is one simple fact which gives you a reason to be especially particular about keeping floor coverings well vacuumed or cleaned. The greatest enemy of wool carpeting is the sharp edges of sand and dirt tracked in over it even in ordinary weather by ordinary feet. The gritty particles get down to the base of the pile in a carpet and, as they are ground in, actually cut the wool threads. Carpets, of course, are made to be walked on and will wear indefinitely, if attention is given to this detail.

Carpet, cut to room size, is obviously flexible in use.
MINNEAPOLIS-HONEYWELL ENGINEERS

Scatter rug provides contrast to completely carpeted area.

Parquet can be used with Modern.

GREEFF FABRICS, INC.

Cork is effective here on floor and wall.

Oriental runner blends well with Classic.

DAVISON ART CENTER, WESLEYAN UNIVERSITY

White glazed tile complements wrought-iron furniture.

MC COBB WROUGHT IRON FURNITURE

Cotton twist is fitted from wall to wall.

DREXEL FURNITURE COMPANY

Plastic squares in living room strike a dramatic note.

HAROLD FOWLER

White unfinished plaster will never look like a temporary condition if it is incorporated into the color scheme of the room. The red-and-white chintz here does just that. The red sofa and green chair carry on.

Interior Walls

Appropriate Treatment and Materials

In an empty room there is more wall space than anything else and our plans for wall treatment seem to be the most important decision to make. This is partially true because what we do to the walls will make them recede to make a larger room or approach to decrease its size; will make the whole room busy or restful; will determine the pace of the other furnishings. However, in a finished room the walls retire to their proper place and go unnoticed unless something very special or startling has been done to them.

Early in our plans we decided whether we liked paint or wallpaper, paneling, mirrors, or fabric for the walls. Now is the time to consider some of the practical aspects of these wall treatments. In most new houses the walls are finished in white plaster and we are cautioned not to paper or paint them for several months, or even a year until the house is thoroughly settled. This is not necessarily a drawback to our decorating plans as plain white walls can be very attractive and keynote the tempo of a whole room, formal, casual, or just for everyday living with no defined interest in style. On page 126 the white walls are effective and a part of the plan of the room. They could be pale green or a soft rose eventually, but perhaps this would reduce a charming room to mediocrity. In this problem there is no choice, but white walls have proved so effective in lightening a room and providing an excellent setting for almost any color, that those who do not have them originally often choose them.

Good plaster may be left unpainted, or eventually painted a plain color or papered at will. Very old patched or broken plaster presents quite another problem. If your heart is set on painting old plaster from which wallpaper has been removed or which has suffered from leaks or settling, do not be discouraged. It can be done with a little patience and enough coats of paint. Fresh plaster patches have a tendency to absorb paint differently from old plaster and may show through the first coats, or you may have to wait for the new plaster to age a bit before you attain completely satisfactory results, but it can be done. The problem of removing every tiny trace of wallpaper paste from plaster in order to paint is even more difficult, but it also can be done. Occasionally when your heart is set on a plain color and a wall is in bad shape, or you are so anxious to be done with the walls, you will settle for the simplest solution—a plain-colored paper of which there are hundreds on the market. Your final result will give much the same effect as a painted wall. However, one word of warning about this simple solution, in case you are planning to do your own papering. It takes a very neat and careful workman to use plain paper with nicely pressed-out seams and no paste or finger marks on the right side. Unless they are exceptionally skilled with handwork, amateurs do well to get a little practice in their wallpapering with patterned papers in an all-over design which will conceal slight errors or ineptitudes.

When it comes to painting, the mechanical problems are somewhat easier. You have chosen a color for one reason or another, but your task is to achieve the exact shade that you desire. In the old days you started with a bucket of white paint and a few tubes of color—sienna, cobalt, madder, lamp black, verdigris or others—and put a few dabs of each in your bucket, stirring madly and wondering what color the wall would be when it was dry. That is still lots of fun and full of surprises. However, from a strictly practical point of view, you will be better off buying mixed paints from one of the many lines of colors now offered by most manufacturers. Attic pink, dormitory buff, oyster white, cream, sky blue have given way to hundreds of colors and shades. Now you can buy that exact shade of peacock, chartreuse, or cocoa already mixed and know how it will look when it is dry. For general use a semigloss on the woodwork and a flat finish on the walls are most satisfactory.

Whether to paint or to use wallpaper is a constantly recurring question, but there are a number of other things you might like to try for all or some of your walls. The use of wood as a wall finish dates from the earliest houses in this country. We remember the type of pine sheathing that the earliest settlers used, the very handsome paneling of the eighteenth century which was almost always painted, and the mahogany and walnut libraries of the last century. Currently there are a number of plywoods and wall sheathings in wood which, though designed as a background for modern rooms and furniture, are well adapted to all sorts of small houses, apartments and ranch houses. Some of these come finished with grooves and are ready to install. Others can be pickled, stained, rubbed down with potash or a little color to give charming or interesting effects.

Our ancestors used velvets, brocades, satins and leather on their walls. We are more apt to use printed cottons or chintzes and plastics resembling leather when our decoration calls for something of this sort. If fabrics are used on the walls they should be mounted on frames which fit each wall section for easy removal and cleaning. Plastics may be glued directly to the wall in the manner of leather or wallpaper.

For quick inexpensive freshening in a room, it is well to investigate paints that are applied directly over wallpaper, giving a new color and obliterating the pattern entirely. The same treatment may be given to cover the old grass cloth walls of the last century which seem to last forever, but get exceedingly drab and dated. Color stippled over the latter gives an interesting effect of a textured paper and rejuvenates the whole room. These are, of course, stopgap measures, but often time or the budget makes them a welcome solution until something more permanent can be done. The paint dries overnight and will look even and well done when dry, however amateurish it appears when first applied. Just a hint, if you are going to do it yourself. Wipe up spots on the floor while they are wet.

Mirrors, not hanging on the wall but as actual wall covering, have found their way into many homes of all types, not because they are any particular style of decoration in themselves, but because they add glow to a room and amply reflect its own style. Until recently the prices were prohibitive, or if the glass itself was obtainable, the cost of installation almost duplicated the price. This will still be true for a major installation involving a whole wall with door and window openings, but the home decorator can now install quite handsome large mirrors himself with the brackets which are packaged with each custom-cut mirror. These brackets are equipped with hardware and felt-padded clips which may be fastened to the wall with wood screws, toggle bolts, or other means, depending upon the type of wall.

The lower bracket is attached first, then the upper bracket with the ratchet clips in raised position as in the illustration at the right. The mirror is then placed in the felt-padded lower bracket clips and raised to the wall against the upper bracket. Ratchet clips are now lowered to hold mirror in place.

Mirrored walls may be of clear glass, fogged or smoked—each name describing very well the appearance of the glass itself. A gay lively room or one that needed a bit of these qualities added to it would call for the first type. Fogged glass could be used where the light was a trifle too strong and the smoked type is most at home in a very sophisticated room.

There are a few household hints concerning walls which may be useful. We always save leftover wallpaper for a possible replacement in case of accident to a room. However, unless this accident happens within a few weeks of the original hanging of the paper, the remnant will no longer match and will make an ugly patch where you have tried to use it. Sometimes wallpaper will tend to peel off in dry spots or on large areas. If you do not have wallpaper paste on hand, mix a little flour and water and stick it back immediately before it really tears or breaks off.

Brackets are installed to hold large wall mirror.

PITTSBURGH PLATE GLASS CO.

Before repainting a kitchen the walls must be scrubbed, as paint will not adhere to grease or oily surfaces. Often a mere scrubbing will so improve the room that painting will not be necessary—often, but not always.

In bathrooms and halls you can protect your wallpaper with a colorless wallpaper lacquer which may be wiped off with a damp rag. There are several good lacquers on the market which do not change the color of the paper, but they are not recommended for plain papers, or those with a black background.

Wood paneling should be thoroughly waxed once or twice a year to preserve the finish and discourage cracking.

Do not be timid about trying something new on your walls. It is an age of experiment and much of the fun in decorating today springs from the loosening of the bonds of traditional usage.

A strip of wallpaper is used between two windows.
KATZENBACH AND WARREN

One wall is pine sheathing, others are papered in stripes.
MONSANTO CHEMICAL CO.

Styrene plastic tile used in vertical, horizontal strips.
MONSANTO CHEMICAL CO.

Mirrored fireplace and doorway have indirect lighting.
LIBBEY-OWENS-FORD GLASS COMPANY

This enchanting needlepoint rug, at the bottom, made by the associates of the British Women's Home Industries, Ltd., was the inspiration for the needlepoint chair seats illustrated. It may be hung on the wall like a tapestry, or cover a table in the manner of our ancestors. Beautiful on the floor, it could provide a center of interest for any room.

HAROLD FOWLER

Pictures and Mirrors

Selection, Hanging and Arrangement

Pictures come under the general heading of accessories, yet must be considered separately because they play such an important decorating role. The selection of pictures, almost more than any other furnishing, provides a clue to personality, artistic taste and individuality. The way they are used forcefully adds or subtracts from the decorative rating of a room. Pictures call attention to an important furniture piece, provide interest for a drab corner, brighten a dull hallway, dress up a bare wall. They either key or carry out a color scheme. As for atmosphere, pictures create it, since their subject matter sets the mood, be it formal or informal, masculine or feminine, gay or serene. Considering these points, you will easily see why pictures should be selected carefully.

The choice is a very personal one, so don't let art connoisseurs embarrass you into purchasing a "good" picture because you think you should like it. For the purposes of home decorating, a picture is as good as you think it is. The work of the greatest master is not a suitable addition to your home unless it holds meaning for you. Pictures should fit in with your decorative scheme, wear well, and you should get true enjoyment from them.

The field of selection is wide. Original works have a special charm because they are one of a kind. There is a pride of possession that comes with knowing a painting belongs solely to you. Nor are originals always beyond the reach of the average-income family. Talented young artists, who have not yet received recognition, frequently place a modest price tag on their canvases, or you may do some art work yourself.

However, it is wiser to hang the reproduction of a worthy painting than to display a poorly executed original. Some reproduction processes are so excellent they faithfully duplicate even the slightest brush mark. The best of these you will be able to purchase through art museums and shops. The only word of caution needed is to avoid fads. In recent years, for example, Van Gogh has enjoyed such popularity that few living rooms seem to be without at least one of his paintings. This overuse detracts from the individuality of a room, makes it seem like an unimaginative copy of others.

In selecting pictures, also consider woodcuts, prints in black and white or color with bold lines; etchings, ink impressions from plates engraved by lines eaten out with acid; steel engravings, which have line and wash effects; lithographs, chalklike drawings in black or colors, mezzotints, lineless designs in velvety black and white; or aquatints, noted for their subtle and delicate coloring. Among other suitable wall decorations are photographs, maps, tapestries, petit point embroideries and samplers.

The subject of a picture is of prime importance, since it tells a great deal about the owner. A person of simple taste may like an appealing landscape, while the more complex individual finds pleasure in a bold abstract drawing. The subject should express personal tastes and interests and, at the same time, suit the room in which it is to hang.

Pictures for the living room of the average home should not be too startling in subject, color or composition. This is a restful room, one in which the family spends many hours. The selection, therefore, must be one that will be pleasant to view every time the room is entered. The enjoyment of a well chosen picture increases, rather than diminishes, with time. For the living room, then, consider landscapes, marines, portraits—not necessarily of family members—flower prints or figures.

Pictures for the dining room can be gayer and bolder since you will not have the opportunity to tire of them as readily. Vividly done flowers, still lifes and landscapes provide a pleasing background for dining. Nor should the kitchen be forgotten. A few bright pictures bring it the decorator touch you have taken care to achieve elsewhere in the house. Fruit and vegetable prints or other subject matter related to homemaking or cooking, or a gay cartoon may furnish just the needed note of kitchen color. A bulletin board for posing pictures and memos that occupy passing fancy is a very useful wall decoration here as well as in teen-agers' rooms.

The bedroom is the place to display family photographs, or those which have personal significance. Godey prints or florals create an unmistakably feminine atmosphere. Sport scenes, dogs or horses bespeak a man's room. Storytelling pictures delight young children, while teenagers prefer cork boards which permit quick and frequent changes of snapshots, dance programs and other miscellany. In a rumpus room, anything goes—travel posters, cartoons, hobby groupings, whatever strikes the fancy and is colorfully amusing.

Color is the first thing you notice about a picture. Decorators oftentimes use a painting to set the scheme for an entire room. Pictures can repeat upholstery, rug or drapery shades. They may also provide needed contrasting color accents. Always the colors of a painting are on friendly terms with the rest of the room. Never should they clash. Generally speaking, bold, warm colors brighten gloomy corners or have the power to make a large room appear cozy and intimate. Cool shades, found in sea and landscapes, help push back the walls of a small room, giving it needed vista.

The purpose of a frame is to enclose and add beauty to a picture. It should never be a dominating feature. The frame you choose will depend on the subject and type of picture. A period oil painting demands a rich, heavy frame. Antique frames may also be used for modern oils, though these are more frequently enclosed in simple wood designs which blend well with contemporary furnishings. Frames that have a worm-eaten or weatherbeaten look of age are increasingly in demand, as are those which play up the natural beauty of the wood grain. When framing a reproduction, it is advisable to invest in a good frame so that it does not appear cheap. Oils are invariably framed without mats or glass.

Because of their delicacy, water colors are simply framed. This is also true of pencil sketches and other pictures which a bold enclosure might easily overpower. Black or colors (always in keeping with the room scheme) are effective for prints, etchings and lithographs.

Pictures come ready to hang on the wall, but it is occasionally difficult to find just the right happy combination of picture and frame. Your alternative is to make separate purchases. Select the print, painting, photograph or magazine illustration that suits your needs and have it mounted. There are shops that make a specialty of this. You will find they offer a wide variety of framing choices. In addition to wood, frames are made of glass, mirror, chrome, cork, fabrics, plastics and numerous other materials.

For very casual settings, such as rumpus rooms, children's rooms, and for pictures of temporary interest, you simply use heavy cardboard on the back, glass on the front, and secure the whole with adhesive tape or black plastic Scotch tape with a patent-leather finish.

Take the size of the frame and the wall into consideration when selecting the mat for a picture. A square frame calls for top and side margins of the same size with a wider margin at the bottom. A rectangular frame hung horizontally will have a narrow margin at the top, wide at the bottom and medium on the sides. An upright rectangle needs a medium margin at the top, is narrowest at the sides and widest at the bottom.

Use a wide mat to make a small picture appear larger. It is also the best choice for pictures crowded with objects or action, or those to be hung on a patterned wallpaper.

White mats are a desirable choice because they accentuate the colors in a picture. For subdued effects, use gray. Mats may be any color, however, as long as they do not overshadow. They are often chosen to pick up upholstery

Venetian mirrors which clip to your doors are made in standard sizes to fit interior millwork doors.

PITTSBURGH PLATE GLASS COMPANY

Picture of this type may be framed with or without a mat.

MONSANTO CHEMICAL CO.

or drapery shades or to contrast or harmonize with the picture itself.

In addition to standard mat paper, which is a rather thin cardboard, mats may be mirror, glass, handmade or metallic paper, plywood, fabric, wallpaper, or whatever material your ingenuity and decorative sense dictate.

Once the right picture has been selected, you must give thought to proper placement. Never hang a picture merely to fill up an empty wall space. Pictures do not stand alone but must provide a connecting link between backgrounds and furnishings. Thus, hang pictures over sofas, tables or desks that are placed against the wall to provide an anchor. You may also relate pictures to architectural features, arranging them at the sides of doors, archways, even windows. Try to make your pictures form a unit with other furnishings.

Common sense will tell you what size picture to use. Since it is part of a unit, the picture must be in proportion to the furniture it hangs over and the wall it hangs on. A small print is forlorn and out of place on a great expanse of wall over a huge sofa. Instead, one large picture or a group of several small ones should be hung. By the same token, a massive oil painting does not belong over a fragile end table. For harmonious arrangement, shape must also be considered. If furniture has horizontal lines, the pictures over it must correspond to present a pleasing combination.

Balance and rhythm are important factors in picture placement. A picture should be well centered for a formal effect. Off-center arrangements can be achieved by proper spacing and effective distribution of other accessories. A picture, for example, may hang to the left side of a buffet if a tall lamp is placed at right.

Groupings of small pictures are sometimes more decorative than one large picture would be. They should hang close together as a unit to avoid a helter-skelter look. Formerly it was thought that subject matter, color values and frames in groupings should be fairly closely related. The modern trend, however, permits a great deal of leeway. The adventurous combine water colors, oils and prints that are square, rectangular, oval and diamond-shaped with strikingly attractive results. This is chancy, so unless you have a keen artistic sense it's safer to stick to more conservative groupings. Before you hang groupings, plan the arrangement on paper or cut out patterns of the frames and try them on the wall. The same rules of size (here the size of the entire grouping), choice and placement which govern a single picture are also applicable to the group unit.

Groupings are extremely versatile in their uses. They can circle an oval dressing-table mirror or frame a square one. Use them to turn a corner with a sectional bookcase or to march up a stairway. This, by the way, is the only proper place for a stepladder picture arrangement. Groupings can cover a screen, a door, or even an entire wall, creating a wallpaper-type pattern.

Pictures are best hung on painted walls but may be mounted against wallpapers which are not overly patterned. Scenics and papers with busy and intricate designs make confusing backgrounds, however.

For emphasis, isolate a picture on a large expanse of wall. Don't let a lamp or vase hide it. Utilize lighting to create importance. Paintings should always be lighted from the side. A light from the front will cause a glare on the oil or glass and obscure the subject. Hence, choose your picture placement with a view toward lighting from side windows, lamps or concealed spotlights.

Don't hang pictures too high on the wall. Small paintings should be placed so the center of interest is at eye level. Oils, which are meant to be admired from afar, may be slightly higher. All pictures, however, should be arranged so they may be easily viewed on close inspection.

Crooked pictures, which superstition has it, mean bad luck, are the result of poor hanging. A single nail is not a good anchor. It is best to use two nails or picture hooks. Space them a little less than the width of the picture apart. Picture-frame wire, heavy string or light cord will not slip when placed over these nails. Make sure pictures hang flat against the wall and conceal hanging fixtures. Before driving in nails, place a tiny piece of Scotch tape over the place marked for the nail. This will keep plaster from chipping or forming an unsightly hole when the nail is driven home. Use the special nails with attached hooks

For very casual settings such as rumpus rooms, children's rooms, and for pictures of a temporary interest, it is easy and practical to frame pictures between sheets of glass.

that are sharp and go in at a slant, or hammer regular nails in at a downward angle so that the weight of the picture tends to push the nail further into the wall and provides good anchorage for the wire.

Very large pictures are usually hung from the picture molding, or your walls may make this more advisable for any type picture. When this treatment is used, make the hanging as inconspicuous as possible. Parallel wires attract the least attention and conform to the rectangular lines of most pictures. Hence two wires hung from two molding hooks will look better than a triangle wire from one hook to each side of the picture, except in the case of an oval picture when the triangle is better. You may be able to find hooks the same color as the woodwork or wall, but if not it is merely a matter of planning ahead to paint a few when a room is being painted. Avoid silk cords and tassels unless a room is very stylized and calls for such treatment.

Framed mirrors, except that they are not hung in groups, follow very much the same rules as those suggested for pictures. Mirrors should be in proportion to the piece of furniture over which they hang, both in size and style of frame. They are almost a necessity to decorating and, if wisely used, can provide great interest and variety to our wall decoration.

The section on mirrors as wall covering and the one on styles in frames tell most of the story. There are a few practical suggestions which may give you the clue as to what is right and what is wrong with your mirrors. For instance, if a room is long and narrow, you can make it seem wider and in better proportion by hanging a long oblong mirror horizontally on one of the long walls. A mirror on the short wall will make the room seem even longer and narrower. If a fireplace is tall and the mantelshelf high, a long oblong horizontal mirror will look better than a tall narrow mirror reaching for the ceiling. A vertical oblong mirror between two small windows will tie them together as an attractive unit. In a hallway, the shining reflection in a mirror of sun- or lamp-light has a welcoming look, and a mirror here also serves the woman who likes to give her appearance a last-minute check. Mirrors are strategically placed to reflect the view of a picture window or to echo some particularly pleasing furniture arrangement or decoration. They can also be used as the center of interest around which pictures are hung.

A mirror intended for use, such as one in a bedroom or hallway, should be hung at a height to allow a good full view. Such mirrors should also be well lighted.

Like pictures, mirrors come in a variety of sizes and are framed to complement other furnishings in a room. It is best to buy a good mirror, since a poor quality may spot, chip or cloud. The frame is another matter. Mirror glass is heavy and takes a fairly strong frame, but some of the old-fashioned picture frames that go for a song in a secondhand shop or at an auction make very interesting and different mirror frames. If you do not care for the plain unframed mirrors which are used so widely with modern furnishings, or if your room is not that modern, frame a mirror in the unfinished, bleached or pickled woods that are used for modern pictures.

By covering the wall with burlap—in this case it's calcimined—nails may be driven in without damage and new picture arrangements can be worked out as desired.

There is nothing really mysterious about picture hanging if one keeps in mind a few simple rules. Large pictures are placed over a fireplace and should be in proportion to the furniture; small pictures may be grouped to make a large unit. Pairs of pictures can be arranged symmetrically. These are examples of simple improvements which your eye will catch at once.

DRAWINGS BY MICHAEL SENICH

No

Yes

No

Yes

No

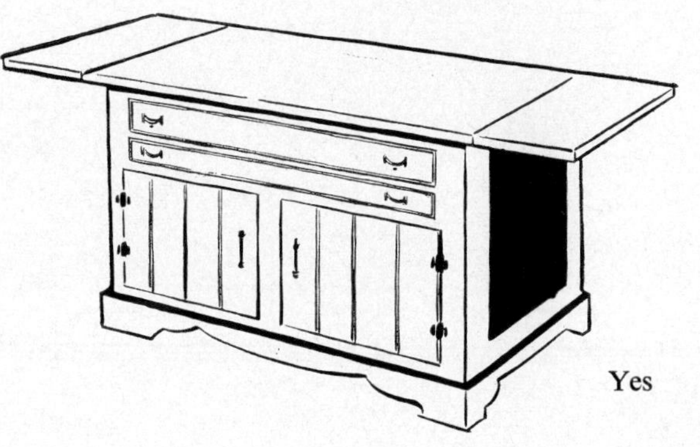

Yes

HAROLD FOWLER

Japanese lanterns, long an established and delightful feature of alfresco evening entertainment, have now come indoors to add a piquant note to the casual and informal room.

Lighting

Distribution and Installation

The eight point black wrought-iron pin-up lamp shown on page 138 provides light in any desired direction by the simple device of hanging the lamp on any of the eight points required. You can have light up or down, oblique or slanted for general illumination yet concentrated in any preferred direction. The shade is of molded Fiberglas that is washable and unbreakable. The circle measures 14½ inches and the lamp protrudes 9¼ inches from the wall. It will hardly make a pinprick in your budget.

Here we have an example of the attention designers are paying to the efficiency required today in lighting, as well as good design and new ideas. With the exception of candles on a dining table or mantel for a special party, no one considers lighting any more except in terms of electricity with all its new developments and intensities which can actually give us an opportunity to change night into day indoors, if we like. However, most of us understand that our houses would have an artificial air indeed if we took this possibility too literally. Instead, we capitalize on the difference between day and night lighting to give our rooms a welcome change of aspect by evening. A living room may appear sunny, bright and cheerful by daylight. By night we can really change the appearance of the colors entirely to make it cozy and warm, gloomy and austere, or give it dramatic interest depending on how it is lit and which lights we will use to create different moods in the same room.

Artificial light changes everything, especially drapery, upholstery, and slip-cover fabrics and can also bring out different hues in each, so that it is well in selecting home furnishings to try them by daylight and in the evening. Filament lamps emphasize reds, yellows, and warm shades, but fluorescent lamps dull these shades and make the cool colors such as blue and green important. Hence colors and light are interdependent and must influence your choice in both fields.

There are numerous ways in which a home may be lighted. Ceiling fixtures, wall brackets, built-in concealed units, and floor and table lamps are among the most practical aids which may be combined in various ways for serviceable and decorative lighting. The eye works best when there is not too much contrast between the immediate task and the surrounding area. For this reason, the proper illumination lights a room generally and in specific spots.

Ceiling fixtures are possibly the most common form of general lighting, but they are far from the only means of obtaining it. Among the more decorative installations are window lighting units with the drapery valance concealing the lighting fixture. These can be elaborate or simple and inexpensive and even made at home with very little trouble. The fixture installed over the window is plugged in at floor level by means of a cord which is hidden by the draperies. General lighting may also emanate from a curved cove or straight trough installed at the top of the wall or over doors. Modern installations also utilize glass wall or ceiling panels for over-all lighting. It should be remembered, however, that architectural installations, which are efficient, inconspicuous, and decorative, are best planned when the house is being built. Lamps equipped with reflector bowls will also throw light on walls and ceiling for general lighting and diffuse direct light downward at the same time.

Special lighting, required for specific tasks such as sewing, study, or reading, is usually obtained from table or floor lamps, which can also be decorative. Special lighting is also achieved with built-in units over work or reading areas.

When planning general and special lighting for a room, work out a scheme of balanced, diffused illumination. Remember that the eye is not equipped to cope with both brightness and darkness simultaneously. Contrast and glare are often the same thing, as when a sharp spotlight pierces a dim room. Both should be avoided. Direct glare may be caused by raw light striking the eye. It can be sidestepped by using properly placed, diffused, and shielded light sources. Indirect glare, also a menace to eye comfort, may be caused when light bounces back from shiny surfaces, such as mirrors, gleaming metals, or glass-topped desks.

In a room where brightness is important, you can intensify your lighting by using a pale color scheme throughout the room. The ceiling should be white. Light-colored mat-finished walls and light floor coverings will bring about greater reflection and diffusion of light. Dark ceilings and walls will naturally require additional illumination.

Each room in the house has its own particular lighting requirements. The living room need not have a ceiling

Eight-point black wrought-iron pin-up lamp provides light in any desired direction by the simple device of hanging the lamp on any of the eight points. You can have light up or down, oblique or slanted.

FORETRENDS LAMPS

fixture, since general lighting may be obtained from lamps with reflector bowls or with concealed installations such as the valances and coves already illustrated. Wall brackets may also supply general lighting, but they do limit furniture and picture arrangements. For specific lighting, lamps should be arranged on end tables at the ends of the sofa and on tables next to chairs in conversational groupings. The lamp arrangement should be balanced so that lighting effects are even and the eye does not have the strain of adjusting from light to dark. Even TV should not be viewed in total darkness. The brightness of the screen will hurt the eyes unless soft lights are kept on. For

TV, place lamps with opaque shades out of the range of the screen.

In the dining room, soft lighting effects are generally favored since they are conducive to relaxation and leisurely enjoyment of meals. While ceiling fixtures are generally chosen to be inconspicuous, a dining-room ceiling light may be an elaborate period piece in keeping with the room decorations, which is centered over the table to throw a pleasing glow on the setting. Cove lighting may be used in this room or light may be reflected from a pair of floor lamps or buffet urns. Costly but most effective lighting schemes for dining rooms sometimes feature lighting panels set under frosted glass in the table itself or in cabinets and buffets. Flickering candles are always a romantic and friendly way to light a meal. Be sure to provide a sufficient number of candles to light the table, and see that they are tall enough so as not to shine in the eyes of the diners.

Since kitchen and laundry are work areas, lighting must be utilitarian. Usually fluorescent fixtures are favored. In addition to a ceiling installation, special lights should be provided over sink, stove, washer, dryer and work counters. De luxe installations also flash lights on when cabinet doors are opened, making contents immediately apparent. For safety's sake, workbenches, which are usually located in basement or garage, must also be properly illuminated.

An overhead light and mirror lights are generally all that is required for the bathroom. Mirror lighting should be arranged so that your face is fully lighted as you look at its reflection. Lights on either side of the mirror will do this.

In a bedroom, dressing-table lamps should be placed about a yardstick apart from shade center to shade center on either side of the make-up mirror. They must be tall enough (usually about 20 inches) to bring the shade to cheek level. Uncolored shades which are at least 8 inches in diameter are preferable, since they give true light for cosmetic application. The right size bulb is a flexible one which may be turned on at 30 watts for a pretty glow or switched up to 100 watts for make-up sessions. If your lamps have one-way sockets, use at least a seventy-five-watt bulb. A bedroom usually has an overhead light and a special reading lamp, perhaps on a bedside table, where it should be placed so light will shine directly on the book. Pin-up lamps are frequently used for in-bed reading. Hang them at opposite ends of the bed headboards with shade bottoms 30 inches above the mattress. Shades should be white, at least 12 inches wide and opaque so as to avoid bright-spot contrast, which is bad for the eyes.

CLAY TILE FIREPLACE

GENERAL ELECTRIC COMPANY

Above, lights are behind lower molding and reflected by white cove. Below, general lighting comes from bulb in valance of curtain; direct light from ceiling spotlight.

Paint cords to match the walls and they won't be too conspicuous.

Halls and stairways require lighting, which may be subdued. The main need here is the avoidance of accidents. It is well to keep a small night light burning on the stairway for late homecomers or family insomniacs.

When planning lighting for a home, do not overlook the advantages of installing a remote-control wiring system. The conveniences of such a plan are countless. Key switches enable you to operate lights and electric appliances throughout the house. Think of the desirability of flooding a darkened house with lights as you enter late at night or the advantages of being able to turn off forgotten garage or entrance lights from a bedside switch.

Lamps are possibly the most important of all lighting fixtures because they figure so prominently in the decorative scheme and are portable, whereas ceiling and other installations are permanent and are less likely to be changed by those who rent apartments or homes. For these reasons lamps must be carefully chosen to harmonize with the decorative scheme and to fulfill lighting needs.

Lamp-design variety is seemingly endless, and it should not be difficult to find lamps that are the proper size, style and material for a room by day as well as by night. When selecting lamps, even if you are not doing a whole floor plan it is a good idea to make a rough plan of the room, circling groups of furniture which need illumination. This will enable you to determine the number and type of lamps needed. Use table lamps where possible, substituting floor lamps in areas where there are no tables or cabinets, but taking care not to create a forest of ironwork.

A table lamp should, of course, be in proportion to the table on which it is to be placed. A massive lamp does not belong on a delicate table any more than a tiny lamp belongs on a huge buffet. Some lamps bear a CLM (Certified Lamp Manufacturers) tag which takes the guesswork out of purchasing since they meet various standards insuring lighting performance for specific needs, mechanical soundness and electrical safety. Thus, certified end-table lamps are designed for the average end tables and will be the proper size, but if you are measuring your own, or making new ones, the rules are simple. The base of a table

Overhead light is for general illumination and side lights for direct use.

GENERAL ELECTRIC COMPANY

Built-in fluorescent fixture is fine over working area.

GENERAL ELECTRIC COMPANY

lamp should be tall enough to locate the lower edge of the shade nearly level with your eyes when you are sitting in a chair. For the best placement, the lamp should be not more than one foot away from you and in line with your shoulder. In this way, light does not glare into your eyes but will be focused on reading material, sewing or whatever task is at hand. Because floor lamps are much taller than table lamps they cannot be placed at the side of your chair since too much light would shine into the eyes. Arrange them so the base of the lamp rests as closely as possible to the rear side of the chair leg. For reading, it doesn't make any difference at which side of the chair the lamp is placed, either left or right will do. For specific purposes, such as sewing, piano playing or study, adjustable or swivel lamps are especially useful if not as decorative as other types.

Lamp bases are made of a variety of materials—china, pottery, wood, metal, and plastics to mention a few. In selecting shades, consider the base material, size, and shape. Obviously the lampshade must be in accord with the base. A square base looks best with a square shade; an oval or round base takes a circular one. Bell-shaped shades, either square or oval, go on lamps of curved lines or for a soft effect. Drum and cylinder shades complement modern and straight lamps for a tailored style. Exotic pagoda, umbrella, or hourglass shapes are eye-catching, but in questionable taste, except for a passing fancy. As for size, the shade cannot be too large or it will dwarf the base; too small or it will make the base appear huge and heavy. A well-proportioned shade has a diameter across the bottom that is about two thirds the height of the lamp. The chart at the end of this chapter will give you a check list of shade sizes for various lamps.

Aside from concealing the mechanism of actual lights, the shade's main purpose is to shield your eyes from the glare of naked bulbs. Generally speaking, shades should be as plain as possible in solid colors, though occasionally a patterned shade is permissible, especially on an opaque shade. To tie a lamp in with the color scheme of a room, you might use a simple trimming which repeats one of the main or accent colors of the room. It is best to avoid strong colors in transparent shades because the colored light that filters through them will distort your color scheme. When you want accent color, use an opaque

Fluorescent lighting hidden in a ceiling cove provides dramatic effect in this bedroom.

PITTSBURGH PLATE GLASS CO.

shade, which is also the best choice for a lamp against a dark wall, as it will not stand out in contrasting brightness as a luminous shade does. Transparent shades of silk or cotton, plastic, and thin paper or parchment give more general light in a room and make it brighter and gayer. Opaque shades of heavy dark paper, leather, and metal throw the light downward in a more dramatic effect and are useful where the room arrangement is such that many lamps are required.

Sooner or later almost everyone has the desire to turn some *objet d'art* into a lamp. It may be a treasured vase, a piece of driftwood brought back from the beach, an old-fashioned coffee grinder, a duck decoy, or a tea canister, army boot, or baby shoe. The list is as endless as the imagination. Some of these tendencies should be curbed, however, by giving a little thought to the placement of the lamp after its creation. Beware of the extreme and the overcute. The same rules of good taste that govern the rest of your decorating scheme apply to lamps you create yourself. Therefore, before you go ahead, decide whether the article in question will be improved when it is turned into a lamp and consider whether there is really the right place for it in your home.

There are special shops which will mount the lamp for you or will supply the materials you need to do the job. With the majority of lamps, the first step involves drilling a hole in the bottom for the wiring. If the object is of china it is not something to tackle unless you are thoroughly experienced or very lucky. It is hazardous and even professionals will not guarantee not to break the piece, although actually they rarely send prize china back in pieces. If in doubt, be content to run the wire on the outside of the piece and secure it close to it at the base.

For purposes of illustration, let us assume you are turning a vase into a lamp. Once the hole has been drilled through the bottom, the vase is placed on a decorative base. This can be made of wood, brass, gold or one of any number of materials and finishes. Next comes the cord which is best run through a thin pipe extending through the base and vase and secured underneath with a lock nut and washer. At the top of the vase, a metal cap or cover fits over the rim of the vase with a hole in the center to carry the cord. Next, a harp, which is a metal frame designed to hold the shade, is slipped onto the pipe. Finally the socket is attached. This may be for a single or three-way bulb and is screwed to the top of the pipe with the electric wire connected to it. The shade is then fitted on top of the harp and secured with a decorative finial. If you use a clip fixture on the shade, no harp is necessary. For a two-bulb lamp, instead of a harp a longer pipe may be used with a cluster at the top. This type of fixture which also may be purchased complete has a swivel at the top allowing you to tilt the shade to suit your reading needs, and also an adjustable top set permitting lowering or

28-inch table lamp has textured white parchment Drum shade.

Tissue shantung Bell shade placed on a 33-inch alabaster lamp.

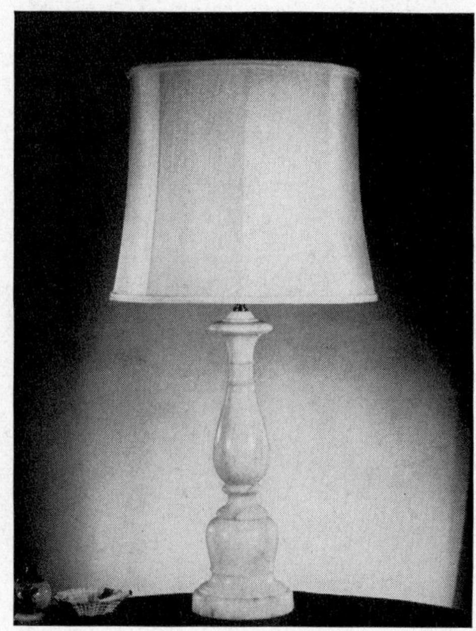

24-inch wicker lamp has a plaid plastic Flared shade.

LAMP AND SHADE INSTITUTE OF AMERICA

raising of the shade an inch or so. Again you will have a decorative finial to hold the shade in place.

The fundamental shape of some objects makes it impossible to drill a hole and run a wire straight through them, in which case the handling is slightly different. A figurine, for example, would be cemented to the metal or wood base. A bent pipe would run through the base at the back of the figure, straight up and close to the back of the figure, where it would be bent up and over the head, so that the socket, harp and shade would be centered over the lamp.

With the mechanics of wiring completed, you may wish to make a new shade or re-cover the frame of the old one. Shantung, taffeta, organdy, china silk, raw silk, textured cottons, and many other fabrics are suitable and easy to work. They can be sewed in place over the wire shade frame and a self-welt, braid or gimp applied to cover the stitches and for trimming. When working with plastics, paper or parchment, glue the shade together and cover edges with sticky tape, or lace onto the frame as in the plaid shade shown on the opposite page.

Tall lamps usually take open-top shades, since these are best for distributing light. Low lamps, with shades below eye level when you are standing, however, should have baffles or some arrangement to diffuse the light and conceal the bulbs and fixtures which are most unattractive to view. In all cases, shades must be deep enough to cover the bulbs and fixtures and wide enough to prevent any possibility of the bulb touching the shade and causing an unsightly or dangerous burn on the shade. Translucent shades should be heavy enough to keep lighted bulbs from showing through. This can be done with a lining, either white or matching the outside. White linings, even for dark opaque shades, will reflect much more light than dark ones.

Although a pair of lamps is often excellent for balance in a room, it is not necessary or even advisable to do too much matching of lamps. Variety is achieved by using several single lamps which harmonize with each other. Shades may be related without being repetitious or monotonous. You can also use both transparent and opaque shades in the same setting with good decorative results, especially when considered from the point of view of daytime appearance. Dark shades go well in a room that is predominantly dark in background, while light shades are more in keeping with a pale color scheme.

Whether you purchase your lamps or make them yourself, remember that the light they provide must be easy on your eyes. In some places the local electric company will send an advisor to your home to check lighting and see that it is sufficient for the family needs, but you can easily do this yourself. Light is measured in foot-candles, which is the light intensity one foot away from a candle; and your needs will vary from 35 foot-candles from a senior

China jar mounted on brass base carries textured fabric shade.

HAEL MILLER, LAMP AND SHADE INSTITUTE OF AMERICA

Dark paper shade is placed on this "Study in Potato Mashers" on wood base.

BEAR NEWMAN STUDIOS

Modern lamp, made of 4 Masonite panels, is independently adjustable.

THE HEIFETZ COMPANY

floor lamp 58 to 60 inches from the floor with a 100-200-300-watt bulb in the living room to 20 foot-candles of light at your dressing table with a pair of 15- or 16-inch lamps using 100-watt bulbs. You will also want to check the number of electric outlets which are important not only for lighting but for using all electric appliances which make modern homes so efficient and comfortable. Running extension cords to various parts of the room from one outlet is not only unsightly but dangerous from the point of view of overloading a circuit, or simply something for someone to trip over. Outlets can be installed in baseboards for lamps and appliances, but will look better and be more efficient for mantel lamps and curtain cornices if they are installed in the wall, out of sight, but fairly near the fixture to be lighted.

Not everyone has the opportunity to plan for good lighting. Those who rent homes must make do. You who are building homes, however, should make sure that your architect studies the problems of illumination and plans on lights for comfort, decorative beauty, and health.

Check List for Lamp, Bulb, and Shade Sizes

Lamp Types and Uses	Lamp Height Measured to Bottom of Shade (in inches)	Shade Diameter Measured Across Lower Edge	Inner Bowl	Total Bulb Wattage	
				Filament Lamps	Fluorescent Lamps
Lamps for Flat-Top Home Desks	14-15 in. above desk top	14-18 in.	Diffusing bowl essential for study	100-150 w.	
	(Fluorescent) 14-15 in. above desk top	Shielding full length of tube	No bowl		Two 20-watt tubes
Lamps for End Tables (Based on tables 26-in. high)	40 in. from floor	14-16 in.	Diffusing bowl preferred	100-150 w.	
Table Lamps (Large)	40 in. from floor	16-19 in.	Bowl preferred	150-250 w.	
Bridge Lamps (Used beside—toward rear—of small-scale chairs, or with small secretaries or flat-top desks)	46-50 in.	10-14 in.	Diffusing bowl preferred	100-150 w.	
Floor Lamps (Placed at rear side of davenports, chairs, and at keyboard side of pianos)	46-49 in.	16-20 in.	Diffusing bowl much preferred	150-300 w.	
Pin-to-Wall Lamps (1. For use in kitchens, at telephone tables, at each side of mirror with center of shade at face level)	48-56 in. above floor except 56 in. at mirror	8-10 in.	No bowl	60-100 w.	
(2. For longer use of the eyes at sewing machines, chairs, over beds, davenports, dinette tables, or used in pairs at desks)	55 in. above floor over beds, 45 in. at desks, 48 in. for other uses	10-13 in.	Diffusing bowl preferred	100-150 w.	

LAMP AND SHADE INSTITUTE OF AMERICA

Brass floor lamp is light, graceful with adjustable arm.

Adjustable desk lamp has plastic cone-shaped shade.

SHEAFFER PEN COMPANY

HAROLD FOWLER—LADIES' HOME JOURNAL'S MORE HOUSE FOR THE MONEY PORTFOLIO NO. 1

This charming living room relates the skillful use of accessories—books, flowers, pictures, desk appointments—to the warm and inviting personality of the room. The room at right shows how it is possible to combine pictures of various sizes and shapes for an attractive wall arrangement.

Accessories

Decorative and Functional

Accessories are the little things that count in your decorating scheme, the finishing touches that stamp a setting "yours" as clearly as any trade-mark. A hotel room, attractively furnished and well decorated, has an impersonal look simply because it lacks individuality. Add a few accessories of your own choosing, and such a room takes on personality and reflects the interests of you and your family.

Though we have given some examples in this book, there is no limit to the things that might be called accessories. They range from ash trays and antimacassars, through candlesticks and toss cushions, to mugs and maps. Each decorating period has reflected itself in its purely decorative accessories, though the actual term is a modern one. Pewter mugs, candlesticks, Delft china, and pottery marked the colonial era. The eighteenth century shone with the elegance of Chelsea statuettes, crystal lusters, salt-glaze wall vases, and epergnes. The Victorian age brought with it bronze Neptunes, replicas of the "Dying Gaul," cut-glass bowls, and wax flowers under glass. Today when we go modern our accessories run to mobiles and abstract sculpture.

Other accessories came into being through necessity or for comfort. The Pilgrims needed warming pans, candle molds, guns with racks to hold them, and cooking pots and had them around as accessories because there was no place to store them. The great houses of the Chippendale era boasted beauties designed to meet their own luxuriant needs—elegant silver tea services, enameled snuff boxes, fine china, quill pens and their accompanying paraphernalia. Decorative articles, such as ivory elephants, souvenir coffee spoons and hand-painted china, seemed more important to the Victorians than utilitarian accessories, yet we can think of such things as footstools, kerosene and oil lamps that were characteristic of their needs. Today, we seek comfort for ourselves and our guests in numerous ash trays, cigarette boxes, matches, lighters, and toss cushions.

This convenient kitchen counter is fine for keeping much-needed accessories within easy reach.

In addition to the definite styles which characterized each period, their method of display is important. The Victorians loved clutter and left few empty places. Today, even in doing a room of a definite period, unless we are trying to re-create another era to the last detail, we tend in the opposite direction and strive for simplicity and lack of clutter. We express our good taste with several important pieces—a figurine, a pair of statuettes, a beautiful bowl. We prefer a few large pieces to a group of small ones, partly as a matter of taste and partly in the interest of saving time in dusting.

While accessories offer opportunity for self-expression, still they must conform to the basic rules of decorating. This means that in addition to being pleasing to you, they should harmonize with the room in design, color and feeling. The chart on pages 100-101 offers some general suggestions for selecting the proper accessories for rustic, casual, informal, semiformal and formal rooms.

Placement is also important. Accessories must fill a decorating need, not merely be displayed because you happen to have them. Many of them we collect as wedding, birthday and anniversary presents or as the result of travels or hobbies. Seldom is there a shortage. More often, it is a surplus that creates the problem. Instead of displaying all at once, it is wiser to stock some away, bringing them out oc-

HAROLD FOWLER

casionally to give your room a welcome scenery shift. A charming china figurine retains its interest far longer if you retire it from view occasionally. When it makes a return appearance, it will be novel and intriguing all over again.

When selecting accessories, color is a big factor. Choose them to introduce a needed contrasting color or to echo a major theme. Never let an accessory strike a lone color note. A small object is not important enough to stand alone. If you wish to add a new shade to a setting, do it with several accessories rather than with one.

Avoid the temporary fads and the "junk" pieces which capture the public eye. Seek accessories which hold personal meaning for you. Let them reflect a hobby or an interest but be sure it's yours. The teacup collection, which makes a charming conversation piece for a friend, would mean nothing in your home if your interests lie elsewhere. Your accessories should not be carbon copies of others but originals with you. The right ones give a room style and individuality; the wrong ones make it tacky and unattractive.

Functional accessories are our first thought because they are necessities which will be found in almost every home. They should be attractively designed but, more important, fulfill the need. A beautiful clock has very little value if it doesn't run.

Clocks are among the more useful accessories. Where would we be without them? The designs are varied and it is an easy matter to find a simply framed clock for the kitchen, a more delicate design for the bedroom, and a period piece that fits into the living-room scheme. Numerals should be easy to read. A bedroom clock is preferable

Accessories used in unusual ways add character and charm to a room. Above left, the polished brass weather vane reflects light from the fireplace. The graceful selection of Victorian silver objects on the table, above right, add sparkle and interest. Holding foliage on the table above is a familiar friend, the Victorian water pitcher.

if it has a luminous dial that can be seen in the dark. The alarm should be sufficiently loud to rouse you in the morning. Combination radio-alarm clocks, available in decorator colors, offer something extra in functionalism.

Kitchen clocks are generally framed in plastic. White is a popular choice, but frames also come in colors to accent the kitchen scheme.

Well-designed living-room clocks may be purchased to suit any period room. Cases range from gleaming mahogany and blond woods through porcelains, marbles, and metals in styles for mantel, table, wall, and floor. If you select a chime clock, be sure its notes are pleasing to your ear. The melody must be an appealing one, since you'll hear it at the quarter and half hours plus the full measure when the hour strikes.

When you arrange a clock in a grouping, be certain it is related to the other objects and see that it is placed where the time can be easily seen.

Ash trays also figure prominently as functional accessories. Their color and design are a matter of good taste and personal preference. For general use they should, as any

DAYSTROM FURNITURE

HAROLD FOWLER

The fish mobile, left, is an interesting accessory with modern satin-finished metal furniture. Glass shelves in a window, right, can be used in many attractive arrangements. This collection of Victorian blue glass is shown off to best advantage, and the addition of a nostalgic bouquet and leafy vine increases its interest.

American kitchens and cellars in the 1800's were plentifully supplied with stoneware churns and pitchers, butter crocks, jars and water coolers of the type shown, right. The cobalt-blue designs were put on by hand, as also was the incised decoration on the water cooler. Ducks are salt and pepper shakers and at the right is a flask dated 1855.

husband will tell you, be man-size. Small ones tend to overflow and may result in badly burned table tops. Reserve small ash trays for bedroom night or dressing tables or for dining-room tables, where they will not get quite so much use and their daintiness will be a decorative asset. Ash trays for the dinner table should harmonize with your china pattern or may be silver or glass to complement your other tableware. Actually, every room in the house has a need for ash trays. In the living room, be certain there's one within easy reach on every table. Even nonsmokers should think of guests and keep this accessory accessible. Cigarette boxes and lighters, also functional but not quite so vital, make charming tabletop accessories too.

The list of useful accessories is a long one. Such things come to mind as scatter pillows, which are colorful accents and especially serviceable in TV rooms. Then there are book ends to keep desk and table libraries in neat groupings. Care should be taken that book-end bases are weighted so they won't slide, causing books to slant or fall over sidewards. Trays—and every home needs at least one of these—can be most attractive when placed on end as background for a figurine, flower arrangement or other accessory.

In this electrical age, candles are primarily for show; nothing else has quite the glamour of their soft, flickering light. In an emergency, when a fuse blows or a storm causes power failure, they prove their original purpose. Magazine racks are useful but, these days, many end tables are dual-purpose designs with special shelves for periodicals. On the ornamental side, screens are invaluable for concealing an unpleasant view or an architectural defect.

Antimacassars, those white doilies which dotted chair backs and arms not too many years ago, are useful if not alluring. Their modern counterpart is the chair and arm covering made of extra pieces of the upholstery or slipcover fabric. It matches the chair and is delightfully inconspicuous. Keep this in mind and have some of these pro-

FROM THE COLLECTION OF GEORGE S. MCKEARIN

A few American potters attempted white earthenware and porcelain of this type before 1850. Large bowls and pitchers were printed with historical scenes or portraits of war heroes to commemorate patriotic events. Pitchers shown depict the Battle of Stonington, Tyler's presidential campaign, and Lafayette landing at Castle Garden.

tective coverings made next time the furniture is done over.

No list of functional accessories would be complete without mention of mirrors or fireside aids, both of which are described extensively in the chapter on Accessories. This also deals with decorative accessories, which are numerous, varied, and have one purpose—to delight the eye.

Whether decorative or functional, accessories must be properly placed. If grouped together, each must have something in common with the next. It may be size, shape, material, or color. The important thing is that the group present a united appearance.

Table tops are the logical place to display accessories, but don't overdo it. The table should not appear cluttered. Half its beauty is the fine finish of the wood; don't cover it up. A good arrangement for a table might feature a lamp and ash tray plus some third accessory—possibly a flower arrangement, an orderly magazine grouping, a figurine.

Coffee tables are not to be taken literally. There is no need to keep your coffee service on them unless you are actually pouring. For display purposes, a low flower arrangement, a cigarette box and lighter, and a huge ash tray are good and useful choices.

Generally speaking, leave the top of the piano free. A lamp or a flower container is an accessory which would strike the right note here.

The mantel is an obvious display place. Avoid the trite arrangement of a centered clock and a pair of candlesticks. Strive for the original. Try a pair of wall brackets filled with ivy or settle for one huge centered bracket flowing with greenery. Think in terms of sculpture or figurines. Use the mantel to show off a hobby grouping of china pieces, or mount a clock collection on brackets over it. Your mantel arrangement need not be balanced. Use a

This little tree blossoms the whole year round. Small bunches of flowers from the dime store are wired to a well-shaped branch which is stuck in a pretty jardiniere.

Here a few fake flowers are used to brighten up foxtails, bulrushes and ferns.

pair of candlesticks at one end, a low arrangement of flowers at the other. The fireplace is a focal point, make it one of interest.

Bookcases also provide accessory space. The books themselves are decorative. It is not necessary to fill a home bookcase as though it were a library shelf. Some very attractive effects are achieved by leaving bare spots or filling in shelves with china or pottery figures or plants.

Desks above all should be free of jumble. Don't crowd the work area. Choose functional accessories first—a blotter, desk pen, and memo pad. If there's room, let a figurine grouping, a globe or several family photographs add the personal touch.

In the dining room, china stored in a glass-front cabinet comes under the heading of accessories. The most frequently made mistake here is overcrowding. If your cabinet is bulging with china and glassware, the effect will not be pleasing. For the sake of appearance, store the surplus out of sight. Sparkling glassware and fine china are beautiful if given the proper space in which to shine.

A buffet top is another excellent spot for accessories. A tea set looks well on it, or group a fruit bowl or chafing dish with candles. Try displaying an odd piece of china. The unmatched soup tureen of grandma's may make a surprisingly beautiful flower container. It's worth a try.

Bedroom accessories tend to be personalized. The feminine woman will display a collection of crystal perfume bottles on dresser, vanity or specially built glass shelves. The teen-ager will have trophies decking the walls or bookcase tops. A bachelor may limit his accessories to a handsome comb and brush set on the dresser or a hobby collection of model autos or sports gear on shelves. Bedside tables can be used for everything from ash trays and memo pads to the latest best seller.

The bathroom, so frequently neglected by home decorators, can be enhanced with a wrought-iron shelf filled with a stack of colorful terry guest towels, a pretty container of dusting powder, a perfume bottle or two, a figurine or a bit of greenery.

Kitchen accessories tend to be practical but this does not make them less appealing. There's gleaming beauty in copper pots hung on racks. Use a wall planter or put up a shelf for cookbooks and gay spice containers.

There's room for accessories throughout the house. Use them selectively. Place them rather than load them on tables and other furniture tops. Accessories should stand out, not be lost in crowded confusion. The suggestions given here are not meant for you to copy. Their purpose is to point the way, to start you thinking of how and where you can use your own prizes. The things you treasure have a place in your home; it's merely a matter of finding the right place.

Plants, flowers, and flower arrangements with their containers are also accessories in decorating. In planning to use flowers consider first where you will place your arrangement. If it is for the dining-room table, the lines must be low enough to permit conversation. A hall table arrangement might be high to fill the wall area below a mirror or picture. Your type of room and the use to which you will put your flowers determines the type of arrangement—formal or informal, viewed from one or two sides, or for a low table where they will be seen from above.

Balance, focus, and harmony are the three requirements of an artistic arrangement. *Balance* means a pleasing grouping that is neither top-heavy nor lopsided. *Focus* is the eye-catching part of the grouping. This may be the use of contrasting or harmonizing colors, or a change in texture, or the use of an unusual flower. In most arrangements the focal point is low and near the center of the design. *Harmony* is the pleasing complement of flowers to each other and to the container and setting in which they are placed. Form and texture are important to a good arrangement, but take second place to color. Generally speaking, one key shade should predominate.

Nearly anything that will hold water can be used as a flower container—soup tureens, goblets, compotes, pitchers, and shallow dishes—in addition to the accepted vase. Your collection should include a large open-necked vase for long-stemmed flowers, a shallow low bowl for the dining-room table, a small bud vase, and, if possible, a versatile wall vase.

Trinket boxes, above, were great favorites in the Victorian era. These are charmingly grouped to set them off.

Ornamental Parian ware, left, was made in imitation of marble before 1875. The rose-pattern pitcher is rare.

There are numerous books on the subject of arrangement if you want to become really expert. However, a good general rule is to work from the outside toward the center. Heavy flowers, or those which are dramatic in color, shape, or texture, should be placed at the center of interest. Use small flowers and airy foliage to outline the arrangement.

Flower arrangement can be a fascinating hobby. Flowers suit every room in the house and give tremendous variety and interest. Arrange them high on the mantel, low on a coffee table. In summer, fill the fireplace with a huge vase of greenery. Let them bring color to bookcases and hang them in copper wall containers in the kitchen. They provide natural beauty for a dressing table and add pleasure to the business of a desk. On a bedside table, a single rose will be the last thing you see at night, the first thing in the morning. A little trouble and interest in this final touch for your house is very rewarding.

A good way to achieve balance in a room is to have a slip cover match the draperies.

Upholstery and Slip Covers

Variety in Methods, Fabrics and Materials

UPHOLSTERY

To many people there is still considerable mystery about the insides of an upholstered chair and why one piece seems exorbitantly priced while another piece which looks much the same from the outside is relatively inexpensive. As a matter of fact, there is a great and honest difference in upholstered pieces and you almost always get exactly what you pay for in quality, looks, and wearing probability. However, not everybody can afford, or wants, a limousine and will settle for a durable dependable medium-priced car, content if he is getting his money's worth. So it is with upholstery. It is not necessary to have only pure horsehair, the finest of down cushions, or a completely hand-finished piece, but there are certain fundamentals which insure good wear and which we would like to have if we can manage it.

In buying a piece of upholstered furniture, having an old one done over, or doing it yourself we might start with the very finest construction and materials and then take note of possible compromises to bring the price within a figure reasonable to our own budgets.

Every upholstered chair, love seat or sofa starts with a wooden frame made in the general size and lines of the finished piece. This frame should be of hard maple, ash, or birch, free of defects and well put together with doweling glued in, hardwood reinforcements screwed into the corners, and any exposed parts which are of a different furniture wood like walnut or mahogany should be securely attached to the frame. Medium-priced furniture may be constructed on frames of elm, gumwood or poplar and the least expensive frames will be made of pine. The latter is not hard enough to hold the many tacks and nails that are required in an upholstered piece and will become almost impossible in a reupholstery job when fresh holes are needed. The frame must be at least 1½ inches thick for strength and to give enough surface for tacking. The exposed wood on an upholstered piece will be as well finished as any fine wood piece.

Every upholstered chair of any pretentions at all will be finished on the bottom with a dust cover of percale, muslin, or cotton of some kind. Working from the bottom up, the next layer will be the webbing. The best quality is about 3½ inches wide, is heavy jute, and interlaced across the bottom of a chair so that the edges almost touch each other. It is stretched tightly and each strip nailed in 3 places, then turned over at the edge and nailed again. A less expensive method is found in the use of lighter webbing or a burlap tacked to a spiral wire frame. There is also a steel webbing which holds very well, but does not stretch, making for a fairly hard chair.

The next layer is composed of steel spiral springs which come in various weights and qualities. The best are double coiled, oven-tempered and japanned; the poorest are simply steel wire given a few twists. As many as 16 springs may be used in a large chair, not less than 12. You will find chairs with only 6 or 8 springs in the seat which could not be expected to stand the strain of more than a child's weight.

The next great difference in hidden quality comes in the tying of the springs. Properly, each spring is tied 8 times, that is, vertically, horizontally, and on the 2 diagonals—2 knots for each direction. It is obvious that the quality of twine used is important and that the tension be such that the springs will not sag, but return to a normal level when weight is released. The springs must be individually sewed at the bottom to the webbing to keep them from tipping over or moving.

On top of the tied springs a piece of burlap is laid and tacked to the frame of the chair. This evens up any possible slight differences in height and makes a firm foundation for the padding. The burlap should be sewed to each spring for a perfect construction, but this is not absolutely essential. Now a good layer of stuffing is laid on as smoothly as possible and quilted down to the burlap below. In the best furniture this last process is repeated, making a double stuffing. In any case, the stuffing is covered with a layer of cotton felt, or cotton batting, topped with a sheet of glazed cotton for a final smooth surface.

Long horsehair is the best filling. This is sometimes used as a topping over moss or pig's or cow's hair and even palmleaf fiber can be used for stuffing and is superior to short hairs which mat, or the cotton waste, straw and excelsior found in the very inexpensive pieces. Cotton felt varies in quality mostly in length of fibers and number of cotton seeds still in it. These seeds exude a black oil which may come through the top cover, and will show on light fabrics. Most of the imperfections in quilted chintz and silks are owing to the stains from the seeds in the cotton used for padding.

Loose cushions are made of downproof ticking and divided into compartments inside to prevent the down from getting all into one place in the cushion. The best feathers are 75 per cent goose down mixed with 25 per cent goose feathers. All down makes a very light cushion with little or no body. All goose feathers is not quite as luxurious as the above mixture, but makes an excellent cushion. Foam rubber is used widely and makes a good soft cushion, slightly severe in line, but highly suitable for tailored pieces. Chicken, duck, and turkey feathers are used in medium-grade furniture, and cotton and kapok used in the least expensive. Some cushions are filled with spring units which are tied and padded in much the same way as the base of the chair or sofa, and vary in quality in the same way. These make a stiffer, neater cushion than feathers which require constant attention to keep them from looking like an unmade bed, but spring cushions do not offer the same luxury.

One other thing to look for in upholstered furniture is a roll of padding, sometimes cotton felt, sometimes burlap stuffed with horsehair which should be used wherever the wooden frame may come in contact with the outside covering. This is for comfort as well as preventing rubbing. In poorly made furniture cotton waste and even crumpled paper is used to soften these edges.

Finally, before the top cover is applied, a chair may be covered in muslin. This serves as a lining for the top covering and makes a change of top cover comparatively easy.

These are all the hidden values—materials, workmanship, care. How do we know what we are getting when we buy a finished chair? Some of the things can be felt easily through the covering. Feel the bottom of the chair through the muslin cover for the webbing and stitching of the springs. Also you can usually determine whether there are braces at the corners of the legs. For the tying of the springs you will have to rely on the reliability of the place at which you are buying and the honesty of the salesman. For the stuffing, cushion filling, etc., you will find in many states a label, required by law, stating what percentage of each kind of material has been used. A careful inspection of the workmanship and finish of the top cover will give you an idea of the standards and quality of the shop where the chair was assembled. Buy according to your budget, but understand what you are buying and what you can expect from a piece in each price range.

The top cover, which is all that is important to the casual observer, figures in the price of a chair by the cost of the fabric by the yard and the yardage required. Most fine furniture is purchased in "the muslin," a yardage requirement quoted, and you pick out the fabric that fits into your color scheme and decoration and add the cost of the fabric to the price of the piece. Some people count on replacing top covers frequently, in which case they do not have to be too careful about weave or color. However, if you are anxious to choose something that will not have to be replaced soon, you will be guided by the weave as well as the color of your fabrics. Loosely woven soft fabrics will not stand hard wear and threads have a tendency to pull out. Heavy textured and twisted cottons, cut and uncut velvet, frieze, grospoint, firmly woven chintz and linen, duck, matelassé, and leather wear well on upholstered pieces. Simply consider the wear that an average piece will get in comparison to drapery, sofa cushions, or even clothes and you will have no trouble in making a choice for your particular need.

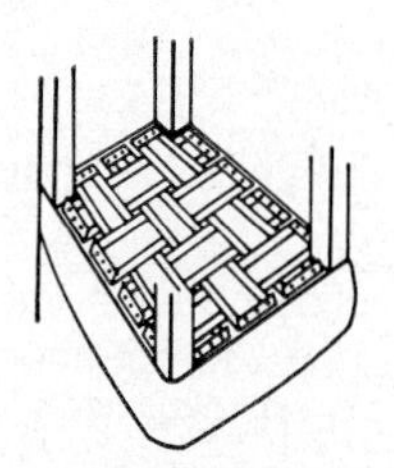

Interlaced webbing—tacked once in 3 places, edge turned over and tacked again.

Springs tied 8 times and fastened to frame.

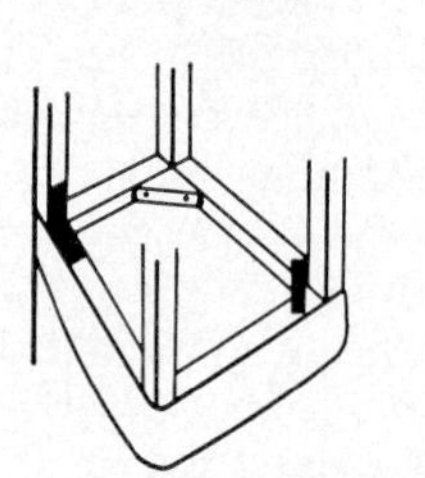

3 ways to strengthen legs—angle iron, wood corner block, straight iron.

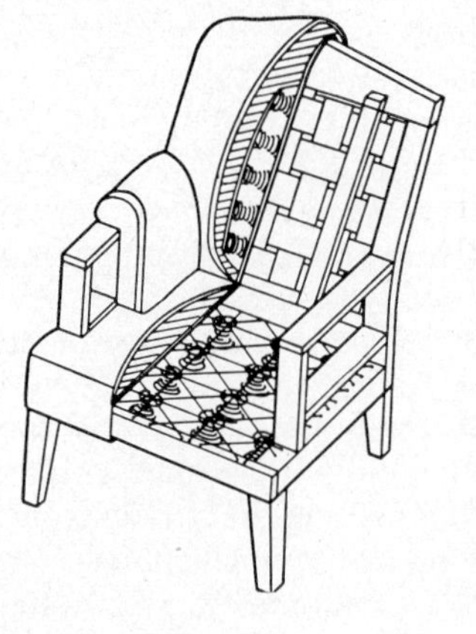

Cross section of upholstered chair showing: webbing, tied springs, burlap, stuffing, padding, muslin, top cover.

All of the virtues that you look for in buying a new chair apply equally to having a chair done over, or in doing it over yourself. If you are debating the question of whether to buy a new chair or do over the old one, there are several considerations which will influence your decision. A favorite comfortable chair will be as good as, and possibly better than, new when it is done over completely, because you can specify exactly what you want to go under the cover. However, a good upholsterer works exactly the way a manufacturer does, and your only saving will be the cost of the frame. If you do it over yourself you could achieve a much better chair for the cost of an inexpensive one, or merely the cost of a new top cover, depending on the condition of the chair, and the quality of materials you decide are merited.

In doing over an upholstered piece yourself, you will follow step by step the building from the bottom up which is outlined in the previous paragraphs on buying upholstered furniture. There are a few suggestions, however, which will help in your success:

1. Take a good look at the chair or piece and decide if you want to restore it exactly as it is, or was when new. You may find that you would like to give it straighter lines, omit tufting, add a skirt, lower the back, or shorten the legs.

2. Provide yourself with a hammer, tack puller, a curved and a straight upholstery needle and, if possible, a webbing stretcher, and some kind of low workbench. None of these is expensive and will save your hands and endless trouble, besides doing a better job. The hammer needs no explanation. You may be able to use the nail puller on the head of the hammer to remove the hundreds of tacks in the old chair, but a real puller with its own handle has a sharper edge to get under tacks and is much easier to handle. The curved needle is essential for sewing all places that you cannot get hold of, and the straight needle for ordinary sewing. The webbing stretcher is simply a block of wood with six or eight sharp nails in one end. It is used to brace against the frame of the chair and hold the webbing taut to insure a firm tight fit. If someone will hold the webbing tight for you while you put in the tacks, the stretcher is not necessary. The low workbench is laborsaving, backsaving and stocking-saving. Upholsterers use a wide sawhorse or two narrower ones with a shallow box on the top lined with burlap. This holds the legs of a chair or sofa, or the arms and seat when the piece is upside down.

3. Strip the top covering from your chair carefully, as you may want to use the pieces for a pattern in cutting the new cover. Turn the chair upside down and take off the dust cover from the bottom. Examine the leg joinings. If any of the latter are loose or the chair did not have corner blocks in the beginning, either supply them or angle irons after drawing the joints as tightly together as possible. Inspect the exposed wood and do any refinishing required before starting on the reupholstering. Check arms and stretchers at this time and make any alterations in the length of the legs.

4. Examine the webbing and if it is torn, has come loose from the sides of the chair, or shows signs of giving way in the near future, loosen the tacks, cut the strings which hold the springs to it and remove the webbing. You can now get a fair idea of the condition of the rest of the chair. If it seems to need a complete overhauling, or you wish to change the fundamental shape, strip the rest of it, leaving only the frame. If, however, the burlap above the springs and the springs themselves seem to be in good condition, leave them alone, checking the spring twine carefully for breaks and worn places. If all the twine is worn, it would be wise to strip the chair, as it is very difficult to do a good job of string tying from the bottom.

5. Now you can see what new materials you will need—twine, webbing, stuffing, burlap, padding, muslin. Do not forget to take note of the size of tacks used in various operations and get yourself a good supply.

6. Make whatever replacements are necessary, using the same quality or better materials. In tacking, try to find new tack holes, as your tacks will pull out of the old ones, especially those holding the webbing and the ends of the spring cords. In a piece that has been done over many times, an antique, or a pine frame, it is sometimes very difficult to make the tacks hold. Rubbing in plastic wood and letting it dry may help, or you may have to add a thin strip of wood screwed to the ends of the bottom rails, or replace the rails entirely.

7. If you decide to use foam rubber, be sure to bevel the edges to the degree that you want curved soft lines. Old horsehair may be cleaned and fluffed up to use over, but cotton padding and felt should be new, as the old will mat down at once. In stuffing and padding allow for matting down and let the arms and back be a little overfull. This applies to the seat also, unless the piece has separate cushions, when the seat or platform below the cushion should be almost level.

8. The muslin cover which holds everything nicely in place is put on very much as the top cover is, except that seams are plain and inside and tacks do not have to be put as close together, as the top cover tacks will help hold it.

9. The final top cover is the easiest part of the job. The guide on pages 166 to 168 will give you an idea of the fabric needed for each type of piece, but it is wise to check the yardage with the measurements of your piece, especially if the fabric you are planning to use has a design which must be centered on backs and seat cushions. In general the muslin undercover is put on and cut like the outside cover.

10. For the top cover, start with the inside back. Using the old cover as a pattern or guide, cut a piece from the

new material and center it carefully on the back of the chair, being sure that the grain is straight. With a pile fabric the nap should brush toward the seat. Bring the material over the back edges of the frame and tack lightly here and there. Now pleat in, or make darts for the shoulders, or any curves, tacking each pleat in place. A number of tiny pleats or darts will fit better over rounded curves than 2 or 3 large ones. Sometimes with stretchy fabric the shoulders can be eased in without pleats. Push extra material allowed, about 4 inches, at seat down into the crease. Some frames make a provision for tacking this to a rail at the back of the top of the chair, others are made to have it tacked to the seat rail or left loose. You will have noticed how this was done when you removed the original cover. Now drive home your guide tacks and fill in between with tacks driven in about every inch.

Next cut the seat cover. If the piece has cushions, you may wish to use your top covering only where it will show and make the actual seat or platform under the cushion of a less expensive material. If so, sew the two pieces of material together, making sure that the substitute material will not show, even when the pressure of sitting on the piece raises the corners of the cushion a trifle. If the arms are squared off with a welting or fringe at the inside edge of the arm, sew these pieces together first. Tuck in allowance at back of arm and seat edge. Usually the stuffing will hold this in place, but it is safer for both the arm and back to tack the loose edge tucked into the crevices with your curved upholstery needle. Make such darts as are necessary to fit around curves and tack firmly in place. If fabric strains at corners, slash carefully, but not too deeply to allow for the curve, or turn.

The skirt, if there is to be one, is your next consideration. The same types of skirts are used on upholstered pieces today as those we have always seen on slip covers—plain, kick-pleated at the corners, box-pleated and ruffled. They give a solidity to a chair with too long or badly shaped legs and relieve that "small forest" look that a room acquires when there are too many legs of chairs, tables, sofas and lamp stands. For an upholstered piece the skirt should be lined. The length depends on the proportion of the piece of furniture and how much of the leg or foot you want to show. The skirt may be tacked on before the front edge of the seat and go under it, or may be left until both inside and outside faces of the chair are covered. It is then finished at the top and applied in the same way as the outside pieces.

The piece is now ready for the front of the arms, the outside arms and the back. If welting is used, it is tacked along all these edges. Welting may be made by covering a cord with bias strips of the upholstery fabric, may be purchased ready-made, or could be a brush fringe. After it is in place, fold back the top cover and tack the edge in place, using narrow strips of cardboard to make a neat edge, pushing the cardboard well against the bulge of the welting, or close to the top edge of the frame, if welting is not used.

You may want to finish a particular chair or sofa with button tufting. Buttons may be covered wooden-button forms, or circles cut of heavy cardboard and covered, or be made like any self-covered dress buttons. For button tufting the shank should be short and sewed on with a corresponding small button on the back to hold it. This is done before the outside of the back is sewed down the sides.

The final step in your upholstery job is invisibly stitching down by hand with heavy thread and a curved needle the outside edges that you could not tack from the underside.

Doing over an old chair that you have dismantled yourself is the easiest way to learn and practice on upholstering. However, many other types of upholstering jobs exist and can be worked out with a basic knowledge of the main ingredients that go into this kind of work. Deep tufting which may take the place of springs and be more suitable for special chairs, starts with a layer of heavy burlap covered with padding and a muslin cover. The pattern of the tufting is marked on the muslin and again on the top cover with chalk or pins, allowing from 2 to 5 inches difference in the spacing of the marks, the larger spaces being in the top cover. The marks are then matched and the slack material in the top cover stuffed and pleated to form the tufting. Slip seats usually start with a wooden frame and are webbed as any chair, covered with padding, muslin and a top cover. As you gain confidence, you may want to try your hand at taking an old wooden chair and making an upholstered side chair, using it for a frame. You may develop some techniques of your own, or make an ottoman by putting legs on a flat fruit box and upholstering the whole thing. Doing your own upholstering is a fascinating hobby.

SLIP COVERS

Not many years ago, perhaps a generation, slip covers were all made of a plain tan or white cotton fabric or the still-available striped tan Belgian linen. They were designed as dust covers for upholstered furniture during the summertime or when the family was away and the whole house was shrouded in cloth—pictures, statuary, piano and furniture. Gradually it was discovered that cretonnes, chintz and percales made just as good covers and were very much prettier and more livable, especially for those who did not close up their houses in the summer. From that time forward, slip covers have come to be part of our fundamental planning in decorating. We use slip covers to change the appearance of the entire house at different seasons of the year. We use them to protect fine upholstery fabrics when they are new and to cover up worn faded upholstery when the exchequer is low. They are used for pieces which take a good deal of hard wear and need frequent cleaning, and sometimes because their softer, less formal lines make for more friendliness and less formality in a room.

Like reupholstery, slip covers can be made of all qualities of fabrics, with many grades of workmanship, and at a wide range of prices. You can also do a very good job on making your own slip covers. There are a number of books and pamphlets on the subject with full instructions and diagrams, and courses in slip-cover making are not difficult to find. However, if you have a sewing machine (and some slip covers have been made even without one) you can turn out a fine slip cover on your first try. Careful planning, cutting and pinning come first and will save you mistakes and adjustments. The actual sewing and finishing is less exacting than dressmaking or that required for well-made draperies.

Whether you are going to make the slip cover yourself, or have it made, your first attention is to the sofa or chair itself. If the piece is new, your only decision is whether you wish to change its degree of formality. A plain slip cover of a formal fabric with a tailored skirt gives formality. A flowered or patterned cover with a flounce looks casual. These are the two extremes. Different materials, contrasting welting, box-pleating, brush fringe and length of skirt can alter the entire appearance of a piece.

In selecting fabric for your slip cover, choose according to use and wear. A living-room chair will get heavier wear than one in your bedroom, and the furniture in the children's rooms most of all. Since slip covers are not taut, they will wrinkle readily, unless you have chosen a wrinkle-resistant material. Very soft loosely woven materials will be hard to work with and tend to lose their shape in use. Hence, a fairly closely woven fabric, shrinkproof, if you plan to wash it, and cleanable otherwise, is your best selection. Linens, cretonnes, chintz, antique satin, textured weaves, and denim or sailcloth are all good slip-cover materials.

When it comes to pattern you will want to decide whether you wish to center a main motif in the back of each section and each seat, or whether you will use it at random, letting the design fall where it will. Designs of large bouquets surrounded by a plain background are usually centered. In planning this, however, relate the size of the pattern and the amount of background on each side to the piece of furniture. Sometimes a center motif will be too large for the back of a chair and lose its significance in being cut off sharply. On a large chair a small pattern that must be centered may appear unpleasantly cut off on the outside edges. Many patterns of diamonds, circles, and the like must be cut to give a symmetrical appearance on the shoulders and sides of a chair and cannot be taken completely at random.

When you are considering slip covers for a brand-new chair, especially if it is to be covered to your order, you might ask to have the chair delivered in a heavy muslin, or inexpensive heavy cotton. You can then have made, or make, two sets of slip covers—one for winter and one for summer.

However, most people become interested in slip covers when they want to freshen up a room or just a chair at a

Tacking the cardboard strip and top cover in place on the upper edge of the back of a chair.

Blind-stitching the outside edge of the back of a chair with a curved needle.

GREEFF FABRICS

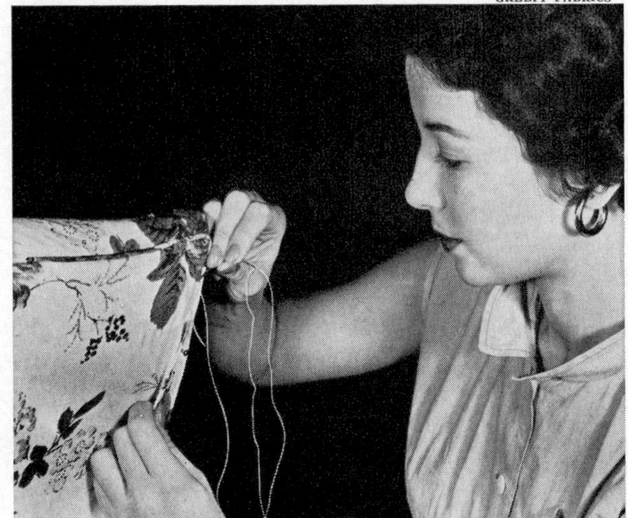

The living room in winter, right, looks cozy and attractive, but the velvet chairs and heavy carpeting make it seem oppressive when the hot months arrive. Notice the difference in the same room, below, when the winter upholstery is covered with cool bright chintzes and the heavy carpeting is exchanged for a small aqua rug.

HAROLD FOWLER

RICHARD WHEATLAND

minimum cost. This, of course, is accomplished by choosing an inexpensive material of reasonable wearing quality, and doing the making yourself. Assuming that this is our problem, here are the steps to success.

Your old chair should be made as clean as you can get it with cleaning fluid or one of the upholstery cleaners. Grease spots on the back and arms may come through if this is not done. If the upholstery fabric is badly worn, enough to show through the slip cover, it may be well to strip it off, hoping there is a muslin cover underneath. If not, a muslin cover is easily made and tacked on. Also check the springs. If they need retying or the webbing is gone, you can fix that up. The chapter on upholstering will help you there.

Now measure your chair: Top of back to seat with a tuck-in allowance of 4 inches, the seat, arms, outside back and sides, skirt. Also check the width at the widest part to determine whether one width of your fabric will be sufficient. Measure the separate cushion, if any, and the amount of boxing needed. The platform under the separate cushion, especially on a sofa, may be made of a less expensive material. If you plan on a self-welt, allow an extra yard for cutting bias strips to make it. Pages 166 to 168 provide average yardage requirements for various types of pieces. By careful cutting and a little piecing you may be able to make a remnant that is slightly short of the requirement do, but it is wise to figure this out pretty accurately before cutting, as a shortage will be a complete waste.

If you are using ready-made welting or fringe, measure all the edges where it is needed and allow a little extra for tuck in and corners.

Slip covers are usually made with an opening either down the back or one side to permit easy installation and removal. This opening is closed with a slide fastener, mechanical snappers, or ordinary large dress snappers. In special cases decorative buttons or lacings are used. The opening should be long enough to accomplish its purpose and prevent stretching and pulling of material. You will need heavy thread and a matching needle for your machine. An inexpensive welting foot with one prong omitted will help keep seams straight and welting in place while

Patterned slip covers contrast with simple background.

stitching. These come in a left and a right, so if you do not like crowding heavy fabric through the center of the machine, it is well to have a pair of them. If you can manage some kind of low table or workbench, it will make the job easier, but this is not absolutely necessary. Most of the job, except for the original cutting and pinning, is not done on the piece. Keep an ironing board and iron at hand, as seams should be pressed open as they are done and before other pieces are added.

At this point some people like to make a muslin pattern, or even a paper pattern, cutting off pieces of the required length for each section, pinning them into place and making sure that they have enough seam and tuck-in allowance. Others are ready to go ahead with the final material.

Whether you use a pattern or not, when you cut the actual fabric you are going to use for your slip cover, lay it on the chair before sewing, right side out. Good slip covers are always fitted right side out, as there is often a slight difference in the arms of an upholstered piece, and if the slip cover was made on the wrong side and reversed, it will not fit as well. Be sure of centering your pattern on the straight of the goods, and pin all edges carefully, as demonstrated in the diagram, right. If your piece has rounded shoulders or arms, or a channel back, pin in the necessary darts following the lines of the chair.

You are now ready to stitch the pieces together. By far the easiest procedure at this point, if not the most effective, is to make a French seam, allowing the seam itself to serve as a line or in place of welting. This is easy because you can stitch your slip cover on the wrong side, just as you have it pinned. Then cut the outside edges a quarter of an inch from the stitching, and press the seam open. Turn the whole thing inside out, crease the seams and stitch again a fraction more than a quarter of an inch from the edge. This will bring the French seam on the outside of the slip cover.

If your cover calls for a more formal treatment, or you want a self-welting, your next step is to make the welting. To do this, cut a square of the fabric, fold on the bias from corner to corner and cut on this fold. You now have two triangles. Stitch the lengthwise edges together and press the seam open, making a parallelogram. Now bring crosswise edges together, with bias edge 1½ inches back from edge; stitch and press. From the tube you have made in this manner you can cut bias strips for welting, starting at the 1½ inch projection and making a continuous strip. Place welting cord in center of wrong side of strip, fold over and stitch close to the cord on the right side.

You may also use bought welting, or cord with a gimp edge, or different types of fringe. With any of these, mark the line on both edges of the right side of the material that is to be sewed together, with either pins or tailor's chalk. Place the trimming directly over the line on one side and stitch it to the fabric. Then place the other piece which joins the slip cover at this point over the trimming and stitch again. The stitching is all done on the wrong side of the slip cover. On straight seams or with careful basting you may be able to stitch the trimming and the two pieces together in one operation. With curved or shaped pieces, however, it is safest to stitch these parts separately.

In joining the pieces of the slip cover together, start by stitching the inside arm pieces to the inside back. These seams may or may not be welted, should fit smoothly over the arm, but be tapered to the tuck-in allowance at the seat.

Now join the outside arm to the inside arm and the front of the arm to both these sections. At this point, it is a good idea to try this much on the chair. Check your line down the back, now made of two pieces, and join back section to the slip cover, leaving the side open for a slide fastener, 18 or 20 inches, unless the chair is very small. Join piece that goes across the front of the seat to the sides and finally the seat section is stitched in on all four sides. Place the cover on the chair, tucking in allowance at back of seat and arms and make any necessary adjustments.

If you are doing an upholstery-type slip cover, mark the place where the upholstery on your piece ends on all four sides of the piece. Measure from the floor, as for putting a hem in a dress. Straighten this line where necessary, turn up a narrow hem and blind-stitch it against the fabric on the inside. If you wish to be sure that this short slip cover stays down and in place, be sure that bottom edge fits quite snugly, or in addition you may attach 2 pieces of fabric, not necessarily of the slip-cover material, to cross under the bottom of the chair, fastened with tapes or snap fasteners. These will run from front to back and from side to side.

For a slip cover with a skirt proceed in the same way, measuring up from the floor all around the piece and

HOPE BRIDGEFORD

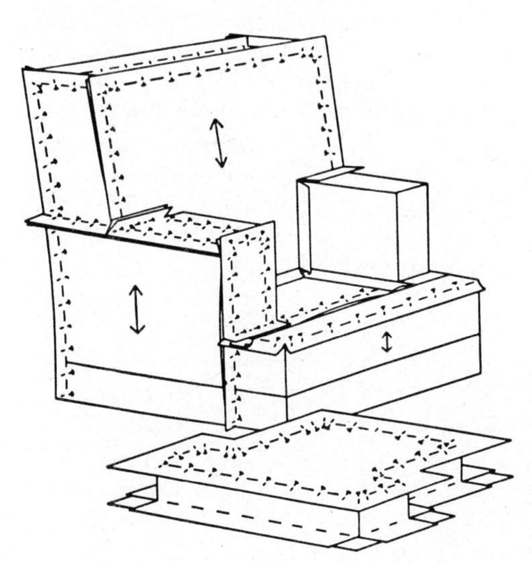

Slip cover is pinned in place, left. Edge for placket is left open with row of pins or chalk mark on each side of closing to show shape of furniture. Upholstery-type slip cover with no skirt, above, is closely fitted and made of upholstery material for the winter. Chintz slip cover with skirt, right, is for summer use.

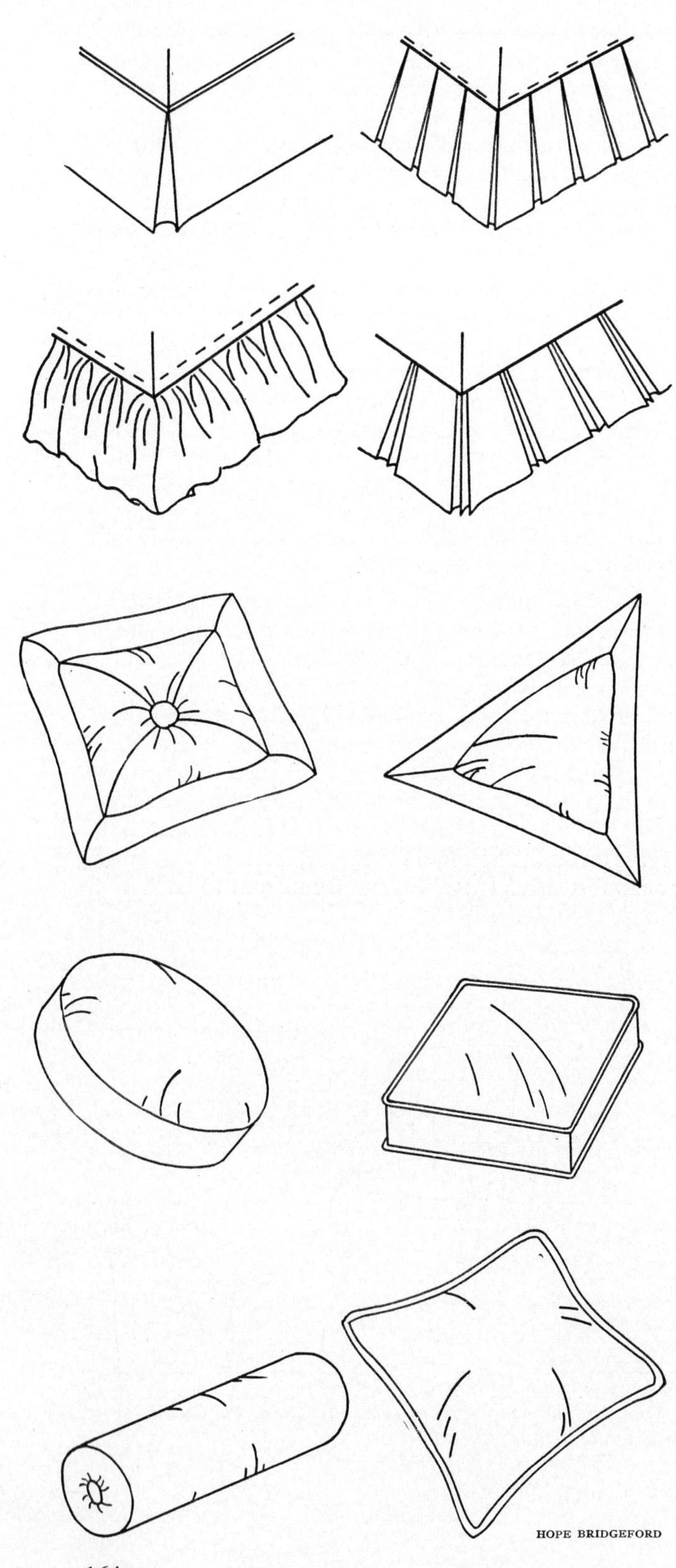

At left are the four simplest types of flounces or skirts used on furniture for upholstery, slip covers, dust ruffles and custom-made bedspreads.

marking a line of pins or chalk to indicate the top edge of the skirt. This height will be determined partly by the pattern, if any, of your fabric and partly by the proportions of the piece of furniture. Usually the skirt goes from just above the upholstery line to the floor.

To make the skirt, cut pieces crosswise of your fabric the length of the skirt, plus allowance for turn in at the top and a hem at the bottom. The number of pieces needed depends on the type of skirt. Measure the circumference of your chair at the skirtline. Box pleats require twice this measurement, closed pleats take three times, and a gathered flounce one and a half times. For a plain skirt with kick pleats at the corners add twenty-four inches. Grouped pleats are measured out according to the number of groups, the number of pleats in each group, and the depth of each pleat. These types of skirts are shown on this page.

When you have found the length of the strip required for the skirt, cut your pieces and stitch them together, matching the pattern as necessary. Press open the seams and put in the hem.

There are several methods of sewing the skirt to the main body of the slip cover. The bottom edge of the cover may be turned under along the marked line and the skirt stitched under it with the stitching showing on the outside. You may repeat the French seams of the body, if you used that method of finishing, or join the skirt with the same welting or fringe used to trim the upper part. The top of the skirt may be turned under and stitched to the outside of the slip cover on the line marked.

The final step in the body of the slip cover is the closing. This shows the least and makes a neat finish when it is run down one side of the back on the edge of a piece. A large sofa cover will sometimes go on more easily if there is an opening at each end, but most chairs need only one. If you use a slide fastener, simply turn in the edges of the opening at the marked line, continuing the trimming used on the front edge. Baste the closed fastener in place with the closed end at the top, and stitch. In selecting a slide fastener, choose a heavy one long enough to extend down into the skirt. For most pieces this will be 18 to 20 inches. When purchasing, remember to get fasteners for the cushions also. These should be as long as the cushion is wide.

Cushions are fun and easy to make. For decoration or comfort, give thought to shape, size, stuffing, boxing, buttons, soft or stuffed flanges, welting.

If you plan to use snappers of any kind, crease fabric along the marked outline, finish the rough edge of the front piece by whipping or a small hem, and blind-stitch rough edge of back piece to itself. Sew snappers close to the edge on this piece and match them on the front. Snappers should be close enough together to prevent any chance of gaping.

There is no rule about when the separate cushion of a chair must be covered. It is the easiest part of a slip cover and you may like to make it first for practice, or to see how the whole thing is going to look. It can be made last, or any time in between. Follow the pinning diagram on page 163 and make exactly as you make the rest of the cover, remembering to clip curves and corners. The slide fastener or other closing goes across the back of the cushion. This can be put in at the edge, but the cushion will be more completely reversible if the fastening is in the center of the boxing at the back. To do this, split the strip for this piece of boxing and stitch fastening in place before you sew it to the rest of the seat cover.

Slip-covering armless chairs, side chairs in which only the seat is upholstered, slip seats, window cushions and ottomans follows the same procedure, according to the demands of each type. You may wish to cover your sofa pillows with a removable cover to match or in contrast to your slip covers.

Many chairs and sofas are made more comfortable or more appealing by the addition of some kind of small or large pillows or cushions. These can take many shapes, be stuffed with down, foam rubber, or kapok. They can be made from all sorts of odds and ends of material, or just a half yard of a beautiful brocade or damask. They should, of course, be in the general coloring and style of the room and the piece they are to adorn. In making such cushions, improvise as much as you like, but always use a separate cover to hold the stuffing to make changing or cleaning the outside cover easy.

In the same category as slip covers come a number of other covers you will need or would like to have. A bedspread is taken for granted, but making it a part of your room, integrated with the curtains, dressing table or color scheme, goes with good decorating. Whether you prefer a simple *throw* which is a plain rectangular cover large enough to cover the top of the bed and reach toward the floor with no fitting, pleats, skirts or embellishment, or really want to dress up your beds, you will find a dust ruffle on the bed improves the look of the whole bedroom. It is easily made by taking a piece of inexpensive fabric, unbleached muslin, sateen or a sheet, and cutting it the

Fabrics are inexpensive, cutting and sewing are simple and everything is washable in this child's room.

CLEANLINESS BUREAU

Fabric and style of slip cover make it suitable as well as practical for its location.

SINGER SEWING CENTER

Yardage Guide

For Upholstery and Slip Covers

Yardages given are for standard-size pieces, plain, small-patterned or striped fabrics. If pattern is large, or must be centered on seats, backs, etc., allow one repeat for each surface, adding an extra inch on all sides for tacking or sewing. For self-welted slip covers, add one yard for bias-cut welting. This is a guide and should be checked with measurements of actual piece if it is out of the ordinary. Calculate other pieces from those shown.

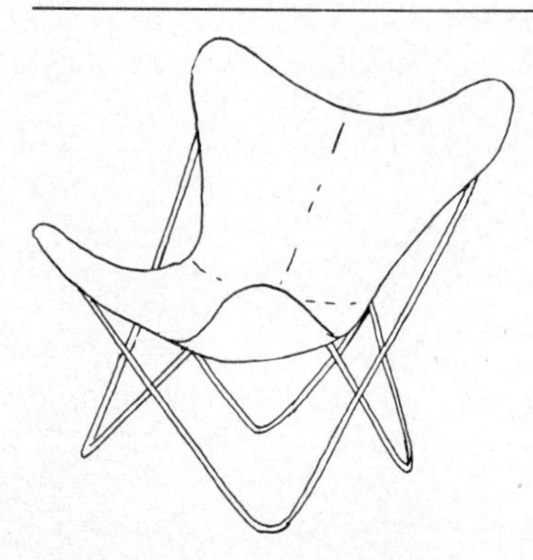

Sling Seat: 50″ fabric, 1⅓ yds.
36″ " 2⅔ yds.
(Do not advise narrow fabric)

Upholstery: 50″ fabric, 2 yds.
Slip Cover: 50″ " 2½ yds.
36″ " 5 yds.
No skirt

Upholstery: 50″ fabric, 6 yds.
(Do not slip-cover)

Upholstery: 50″ fabric, 3 yds.
Slip Cover: 50″ " 4 yds.
36″ " 5 yds.
Skirt: . . . . 1½ yds.

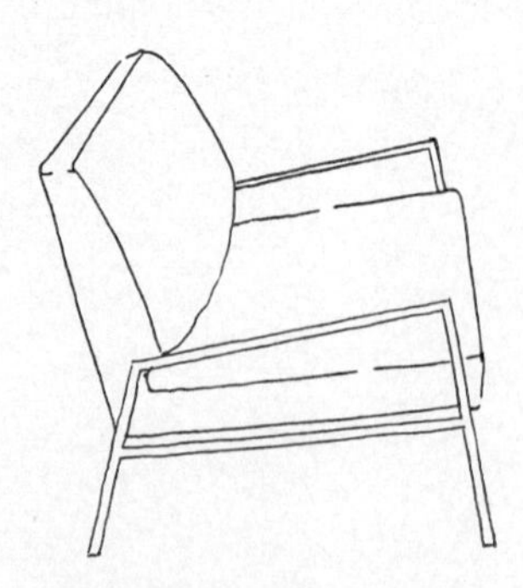

Upholstery: 50″ fabric, 3 yds.
Slip Cover: 50″ " 3 yds.
36″ " 5 yds.
Skirt: . . . . 1½ yds.

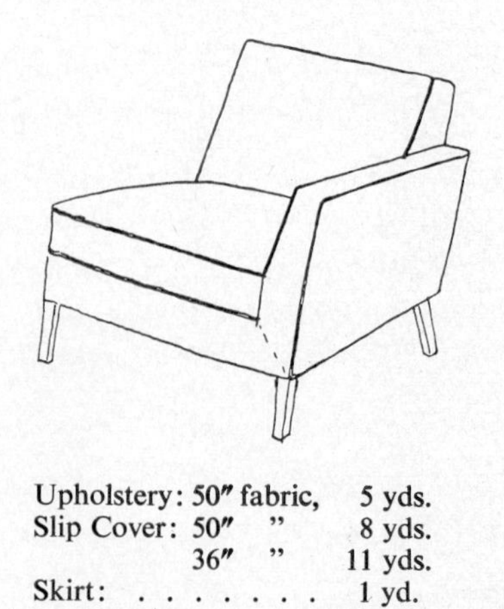

Upholstery: 50″ fabric, 5 yds.
Slip Cover: 50″ " 8 yds.
36″ " 11 yds.
Skirt: . . . . 1 yd.

Upholstery: 50″ fabric, 2¼ yds.
Slip Cover: 50″ ” 2½ yds.
36″ ” 4½ yds.
Skirt: . . . . 1 yd.

Upholstery: 50″ fabric, 5 yds.
Slip Cover: 50″ ” 7 yds.
36″ ” 9 yds.
Skirt: . . . . 1 yd.

Upholstery: 50″ fabric, 3 yds.
Slip Cover: 50″ ” 4 yds.
36″ ” 5 yds.
Skirt: . . . . 1½ yds.

Upholstery: 50″ fabric, 6 yds.
Slip Cover: 50″ ” 9 yds.
36″ ” 12 yds.
Skirt: . . . . 1 yd.

Upholstery: 50″ fabric, 3½ yds.
Slip Cover: 50″ ” 4½ yds.
36″ ” 7 yds.
Skirt: . . . . 1½ yds.

Upholstery: 50″ fabric, 2¼ yds.
Slip Cover: 50″ ” 2½ yds.
36″ ” 3 yds.
Skirt: . . . . 1½ yds.

Upholstery: 50″ fabric, 6 yds.
Slip Cover: 50″ ” 9 yds.
36″ ” 12 yds.
Skirt: . . . . 1 yd.

Upholstery: 50″ fabric, 6 yds.
Slip Cover: 50″ ” 8 yds.
36″ ” 10 yds.
Skirt: . . . . 1½ yds.

Upholstery: 50″ fabric, 5 yds.
Slip Cover: 50″ ” 8 yds.
36″ ” 10½ yds.
Skirt: . . . . 1½ yds.

Upholstery: 50″ fabric, 6 yds.
Slip Cover: 50″ " 7 yds.
36″ " 9 yds.
Skirt: . . . . 1½ yds.

Upholstery: 50″ fabric, 8 yds.
Slip Cover: 50″ " 9½ yds.
36″ " 13 yds.
Skirt: . . . . 1 yd.

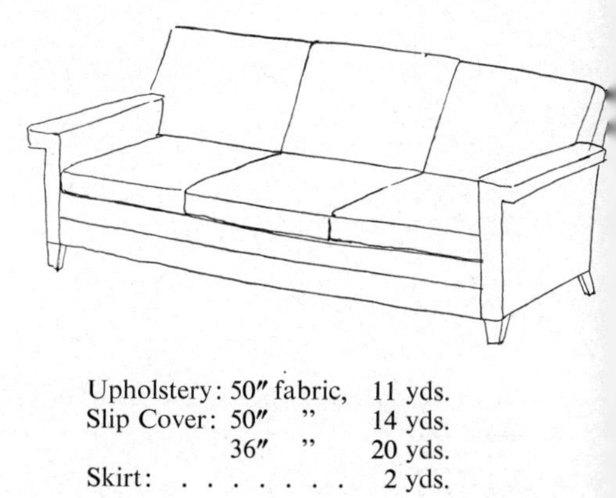

Upholstery: 50″ fabric, 11 yds.
Slip Cover: 50″ " 14 yds.
36″ " 20 yds.
Skirt: . . . . 2 yds.

Upholstery: 50″ fabric, 6 yds.
Slip Cover: 50″ " 9 yds.
36″ " 12 yds.
Skirt: . . . . 1 yd.

Upholstery: 50″ fabric, 8 yds.
Slip Cover: 50″ " 9½ yds.
36″ " 13 yds.
Skirt: . . . . 1 yd.

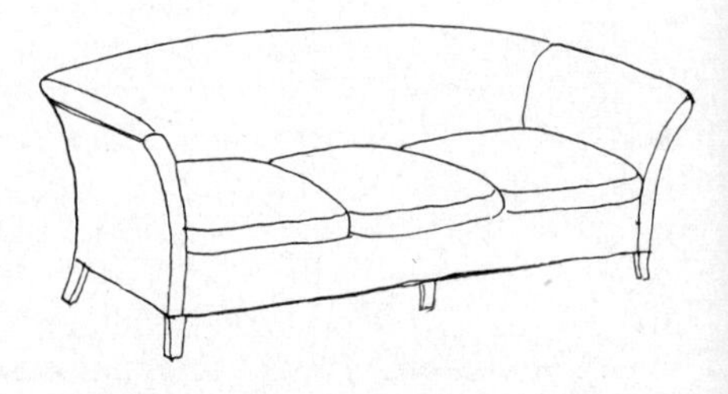

Upholstery: 50″ fabric, 9½ yds.
Slip Cover: 50″ " 12 yds.
36″ " 16 yds.
Skirt: . . . . 2 yds.

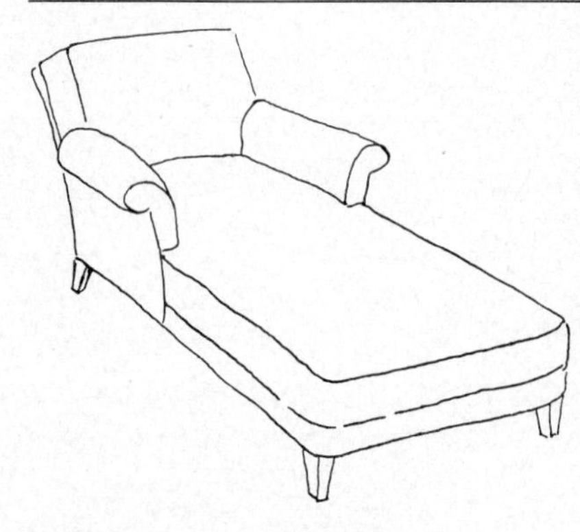

Upholstery: 50″ fabric, 7½ yds.
Slip Cover: 50″ " 9 yds.
36″ " 12 yds.
Skirt: . . . . 2 yds.

Upholstery: 50″ fabric, 8 yds.
Slip Cover: 50″ " 9 yds.
36″ " 11 yds.
Skirt: . . . . 1½ yds.

Upholstery: 50″ fabric, 10½ yds.
Slip Cover: 50″ " 12 yds.
36″ " 20 yds.
Skirt: . . . . 2 yds.

HAROLD FOWLER

size of the top of the bedspring with a slight margin for turning in. Measure the distance from the top of the spring under the mattress to the floor and make a flounce exactly as you would for a slip cover, described on page 164. With the flounce fabric, make a 4-inch top facing on both sides and across the bottom of your large spring cover and sew the flounce between this and the facing. Most beds will not require a ruffle at the head, but the cover should be attached here to prevent slipping. With a dust ruffle you may use a short or long bedspread, fitted or plain. The spring and mattress are covered at all times as well as things that you may have to store under the bed.

Studio couches appear everywhere in a house. Traditionally they come with no head or foot and three oblong pillows to put against the wall. The very simplicity of their outline makes it possible to give them any style desirable by the choice of fabric for the covering and the kind of skirt and trimming used. Do it like the one on page 165 for a little girl's room, or a sitting room. Use a heavy-textured fabric with a plain skirt and kick pleats at the corner for the living room or den. Use two long larger boxed pillows or a long large bolster running the whole length of the couch for greater formality.

A cedar chest makes a good window seat with a little padding on the top, covered with fabric nailed to the inside of the lid, and a skirt tacked to the front and sides. A trunk, which for one reason or another must be kept in one of the lived-in rooms, will look better with a neatly made cover, straight or flounced; and if the height is suitable it, too, can be used as a seat with a padded cushion on the top.

Once you get started with ideas of things you can slip-cover, make on the sewing machine, or use fabric for, your greatest danger is that you will overdo it. The dividing line in decorating between a "good touch" and "too much" is very fine. When in doubt, it is better to stay on the side of a "good touch."

Our first thought in having things made or in making them ourselves is of fabrics by the yard. Sometimes these are hard to match, or we are looking for a short cut. We have found a bedspread we like, but no curtains to go with it. We have no sewing machine or no time. Quite often the answer is to buy an extra bedspread to match the one for the bed and split the second one to make curtains. If you would like a good match for your sheets and dust ruffle, simply buy an extra sheet or two of the same color to make the dust ruffle. Some of the materials that come in ready-made bedspreads are also suitable for slip covers and small cushions. One of the fascinations of working with old fabrics, both fine antique pieces and just old ones, is the exercise given to your ingenuity.

Decorative swag, matching pillow and comforter give point and emphasis to this pretty bedroom.

CANNON MILLS, INC.

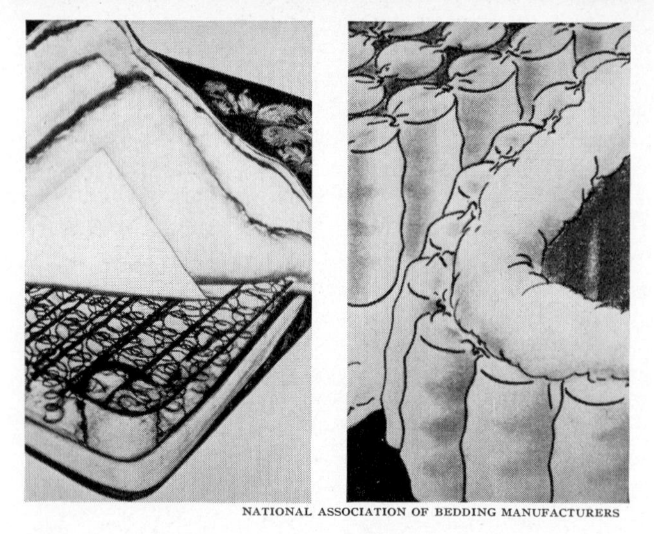

NATIONAL ASSOCIATION OF BEDDING MANUFACTURERS

The room above could be used either as a master bedroom or guest room. Strong greens give it character—the rose touches, softness. Far left is a metal-tied mattress unit. Layers of padding on top and bottom are fastened securely to it. Coils in the cloth-pocketed innerspring mattress, left, are smaller and lighter, but there are more of them.

Beds and Bedding

Selection for Comfort and Style

The average person spends 122 days each year in bed. This is the grand sleep total for those who follow the rule and get eight hours every night. It is an impressive amount of time and makes us realize how very important it is to select bedding carefully. These are home furnishings you cannot choose only for color or design. Comfort and quality come first and it is the hidden values that count.

Bedding is the last place to cut budget corners, the place to buy the very best you can afford. Because of the great variety of springs and mattresses available and the different requirements of various people, when buying new bedding go to a reliable dealer for help in making a good selection. There are special mattresses for short, tall, fat and thin people, for those who have back ailments or allergies, as well as those with definite preferences. The ideal mattress is actually one which conforms exactly to the contour of your body, with equalized pressure at all points. The best test of all in choosing a mattress and bedspring is to lie down on them and test for comfort. You may feel a bit silly doing this in a store, but it is a sensible and smart buying technique.

Make sure your mattress is the right size. Standard-size double beds are 54 inches wide and 74 inches long. Outsize bedding, which ranges from 74 to 82½ inches in length and up to 60 inches in width, is obtainable. Even longer and wider bedding may be had on special order. Ideally, bedding should be 7 inches longer than your height and allow a 39-inch-wide sleeping space. This will give adequate shifting room. Even those who profess to "sleep like a log" will shift position from 20 to 50 times a night.

There are four types of mattress. In an innerspring mattress, the coil unit is sandwiched on either side by insulating material and padding and may be cloth-pocketed. In the latter each individual coil is held in a pocket of heavy muslin. Most such mattresses contain over 800 coils. Another type is the wire-tied coil innerspring. These coils are larger than those used in the cloth-pocketed style and are fastened to one another by small helical springs, wire ties or both. The number of coils used in this construction varies greatly. It is dependent on coil design, assembly method and the quality and size of the wire. There may be as many as 500 coils in a wire-tied unit. The difference in the number of coils used for cloth-pocketed and wire-tied innersprings cannot be compared. Each will make a good mattress, depending on the quality of materials and workmanship. Insulation for such mattresses is necessary to keep upholstery from sinking into the coils and to keep you from feeling them. Metal bands, wire, wire mesh, cotton netting, quilted pads and stitched sisal pads are used for insulating. Suitable upholstery materials include felted cotton, latex pad, curled hair, rubberized curled hair or combinations of same.

The comfort of solid upholstered mattresses without innersprings is based on the natural resiliency of the filling materials. Curled hair, from horse and cattle tails, makes a very firm mattress and is still considered the best. The greater initial cost is offset by the fact that it can be "done over" as good as new many times. Hog hair has less resilience and tends to be stiff and bristly. All-cotton or felt fillings are also used. The best of the latter is long-fibered cotton which has been felted into layers or woven into one large batt. Less expensive mattresses are filled entirely with blown short cotton fibers or have centers filled with these fibers with felted layers above and beneath them.

One of the newest types is the latex mattress, made from the milk of rubber trees or synthetic material whipped into foam and vulcanized in special molds to give it cellular construction. Such mattresses provide airy ventilation during the warm months, wear well, do not need turning and are an especially good choice for those who suffer from special allergies. Latex also adjusts itself to the curves of the body. A latex mattress should be about 4½ inches thick.

When purchasing a mattress, check the ticking. It should be closely woven. If tufting is used, button or tape tufts are preferable. Be sure mattress edges are reinforced to prevent sagging from constant edge-of-bed sitting. Look at innerspring mattress handles to see they are sturdily attached. Handles are made of cord, steel and plastic or, on less expensive mattresses, of cloth. Check ventilators, necessary to air the inside of innerspring mattresses. Look for tape edges (sewing-machine stitching with tape at top and bottom edges of the mattress). A roll edge, which is a round filled edge at mattress top and bottom, is often used on less expensive mattresses. Some stores have small mattress sections for display which will enable you to have a look at the inner construction. Tell the salesman what type mattress you are accustomed to use. This will guide him in helping you make a new selection.

A good mattress is not enough. The bedspring it is placed on must also be top quality for comfortable sleeping. Springs come in three general types.

Box springs are exceptionally popular, both for comfort and because they can be mounted on legs and used to make an inexpensive bed. The coils of a box spring are mounted on a wood base. Cotton felt or hair is used for the top upholstery. Ticking matches the mattress. Top quality springs have coils that are tied to each other, to the base and to the border with special twine, helicals or metal ties, either through the center or across the top. Extra-deep box springs are advisable if you are using a latex mattress, in order to bring the unit to standard bed height.

If you select a metal coil bedspring, double-deck coils are preferable to single deck. Extra long, they are supported through the middle. The upper half of the coil supplies resiliency; the lower half is tightly wound to help support the sleeper's weight. A platform-top coil bedspring can be used with either innerspring or a solid upholstered mattress. It has metal bands which run lengthwise or crosswise or both ways across the top of the spring, making a semiclosed surface. A convolute coil spring has several extra turns of wire at the top of each coil. When the coils are depressed, they make a semiclosed surface. Check for stabilizers which prevent sagging or sidesway. This type spring is suitable for innerspring or solid upholstered mattresses.

There are two types of flat bedspring. One has metal strips which run lengthwise on the frame and are attached to the end with helicals. Good metal band springs are also strengthened horizontally with helicals. The other type of flat spring (link fabric) is made of wire which is woven and attached to the frame with helicals. Such springs are mainly used on cots. They are least expensive and tend to sag with long usage.

Pillows should be light, resilient enough to rebound when pressure is released, buoyant enough to sustain head weight and free from odor, dust, stiffness and lumps. Ticking should be closely woven so feathers do not come through it.

The best pillow filling is a combination of down and goose or duck feathers, which are springy, full, fluffy and have a curved shaft. All-down pillows lack the buoyancy supplied by the curved shafts of the waterfowl feathers. The next quality are made of chicken and turkey feathers, which have straight shafts and must be artificially curved for springiness. Foam-rubber pillows, similar to foam mattresses, are favored by many, especially those allergic to feathers.

These days, sleep equipment is to be found in the living room as well as the bedroom. Dual-purpose sofas and chairs make full use of limited space. In a small apartment, they are a necessary furnishing for the combination living- bed-room. In a home, they may take the place of the disappearing guest room. Our national tendency to more compact living quarters is making them almost standard equipment. Easy to operate, they are styled to fit Provincial, Early American, 18th Century or Contemporary settings. Sizes vary from chair through love seat to sofa

Spring unit with convolute coils around the edge provides a firm base for innerspring mattress. Mounted on a wooden base, padded and covered with ticking and closed with a dust cover, this becomes a box spring.

Below is a metal band top bedspring with helicals at the ends and crosswise for added strength and wear.

NATIONAL ASSOCIATION OF BEDDING MANUFACTURERS

NOWELL WARD AND ASSOCIATES

Bedspring and mattress unit in a steel frame rolled under a storage back provides comfortable sofa seating depth. Bedding is of the best quality to hold up under 24-hour-a-day use.

The beautiful sleigh bed, below, is found in the Denison Homestead, Stonington, Connecticut.

lengths. There is even an ottoman which unfolds to make a bed. You can select a double-duty sofa in single, twin, three-quarter, full or extra bed size. There are sofa beds with arms which drop down to make extra sleeping space. Others come with or without arms, with one arm and a back, or have bolsters. Storage space for linens is provided in some pieces. Others are designed so that linen may be left on the bed when it converts back to a sofa.

The convertible sofa conceals a one-piece mattress in davenport or love-seat width. The studio couch converts into twin beds. The single sleeper is the modern version of the old day bed. Either of these three types is a good choice for every-night use.

A twin-size mattress and bedspring on legs can also serve double duty. Many of these have storage backs so constructed that the bed slides part way under them to make comfortable seating depth. Rollaway cots are also worth considering. They fold in half for convenient closet storage. Opened, many have adjustable back rests which make them ideal for sunning as well as sleeping.

With wise buying, sleep equipment can be comfortable and decorative. Use pretty linens to make your bedroom a restful haven for waking hours and quality mattresses and springs to lead the way to pleasant dreams.

STUART-STEPHENSON

Storage starts in the kitchen. If it is well planned you will save steps, time and energy.

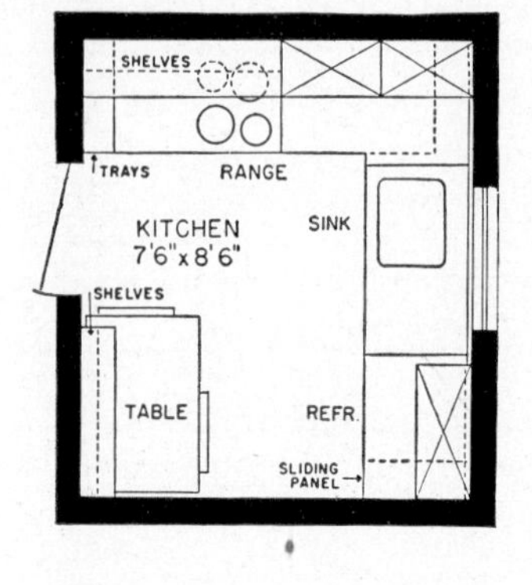

Storage

Planning Efficient Space

PHOTOGRAPH BY THE MAKERS OF ARMSTRONG'S LINOLEUM

This ingenious and inspirational use of space is far more accessible than the familiar, overburdened hall closet of legend and joke.

The well-planned home has a place for everything, and everything covers a wide range of belongings. There are articles we use daily, such as cleaning equipment, gadgets, clothing, linens and the like. There are things we collect—some because they represent an interest, others saved for sentiment, a few put away because we know "they'll come in handy some day." Considering the thousands of possessions even a small family acquires, it is little wonder that we never seem to have enough storage space.

Storage space must be well-planned or improved to meet our needs and to fit space requirements. Ideally, articles should be stored closest to the point of their use. (An orange-juice squeezer does not belong in the dining-room cabinet.) Storage should be arranged so that articles are easy to get at. (Dinner plates should not be at the bottom of a stack of salad plates, saucers and cups.) Wise use of space and efficient planning are important for easier housekeeping.

The kitchen is the big work and storage center of the home. Certainly, it is the one room that is of prime concern to the homemaker. If it is well arranged, she will save steps, time and energy. Among the things which must be housed in this area are food, china, silver, pots, pans, utensils and appliances. Each should be arranged nearest its point of use in a cabinet or drawer designed specifically for it. Serving dishes, pots and pans are best kept in a vertical file with slotted spaces designed to hold each one. Platters and trays may be arranged on slide-out shelves or stored, standing on end, in a narrow vertical closet built into one of the cabinets. Linen units should be partitioned with separate areas allotted for place mats, cloths and napkins. The minor irritation of unstacking a pile of dishes to reach the size plate you need is solved with round revolving shelves sized to fit various plates. The shelves swing out to bring your choice within easy reach. A handful of hooks screwed into a shelf bottom, will give you a place to hang cups. Food cabinets frequently waste space with too-high shelves. Tiny tiered half-shelves built above the full ones utilize otherwise lost space and make the perfect place to store small canned goods or spices. Foods used daily should go on lower shelves; reserve stock can rise to greater heights.

Each kitchen will, of course, present a different problem. Sit down and study your own layout. Plot ways to make every inch of floor and wall-cabinet space count.

Furniture is most frequently used for dining-room storage. A buffet holds silver and linens, even trays. A china cabinet houses dinnerware. Where living and dining spaces form a combination area, a room divider can fulfill storage requirements for both. Storage walls are used in many living rooms. They are made up of numerous units including closets, cabinets, drawers, shelves and sometimes drop-leaf desks. Some have special sections for

TV or radio-phonograph sets. Such units are inexpensively constructed by the home handyman from plywood. Plans are available from lumber yards and plywood companies.

In living- bed-rooms, end tables may be used for storage. Many have cabinet bases for blankets and linens. Some have tops which slide closed over storage bins. There are sofa beds equipped with storage backs or with drawers along the base line. Hassocks are also deceiving. Many open up, revealing a space for magazines, ash trays or other household articles.

The clothing closet is the main storage spot in most bedrooms. Space-saving gadgets permit you to get full use of space. Special hangers take as many as five blouses at a time. There are racks and hooks for ties, belts, handbags and shoes. Deep, narrow closets are best utilized with a pull-out clothing rod which runs the depth, rather than the width, of the closet. This gives more hanging space. Group long dresses at one end of the bar, short ones at the other with shoes or other articles stacked on the floor underneath them. If the closet is large enough, equip it with drawers and shelves for shoes and other accessories. Utilize closet doors for umbrellas, shoe racks, hats and other small articles.

Storage headboards on beds offer further possibilities. They come with shelves and drawers for books, radios, telephones, lingerie, linens, and what have you. Bookcases fulfill a storage need in the bedroom as do flat-top desks which open into fully equipped vanities.

Most bathrooms are badly in need of additional storage space. One small, crammed medicine cabinet is not sufficient to house equipment for the entire family. Two towel bars are invariably not enough. Each member of the family should have a place to hang his towel and face cloth. You can purchase clip-on towel and cloth racks that attach to the edge of the sink or tub. You can mount extra towel bars on the back of the bathroom door. A clothes hamper might also be hung on the door, out of the way. You'll probably find space for additional shelves or a second medicine chest over the water-closet tank. A chrome divider between sink and bathtub gives still further space for towels and soap. De luxe bathrooms provide vanities with cabinets and drawers for storage.

The attic, if you're fortunate enough to have one, is the ideal place for storing little-used articles. A series of drawers and cabinets labeled with contents will bring your attic top storage efficiency.

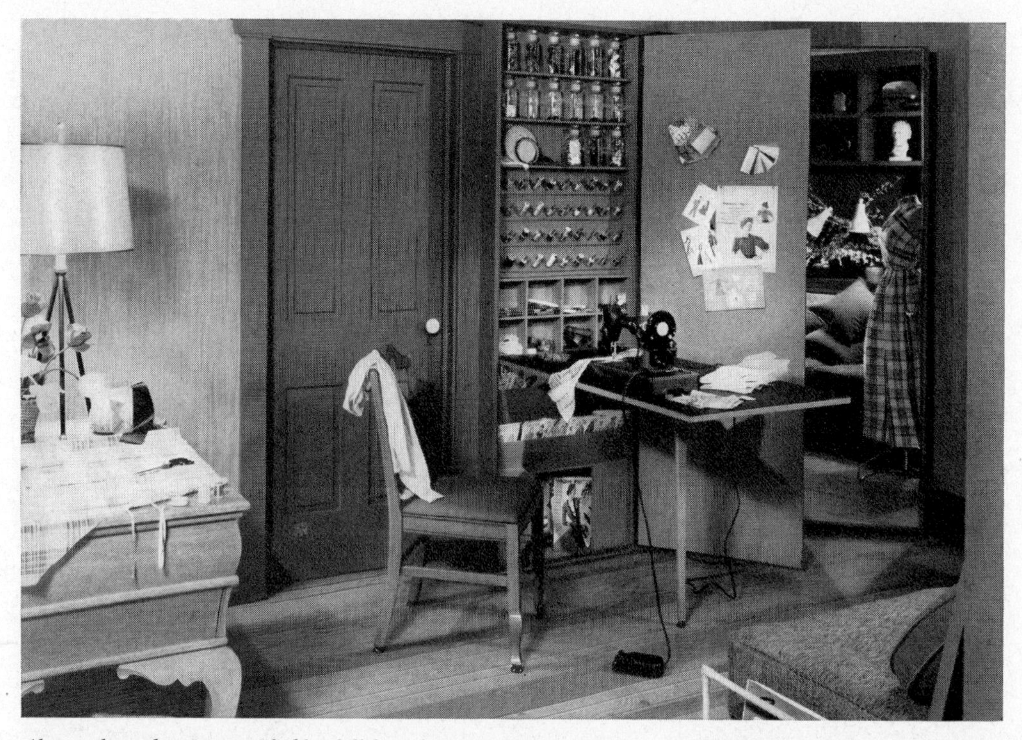

Above, three doors concealed by full-length mirrors open on complete equipment for home dressmaking, including an ironing board and iron. Shelves under the stairway in the living room, left, can be used for storing many objects. The unit is partitioned down the middle to store linens on the opposite side. The roll-away doors in the kitchen, below, cover pass-through to dining room with china and glass shelves above. The closet, below right, is a complete dressing room by making use of the backs of the doors and built-in drawers.

Hand-crocheted place mats and doilies are fun to make. Weight of thread regulates delicacy of finished product. Fine thread for party use, heavier thread for everyday regular use.

Table Settings

Formal and Informal Occasions

Dinner

HOLMES AND EDWARDS SILVERPLATE

Breakfast

HOLMES AND EDWARDS SILVERPLATE

Luncheon

RED WING POTTERIES

Table accessories are among the most important in your home. They're brought sharply into focus three times a day—morning, noon, and night: breakfast, dinner, and supper. They serve a useful purpose and, decoratively speaking, give meals importance, make them more than a matter of mere eating.

Like everything else in the well-planned house, table accessories must harmonize with each other and with the background. A breakfast-nook table is set one way, a dining-room table deserves quite different treatment. The first may combine pottery and a plaid cloth; the second rates fine dinnerware and damask.

In selecting accessories, you may start with silver. Sterling is the homemaker's pride. It is meant to last a lifetime, so choice of pattern should not be hasty. Simple shapes and designs are preferable to more ornate ones; they can be used for formal and informal settings alike. Silver plate, though less expensive, is now made in beautiful patterns. Good grades wear well and look much like sterling. When the backs of forks and spoons are reinforced with additional silver, plate is called sterling inlay.

Depending on your budget and style of living, dinnerware may be beautifully glazed, translucent china; earthenware, or inexpensive pottery. Much of our fine china is imported from Europe, but some—Lenox, for example—is now being turned out by American companies.

Generally speaking, white, cream, ivory, and pale tints are favored for dinnerware. Bright, deep colors have been introduced but not too successfully, since they often clash with the color of the food served on them. Spinach on a green and purple plaid plate or red beets on a brown one are not too appetizing.

Dinnerware can be plain or patterned, mixed or matched. Patterned dishes should usually be mixed with plain ones and placed on a plain cloth. A combination of two patterns is apt to be busy and confused. When mixing

dinnerware, try for shapes and types that are similar. Pottery and china are not used together. Instead, team two pottery or two china sets. One may be patterned, the other plain. Both can be plain but in different colors.

When buying teacups try handles to see that they are comfortable and easy to hold. Check coffeepot spouts. They should not drip after pouring. Keep in mind that open-stock dinnerware has an advantage, as it can be replaced when breakage occurs.

Glassware with its graceful lines and lovely sparkle is another important addition to your table. Crystal is glass that is nearly pure and flawless. Most glass may be plain or decorated in a number of ways. Cut glass, so popular with the Victorians and in vogue again, is cut in facets, which catch the light and reflect it brilliantly. The surface of glass can be patterned with shallow cuts, engraving, or may be etched with acid, or painted. Pressed glass is decorated in a mold.

These days, good design can be found in the least expensive ware. While such glass lacks the sparkle of crystal, there is beauty in its graceful lines. Colored glass is an excellent inexpensive buy, since the color, not the quality, attracts the attention.

Your choice of glassware will be based on your needs as well as your income. Water glasses are essential. They can be tumblers or formal goblets. After that, your choice may range to highball, cocktail, wine, brandy glasses, or others, depending on how much entertaining you do.

Tablecloths and place mats are the background for your other table accessories. White is a favorite choice for formal settings, although charming effects are achieved with pastels and other shades. Generally speaking, patterned cloths and bright colors are on the informal side.

The conventional favorite for a formal dinner is a damask cloth, which may be made from cotton, rayon, or linen used singly or in combinations. Lace, hand crochets, and organdy have an elegance of their own and even place mats may be used. These have become increasingly popular, especially for polished or beautifully grained tabletops, and offer a whole new range of decorative possibilities from conservative linens, embroidery of all sorts, to cotton textures spattered with sequins and threaded with metal. Place mats for formal use are versatile and more practical in any household than large, difficult-to-launder tablecloths.

On the casual side, cloths range through a variety of fabrics including gingham, Indian head, monk's cloth, sailcloth, and linen. Mats may be plastic, raffia, bamboo, cork, even brightly colored dish towels. At remnant counters, you will find a variety of washable fabrics, patterned and plain, which can be hemmed to bring new interest to your table. Cloths should be large enough to hang 12 to 18 inches below the tabletop. Mats are usually 12 by 18 inches in size.

Flowers are always charming on the table, but imposing flower centerpieces are most frequently used to decorate tables for special occasions. Select them to match the floral pattern of a plate, to harmonize or contrast with the color of the cloth. For unusual effects, combine them with sea shells or candles. Place flowers in baskets, beer steins, soup bowls, wooden shoes, or more conventional holders. Scatter confetti around them or circle containers with strings of pearls. Use figurines for accent. Tape feathered butterflies or tiny birds to leaves. Let imagination be your guide. Try fruits and vegetables as the centers of table interest on trays or in bowls and baskets. Arrange parsley sprays in a graceful glass vase. For special occasions, create a centerpiece that bespeaks the event with crepe paper, cardboard and ingenuity.

Consider such accessories as straw breadbaskets, wooden salad bowls, and pottery casseroles.

Set a decorative table. Remember that the completed setting must present a unit with all the various parts—silver, china, cloth, and centerpiece—working together to create a picture that is formal or informal depending on the occasion and the background.

The gleam of silver, page opposite, in this case Victorian silver picked up inexpensively from a secondhand shop, can add warmth and charm to your dining room, while the delicate, hand-crocheted doily, right, is attractive and an addition to any table setting. The buffet table for a children's supper party, below, is imaginative and appropriately done.

HOLMES AND EDWARDS SILVERPLATE

HAANEL CASSIDY

This delightful area transformed for dining is modern in taste.

Ladies' Home Journal

BOOK OF INTERIOR DECORATION

PART THREE : ROOMS FOR EVERY USE AND TASTE

ROOM ARRANGEMENT BY DOROTHY PRATT; PHOTOGRAPH BY EZRA STOLLER

Upstairs drawing room from the Stuart house in Charleston is beautifully furnished for living and accurately reflects fine 18th century spirit.

Introduction

If we have all the knowledge in the world of periods and styles in architecture and furniture, with a good working knowledge of how to go about the details from room planning to cleaning the upholstery on an old chair, we still cannot do any interior decorating without ideas.

We want to develop our own ideas, but seldom find an entirely original one coming to us from nowhere with no background. Actually most ideas of our own are developed through being interested in every house, room, or display we see and taking advantage of every opportunity to see what others have done. Curiously enough, once this attitude is developed, we notice everything in decorating that we once took for granted. We see other people's rooms and our own as a whole and in detail. We see what is effective, how to solve a decorating problem, and learn what we like from this constant observation. Suddenly, by taking one thing from one place and something else from another, we create something quite original and personal to ourselves.

The personality or background of each person makes him find certain aspects of his own or other people's surroundings attractive or repulsive. To some, simplicity and practicality is of paramount importance. Some find their sense of well-being is improved by a certain amount of elegance. Old houses, inherited or acquired, capture the interest of many, while others want no part of this style of living and will sacrifice everything to be up to date. In addition to all the degrees of these ways of thinking, a large number prefer to combine what they particularly like from each one.

Such considerations set the pace, but must be adapted to the circumstances of living conditions—family, location, and budget. All we can do is seek the ultimate satisfaction within the limits of necessary compromises. Fortunately, when we put our minds on it and deliberately seek experience through observation, the compromise aspect disappears and we attain exactly what we want.

The professional decorator's chief asset is having planned and seen the results of hundreds of rooms to every *one* that the average homemaker works over. This is experience. This section of the book is designed to help the inexperienced see what is good and what is bad in various types of rooms, and above all what they like. It will give you some ideas to work on, and may indicate the solution to some problem.

The following pages are devoted to examples of rooms of many kinds. After looking at all of them you will know what type of decoration and arrangement you prefer, if that is your quandary. If you are looking for ideas, you will find hundreds of them. Look these rooms over with a critical eye. There will be many things that you will be glad you do not have to have, or would not want as a gift. There will be others that will start you off at once to make some improvement in your own home. It could be changing the position of a lamp, or might end with redecorating the whole house.

The field of interior decorating is tremendous, with many aspects which are so closely interwoven that it is almost impossible to isolate any one of them and discuss it in a vacuum. Neither is it possible to get all the knowledge on the subject into one person's head, certainly not into one book. There have been volumes written on every subject touched upon in this book and there are people who have made a lifelong study of the work of Duncan Phyfe or the weaving of fine fabrics.

The average homemaker, man or woman, does not have time nor does he care to become an expert. We do feel, however, that our education is really unnecessarily neglected if we know nothing about a subject that concerns us so intimately every day.

Whether you read this book from cover to cover, or use it as a reference book, it will provide the basic knowledge that you need. No effort has been made to deal exhaustively with any style of furniture or kind of wood. A definite effort has been made to bring out information that is most in demand on furniture periods, methods of work, quality, workmanship, prices, and artistic values.

Emphasis has been on good decorating advice which indicates the right direction to follow in each special field and on encouraging each person to follow it as far as he likes, to make his own living interesting and contented.

HAROLD FOWLER—LADIES' HOME JOURNAL'S MORE HOUSE FOR THE MONEY PORTFOLIO NO. 1

The buoyant use of color in the living room above is as practical as it is imaginative. The new materials keep their color, are resistant to stains, scars and scuffs. Living room at right features an unusual fireplace.

Living Rooms

The part of the house set aside for leisure time and living, whether it be a room, an area, or a corner, merits our very best decorating efforts. Here the family live, and here many friends and visitors get their only impression of our taste and housekeeping. Comfort, good lighting, and charm are the essentials. If you do not have enough of all three you may want fresh ideas for a complete change, or a bit of rearrangement. It is fun to pretend you are a visitor in your own house and examine the living area with a new eye.

GOLDING DECORATIVE FABRICS

Wall-to-wall drapery in a screened cotton print adds to the dimensions of the room and provides excellent background for the metal and upholstered furniture in this studio apartment.

HAROLD FOWLER

This fresh flower-patterned chintz fits the relaxed mood of the two big chairs, and blends happily with ice-green walls and gold cotton rug.

LADIES' HOME JOURNAL'S MORE IDEAS FOR THE MONEY PORTFOLIO HOUSE NO. 4

Excellent for family activities and dining is this sunny, informal gallery, above.

The formal setting, below, is enhanced by the mirrored fireplace and good lighting.

LIBBEY-OWENS-FORD GLASS COMPANY

TELEVISION HAS BECOME PART OF AMERICAN HOME LIFE

If you are not satisfied with the use your television set is getting, or are contemplating buying one, you may find it worth while to give some thought to where it is placed and how much comfort you can provide for the audience. When you have selected the best possible place in the house for it, the next consideration is placing it in the room. A television set which is used in the daytime should not be against a window or window wall, causing the audience to gaze into the daylight behind it. A corner or an inside wall is preferable. If this is impossible, the window should have a tight shade or venetian blind.

Seating arrangements are important too. Whether the set is in the living room or playroom, you will not want the room set up always with all chairs facing it as in a theater. The sofa or heavy chairs may be placed to face the set permanently, but a few easily moved chairs may have their backs to the screen and be turned around at will. These might be occasional chairs, lightweight ones, or of a type now being made in many styles with an invisible swivel in the bottom which allows the body of the chair to be turned around without moving the base. Extra cushions and ottomans, small tables for ash trays and refreshments will also add comfort and promote joys of watching television.

LADIES' HOME JOURNAL'S MORE HOUSE FOR THE MONEY PORTFOLIO NO. 5

This corner, above, of a family room neatly includes television along with books and records. A built-in television, below, disappears behind the paneled doors when it's not in use.

SYLVANIA ELECTRIC COMPANY

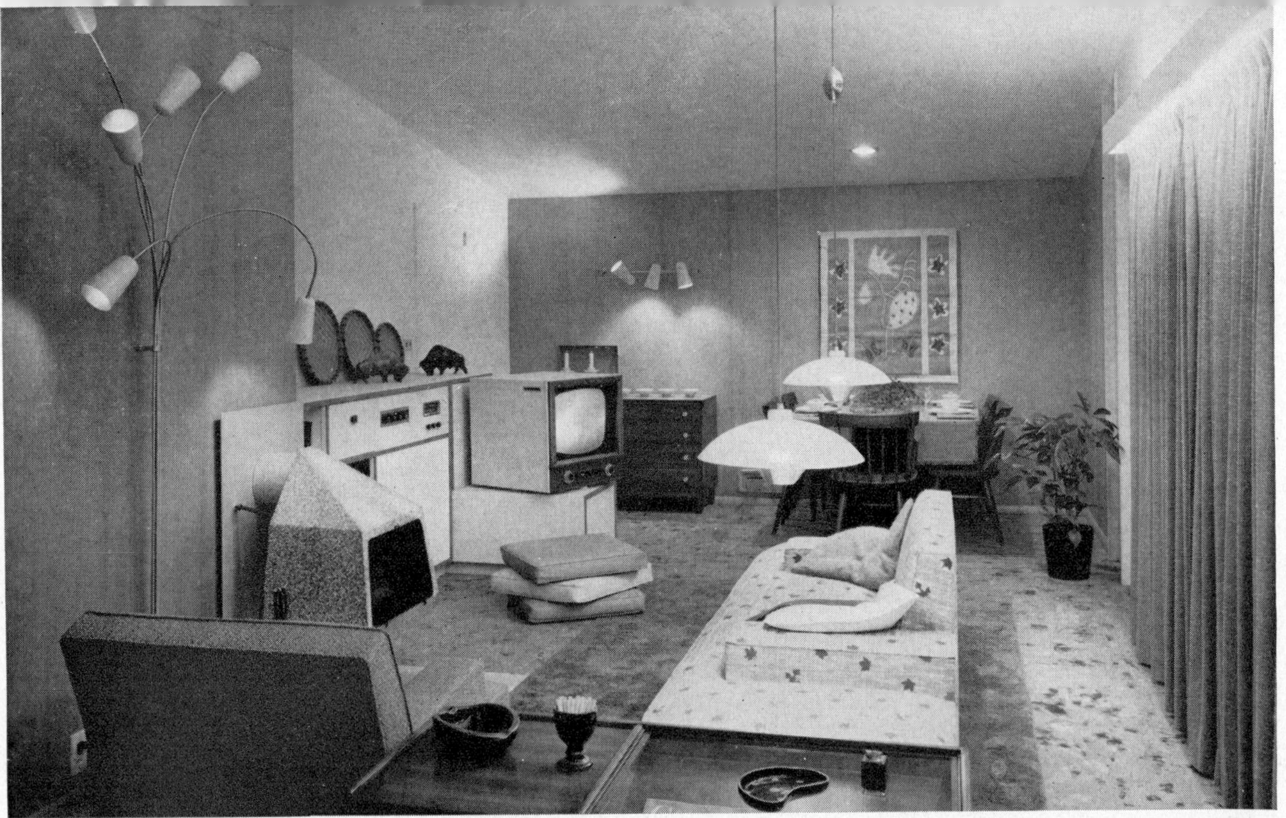

GENERAL ELECTRIC PHOTOGRAPH

Television need never dominate a room but it must be available without a great shifting of furniture. The above arrangement has a good deal of practicality.

In planning a desk or storage unit for a small sitting room, as below, it is simple to allow space for the television set where it will take no floor space and be unobtrusive.

PHOTOGRAPH BY THE MAKERS OF ARMSTRONG'S ASPHALT TILE

Dining Rooms

Ideas about a fixed place to dine at home have undergone many changes in modern times. In this phase of decorating, the word "area" has come into its own. However, no matter how far your plans stray from the stereotyped dining room, comfort and a pleasant atmosphere for eating are still of primary importance. The constant factors, then, will be a good firm table with a top about twenty-nine inches from the floor, adequate chairs with seats approximately seventeen inches high, and carefully blended restful colors. With these three important factors in mind, your choice of location may be unlimited.

Spite House, built in the early nineteenth century in Maine, is part of our American tradition. Its dining room, left, is traditional with Adam woodwork, reproduction of an 1820 carpet from Massachusetts, and a scenic wallpaper—Dufour's Conquest of Peru.

Once the background for hoop-skirted soirees, the Pontalba dining room's elegant simplicity in New Orleans is timeless. Table is set with exquisite antique china and softly lustrous silver.

Beautiful and spacious dining rooms still exist in some of our fine old houses and remind us of long leisurely dinners with excellent food and wines and plenty of service. The excellent food and wines are still served, but few people devote an entire room to the sole purpose of serving meals.

A dinner party or a family celebration may call for a big room or a big table occasionally, but the general trend is toward informal meals served in a room that is used between mealtimes for many other purposes. The breakfast nook in or just off the kitchen is almost standard installation in most houses today; and in apartments all but the inhabitants of extremely large ones plan to eat meals in a corner of the living room, the wide hallway, and in good weather on the balcony or terrace, if they are fortunate enough to have one. This tendency has had a great influence on dining tables, which are being designed to be used for many purposes and change their size as easily as Alice in Wonderland.

When space is very limited, an attractive solution for breakfast and lunch has been found in the counter type of table, which may be merely a shelf at the proper height in front of a window, or part of the divider that separates the stove and sink from the rest of the kitchen.

Happily, our more casual attitude about meals and the obligation to do most of the cooking, serving, and dish washing ourselves has not impaired our interest in nice china and tableware, nor our desire to have a pleasant place setting whether it is on a tray or at a formal dinner table.

LEVITTOWN, PA.

This arrangement for the informal breakfast or supper allows for service from the far side of the counter.

Colonial dining room is given interest with draped curtain of blue-and-white mattress ticking and white muslin.

Blond wood table expands to twice its size in this dining area. Chairs are sturdy in black wood and woven fiber.

STUART

Comfortable dining is possible in the living room when the table and chairs are designed for that purpose.

LIBBEY-OWENS-FORD GLASS COMPANY

Combination Rooms

Any room that does double duty as living and sleeping quarters for one or two persons; living and dining area for the family; or the well-known one-room apartment for living, dining, and sleeping, presents a challenge to the decorator. Arrangements must be made for all these activities in a way that will make each seem adequate and uncrowded when used for the specific purpose, with minimum furniture shifting and commotion to change the scene for another need.

MINNEAPOLIS-HONEYWELL ENGINEERS

Today every member of the family wants a place to be with his own friends at home in some privacy away from the general commotion of the household. An older daughter or a grandmother could be happy in the comfortable bed-sitting room above. The warm friendly room, below, does double duty in living-dining-entertainment plans.

PHOTOGRAPH BY THE MAKERS OF ARMSTRONG'S LINOLEUM

An illusion of greater space can be achieved when sitting room, dining room, study, kitchen, and even bedroom are all open in one large area as in the room above.

The combination room, below, radiates pleasantness with its sunshine, roominess, and comfort.

PHOTOGRAPH BY THE MAKERS OF ARMSTRONG'S CORK TILE

STUART

This happy room, just a step away from the cooking area, can be put into service for dining, entertaining or just plain living. *Plenty of shelf space shows off a fine ironstone collection, and the room is generous enough to hold a big pine table and Hitchcock chairs. The hearth with its black iron stove sends out warming firelight on a winter's night when the family relaxes and the children gather for story hour before bedtime.*

PHOTOGRAPH BY THE MAKERS OF ARMSTRONG'S LINOLEUM

The combination room, above, with its cheerful old-fashioned stove is ready for anything—entertaining guests or general family activity including small fry.

The tiny apartment can be comfortable and attractive and function smoothly when sound planning has used all available space to good advantage.

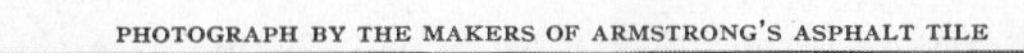

PHOTOGRAPH BY THE MAKERS OF ARMSTRONG'S ASPHALT TILE

Rejoice in your sun porch, if you are lucky enough to have one, and make it gay and useful. It could be the most important room in your home for actual living. Here is your observation post of nature's activities in every season. It is a great place for work or play, a place to turn a simple meal into a picnic, or in summertime to have dinner at a reasonable time without giving up those last outdoor hours of daylight. A small living room doubles in size if you make your sun porch a part of it in color and furnishings; or the out-of-doors comes into your house if you prefer it a garden spot.

Sun Porches

STUART

A sun porch may be a garden also, especially for collectors of geraniums, or any plants for that matter.

This bright and sunny porch-dining area adjoins a kitchen.

The sun porch, above, has an upholstered sofa covered with a fabric with a metal thread. The blinds are also decorated with metal, making this a glamorous corner in the house.

The porch, left, is really another dining room and most summer meals can be served out here in comfort.

The screened porch, right, becomes an extra living room with all the charm of any indoor room. The family can virtually live out here during summer torrid spells.

RICHARD PRATT

Patios

Primary requisites for a patio are informality and ease, a place to play and a place to relax. To some people privacy is of the essence, to others this is not important. The essentials are some kind of a paved or marked off flooring, comfortable chairs, provision for partial shade and for full sunlight. For the more practical, sunfast fabrics, weatherproof furniture and easy care should be included in the planning.

Efficiency is the byword for the kitchen of today. A place for everything and everything in its place. One step from the stove to the refrigerator and two steps from the refrigerator to the sink or vice versa; nothing too high and out of reach, nothing low enough to make extra bending. Kitchen designers and manufacturers of cabinets, storage units, built-in dishwashers, and appliances have worked out all sorts of well-planned kitchens. In fact, if your dream is to have a completely modern kitchen, you may buy it by name like an automobile.

Kitchens

Now that everyone takes a hand in the cooking, from daily meals or baby's formula to party dinners and midnight snacks, strange things have moved into the kitchen. Music, and even television, a telephone, a breakfast nook, a bookshelf, plants and flowers, and perhaps a desk and a toy chest make this room join the parade of versatile uses. Whatever goes on in your kitchen, you will be able to decorate to fill all functions pleasantly and comfortably.

Brick chimney cleaned of many coats of paint makes a fine background for new main cooking center in this old Connecticut house. Range just 30″ wide is complete with full-size oven, storage space, and 4 units with push-button control.

With good planning it is frequently possible to fit laundry equipment into a kitchen. The laundry section, right, can be closed off by the white louvered doors.

Knotty-pine cabinets give a warm, mellow feeling to this kitchen. Dishwasher and garbage unit in sink make short shrift of after-meal chores. Green tile floor is vinyl plastic.

A desk shelf and a stationery drawer are a wonderful convenience in a kitchen. Big help too: a range with oven plus separate broiler.

Even an 1890 kitchen can have its face lifted to an efficient new look, as above.

There is the kitchen which looks like a hospital clinic or a laboratory and the one which may be colorful, but everything is out of sight. Small apartments have complete kitchens in a small closet, or the railroad type with everything against one wall behind a screen. There are still kitchens with modern appliances, but retaining the old-fashioned atmosphere of the day when grandma made six pies on a Saturday morning, and steak was broiled over an open coal fire.

Considering the number of hours that are spent in this one room, it certainly should be the first place to exercise your right to personal preference, and the first on your list of improvements if you are not entirely happy with the setup or atmosphere of your present kitchen arrangements.

In planning changes in a kitchen, cleanliness, convenience, and charm should be considered in that order. Under cleanliness you would eliminate corners that are difficult to clean, counter tops with edges that hold crumbs and dirt; and find a place for the garbage pail and scrap basket, out of sight but easily cleaned. The floor covering

This shoehorn kitchen exercises its ingenuity here as it narrows to make space for a table, while the washer fits against a jog in the wall.

should fit closely around the edges and be of a type that is readily mopped or scrubbed. Convenience is a matter of having utensils at hand, but also as separated as possible so that you do not have to move others to get at the one you need. Charm comes in the lighting, color scheme, and hospitality that your kitchen offers.

Draw curtains of Dacron and cotton are easy to keep looking fresh in the well-planned kitchen, above. The long blue plastic counter is useful for unloading groceries after shopping, or for serving at mealtime. Fan above the cooking top draws off odors, and the stainless-steel hood can be unhooked and removed for cleaning. Push-button switches for cooking top show colored lights to indicate cooking speed.

The ghosts of our ancestors walk in this eighteenth-century bedroom from the Tate House.

Master Bedrooms

Master bedroom is an old-fashioned name which persists in the face of changing times, because it has always described the most important bedroom in a home. A single person decorates as he chooses. For husbands and wives,

LEVITTOWN, PA.

The tailored master bedroom becomes many women, especially if they like modern furniture.

Grandmother's old bed and her piano stool combined with some Regency chests in this room are adequate proof that styles carefully mixed can have great charm.

compromise or lack of it may contribute to a divorce or a happy marriage. Who is to say whether a husband should feel like "a bull in a china shop," or a wife like a Dresden doll in a hunting lodge? Only those concerned can answer this question.

The name, master bedroom, conjures up impressions of large houses, big windows, a system of bell signals in the pantry. Actually it is just what the name implies—the room where the owners or those responsible for a home sleep. The decoration of this room gets very mixed up in personal preferences of two people. A man may leave all the decisions to his wife and trust that she will show some consideration of his masculinity. A wife might have this in mind, but hate to give up her pink-taffeta vanity table. One personality may dominate entirely, there could be a compromise, or perhaps the fact that their tastes were congenial was what made them marry in the first place. All of these questions, though primarily in the field of marital relations, are bound to have some influence on the decoration of the home, especially the master bedroom.

Bedroom furniture is made in every style, just as other furniture, but for some reason, when it comes to styling beds the actual models of various periods are not copied. Contemporary beds may copy the acanthus leaf of Phyfe, or the inlays of Hepplewhite, but if the current style calls for no footboard, it will be omitted—a treatment that neither designer would have considered. The popularity of twin beds decreased the popularity of the four-posters as a model, because two complete testers in a room seemed overpowering.

The latest liberty that beds have taken with period styles is the "Hollywood" bed which consists of a pair of beds placed together with one long headboard. This takes less space than the older style of separating the twin beds with a night table, but needs more room than the average double bed. Headboards are made in every style, but the most popular for this style of bed is an upholstered headboard with or without a frame around it.

JOHN WIDDICOMB CO.

A formal town house sort of bedroom lends itself to a tufted headboard in the French style. The beds pivot away from each other for ease in making.

DESLEY FABRICS

Removing the footboard from an old spool bed makes the room seem larger and doesn't destroy the New England atmosphere.

HAROLD FOWLER

Some second-hand furniture, paint, and inexpensive accessories made this pretty guest room out of the room at the right.

Guest Rooms

Though hospitality comes from the heart, circumstances may contrive to hinder its complete fulfillment in the lack of space for an overnight guest. A little determination on the part of the heart, however, will find a way. The accommodations are not as important as the sincerity of the invitation. Perhaps happiness and peace of mind in yourself on this score depend upon the effort you have made to provide comfort, however much or little space you have to offer your potential guests.

In some households part of the way of life includes welcoming many overnight guests. One, two, or more guest rooms are set aside, furnished and decorated for comfort, but also with an idea of making them a little more startling or dramatic for those who are staying briefly. Here is a chance to use a color that you love, but find too flamboyant for year in, year out use. Here is the place for very delicate or heirloom bedspreads that should not be washed or cleaned too often. Within reason, it is the place for an

CHARLES M. COWDEN

occasional delicate piece of furniture, which is in constant danger elsewhere in the house. A guest room should be comfortable, but need not be as durable as bedrooms used daily. Above all it should be well appointed. Even if you have checked every detail carefully, it is well to spend a night yourself in your guest room to see if you missed anything—pen and ink and a place to write a note, hooks in the closet in addition to the closet bar with hangers. Nobody likes to hang pajamas or a nightgown on a coat hanger.

There are more families who need every inch of space for themselves and cannot set aside a room for occasional use. Sometimes a storage room in the attic can be made into an attractive guest room with very little effort. The one illustrated on page 221, bottom left, is simple, but quite charming with the drapery valance carried across the bed alcove and the slanting roof emphasized with the wooden sawed-out scallop of a darker color. This could be for a guest, or a cozy corner for a member of the family who does not live at home, but visits frequently.

When space or conditions in a household are such that there is no possible place to put up a guest, even on a stormy night, through no fault of your own you will feel like a misanthrope unless you find some solution. The obvious one is the convertible living-room sofa, chair, or ottoman. However, this may be something you would prefer to do as a completely last resort. Another answer is to make some provision for an extra bed in one of the bedrooms. This is particularly useful when the children or young people want someone over to spend the night. There are many variations on this idea for an extra bed, from the studio couch and folding cot to an arrangement like the one illustrated on page 221, bottom right. In this case one of the beds slides under the table when not in use.

Most guests "prefer to sleep in their own beds," whether they admit it or not. If possible, the ideal hostess will try to make her particular overnight guests forget this longing, or ease it with as much comfort as she can muster for them. This might include a light for reading in bed, two pillows instead of one, and somewhere to hang their clothes.

Originally this type of bed folded up under the half canopy—forerunner of the Murphy bed. The decoration remains, this bed is stationary.

CELANESE CORPORATION OF AMERICA

A guest sleeping in the bed, above, may dream he's Napoleon. It belongs to that era.

Sometimes a storage room in the attic can be made into an attractive guest room with very little effort. The one below is simple and very comfortable.

PHOTOGRAPH BY THE MAKERS OF ARMSTRONG'S TEMLOK

It may occasionally be possible to make provision for an extra bed in one of the bedrooms. The bed below slides under the table when not in use.

CABIN CRAFTS NORTH STAR

The evolution of the bathroom from a converted clothes closet to a "salon" has been slow, because it involved architectural planning only possible in new houses.

SYLVANIA ELECTRIC COMPANY

Dramatic lighting is not difficult to achieve. It's attractive and can be a decided safety measure in a bathroom.

Bathrooms

The evolution of the bathroom from a converted clothes closet to a "salon" has been slow, because it involved architectural planning only possible in new houses. The majority of bathrooms today answer neither description. However, most of us will settle for good plumbing and fixtures, efficiency, and comfort. Embellishments and extras are a matter of taste, time, and budget. A beautiful bathroom can be a source of great satisfaction in decorating.

Designing and planning more convenient as well as more glamorous bathrooms has made tremendous strides in the last twenty-five years. It was not very long ago that the miracle of indoor plumbing, hot and cold running water, and drainage was enough. Now the bathroom must have a color scheme, special window treatment, and lighting. If possible everyone wants a shower in addition to, or over, the tub, extra towel storage, plenty of well-lighted mirrors, and a special cabinet for cosmetics.

For color scheme, take any combination of colors, probably not more than two; use them for walls and floor, towels, and in the fabrics. If your plumbing fixtures are in color, pick another color to complement it, or try a bathroom in lighter and darker values of the same color.

There are many wallpapers especially made and finished for the bathroom, but today you can use almost any paper. Simply give it a coating of wallpaper shellac and make it water- and steam-proof. If the wall is tiled part way up, try using a paper above the tiling and on the ceiling, or paint the walls and use a paper only on the ceiling. If the washstand is of a type that is free from the wall, a large piece of plate glass put on the wall with mirror clips will allow the wallpaper to show through and serve as complete protection against splashing.

Pictures are not at all unusual in today's bathrooms, as well as extra hanging shelves, towel hampers that also can be used to sit on and others that attach to the back of the door. The array of shower curtains in a variety of colors and materials is endless. In choosing the latter, imagine how it will look wet and when it has dried in place. If shower takers in your family follow each other quickly without giving the curtain time to dry, the second and third person will be more comfortable if you have selected a fabric that sheds water quickly.

An old tiled floor with broken tiles or dark cracks between them that make it look dirty no matter how much it is washed up, can be covered over completely with a linoleum or one of the smart new flooring tiles of rubber or plastic.

It may be that you do not yearn for black glass and chromium, but your bathroom could stand just a little decorating.

AMERICAN RADIATOR AND STANDARD SANITARY CORPORATION

The dark tile in the bathroom, above, is an effective background for the attractive fixtures.

CLAY TILE

Storage space in abundance is a joy and a delight in any room but particularly in a bathroom. These hanging cupboards, left, provide extra needed space.

CANNON HOMEMAKING INSTITUTE

Extra towels may be stacked on convenient shelves within easy reach, upper right.

MARTEX

Right, wall-to-wall carpeting is not only attractive but may cover old tile that is cracked and chipped.

MONSANTO CHEMICAL CO.—LARRY GORDON

SINGER SEWING CENTER

Taking a tip from the theater, this room at top left would delight the heart of any young active member of the school drama society.

Pink organdy over a deep-rose taffeta underskirt is completely feminine with its "cancan" flounce made with millinery wire.

HAROLD FOWLER

An old-fashioned quilt on this spool bed, happily combined with a gingham slipcover and percale curtains, is delightful in this young girl's room.

Rooms for Daughters

"Sugar and spice and all things nice" may run through your head when you are planning, but which one to emphasize will be determined by your daughter's age, habits, and tastes. A tomboy will not be happy in organdy and lace. A dainty miss will find no use for built-in bunks and hitching posts. Add to these thoughts your own ideal of how the twig should be bent, before you begin the practical planning of both style and color.

Daughters, as they begin to cast around for ways of expressing their own personalities, often find that doing over their own rooms gives them just the opportunity they are seeking. At various stages their ideas take different forms, some of which will last for a number of years, others will have a very brief life indeed. Eventually they will settle down with a definite taste and ideas of what they want to use their room for and how they want it to look. Fortunately there are so many charming ways of treating a girl's room inexpensively that these changes of ideas can be gratified within reason.

As a girl reaches her teens she begins to take more interest in her personal appearance and in good grooming. Everyone is delighted and wants to aid and abet this idea in every way. This is the time for a full-length mirror in her room. It could be put on the wall or decorate a door, but if this seems impractical, a good place for it is inside the closet door. The next demand is for a dressing table. If she wants to go *all out* on the feminine side, it will be dainty and skirted. White or unpainted dressing tables, oblong or kidney-shaped, with or without small drawers and hinged arms to hold the skirt, are available in any store that sells furniture. They usually have a mirrored or plate-glass top. However, a little old table or packing case can be adapted for this purpose as it will be entirely covered with fabric. Vanity skirts come ready-made to standard sizes of dressing tables. To be original the skirt can be designed and easily made at home. The one illustrated

Day bed made from two old headboards, an old-fashioned marble-top table, pink chickens, and china dogs for lamp bases make atmosphere in a glamour room that is extremely budget-wise.

at the bottom of page 226 is completely feminine. The dressing table in the picture above it demonstrates another idea for an easily assembled dressing table for the girl who likes her glamour on the modern side.

Another thing that is dear to the heart of most girls is a place to have her friends in for long afternoons or evenings of playing records, reading magazines, working out a school project. For this a bedroom with beds you can sit on, a large low table, comfortable chairs and cushions for sitting on the floor will make her happy. This type of room could be done with modern furniture, tailored bedspreads, and all personal objects kept out of sight, or it could be made completely feminine with gay chintz and period pieces.

By all means let your daughter plan the decoration of her room, but give a little guidance. Fabrics that are to get hard usage should be easily cleaned, preferably washable. Money to be spent should go chiefly into the fundamental pieces of furniture that she must use for a number of years—the bed, chest of drawers, desk.

A "cancan" flounce made with millinery wire, illustrated on page 226, is fun; a current interest may be expressed in her pictures; but temporary expressions should be recognized as such and be capable of being changed or converted without a complete redecoration.

Here is a bright pretty room, with a pleasant combination of colors, that will please the older girl. Space has been used to good advantage here.

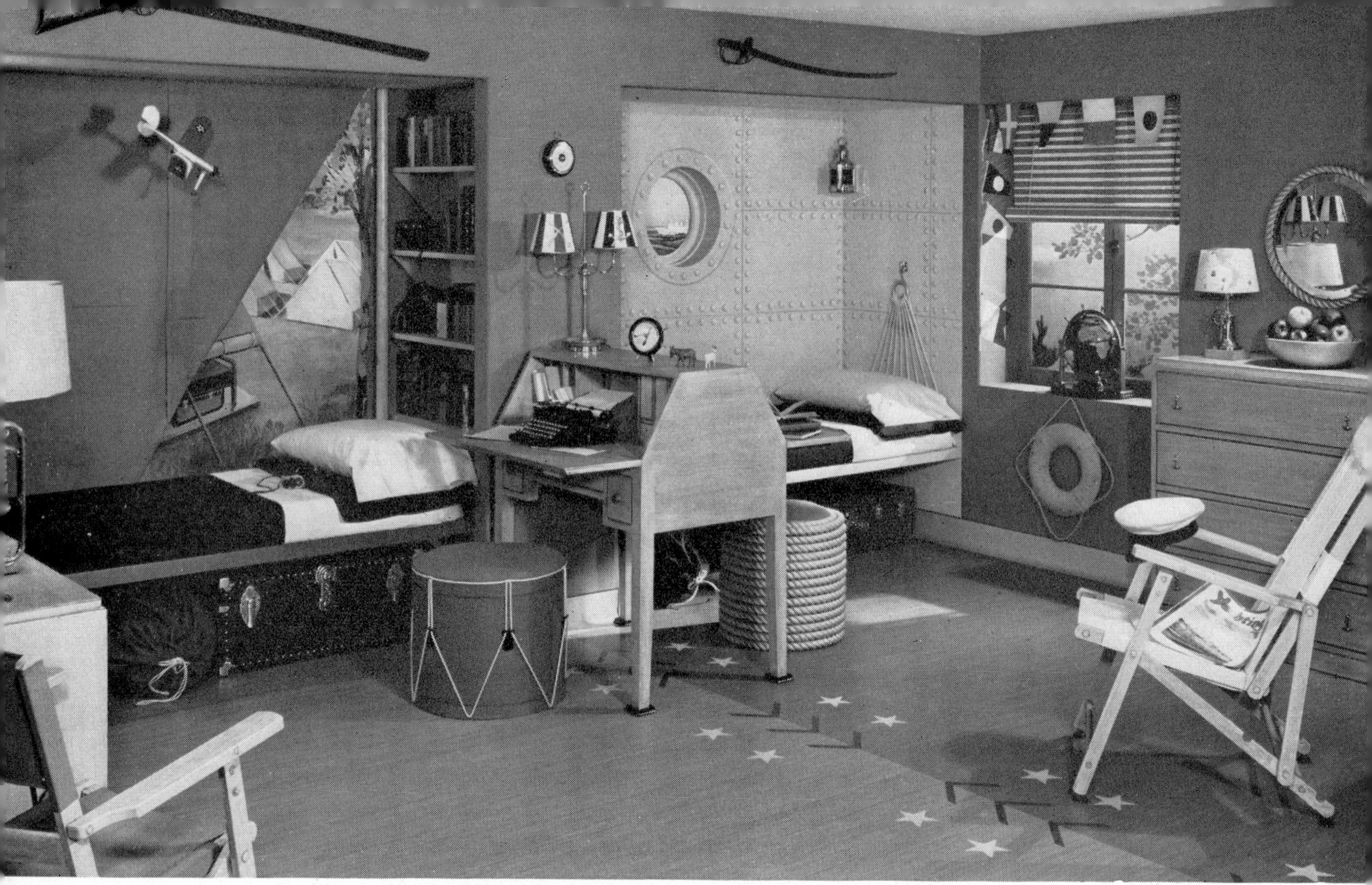

PHOTOGRAPH BY THE MAKERS OF ARMSTRONG'S LINOLEUM

BATES FABRICS, INC.

SHEAFFER PEN COMPANY

The well-planned working space, above, promotes good work and encourages orderliness.

A young salt and an apprentice general could be very comfortable in the inexpensively but imaginatively furnished room at left. Linoleum floor takes hard wear.

The young spaceman's room, lower left, has bedspread and drapery which will stand many, many washings.

Plastic laminate enables an exact match of curtains and coffee table in the bed-sitting room below.

MONSANTO CHEMICAL CO.

Rooms for Sons

"Snips and snails and puppy dog tails" may or may not describe your son at this moment, but most parents suspect that these are the elements in boys of any age that seek expression and will plan their rooms accordingly. Translate your ideas into masculine colors, furniture, and fabrics that will stand even unreasonable wear and tear, and also an atmosphere of freedom where there are few, if any, "don'ts," and you will make everyone concerned completely happy.

A boy is not so apt as his sister to want a say in decorating his room, except that he may be vehement about not wanting anything "sissy." He will, however, appreciate being made comfortable and given a place to give his various interests full scope. He may have definite tastes in colors or just a general idea of what looks all right. Certainly he wants to be consulted.

In planning a boy's room the first thing you will agree on is that it should be sturdy enough to stand a little roughhousing, both as to furniture and fabrics. For your own peace of mind, you will probably want the latter to be dirt-resistant and washable. He will want a place to hang pictures, banners, and the like. You will want plenty of storage space to help keep the room tidy.

On the basic furniture you will be planning for some ten or fifteen years. The chest of drawers, desk, box spring and mattress, and most of the chairs should be of quality and design that will be as good for a college boy or young businessman as they are for a twelve-year-old. If this is too much of a strain on the budget all at once, make plans for the long range, and go as far as you can at the moment, filling in with temporary items.

Boys as well as girls do a lot of living in their own rooms. When they become complete adults they are more apt to use the family living room; but as young people they need a place to study, have their friends, and follow their own pursuits with some degree of privacy and a definite sense of ownership.

CANNON HOMEMAKING INSTITUTE

A sophisticated boy's room may double as a guest room when he is away.

A place to hang banners, set off trophies, and to store equipment and clothes must be considered for the son's room.

In decorating a room for an older boy, or gradually adapting his teen-age room to a more grown-up taste, you realize that the chances that he will use it forever are very unlikely. Whether you expect to stay in the same home yourself forever, or merely keep the basic furniture either to give him for a new home or to make a guest room in your own, an eye to the future is not amiss in making your decisions. This, of course, is true of any piece of fine furniture you buy, but is perhaps more of a factor in rooms for young people whose tastes and needs change as they grow up.

The furniture and decoration of these rooms need not be expensive, but it will have a lasting influence on your children's taste. Therefore, it should not be hit or miss, but definitely planned as much as any other part of the house.

A son who is an enthusiastic hobbyist would be delighted with the section at the right. Ceramics, woodworking, silverwork could be pursued in this full-scale basement hobby area.

PHOTOGRAPH BY MAKERS OF ARMSTRONG'S LINOLEUM

STUART

CONSOLIDATED TRIMMING CORPORATION

KATZENBACH AND WA

The curtain on the window in the room above is one straight piece of fabric for easy washing and ironing. Matching cover on play-box cushion is removable.

The Peter Pan room, top right, was designed for a little boy, although a little girl would love this motif just as much. Enchanting quilt is appliquéd with scenes of Peter and his shadow, Captain Hook, Wendy, Michael and David.

The calico cat in the picture at right is on one wall only, the other three are papered in the background color.

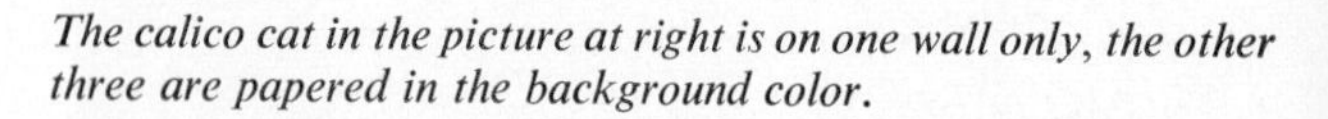

HAROLD FOWLER

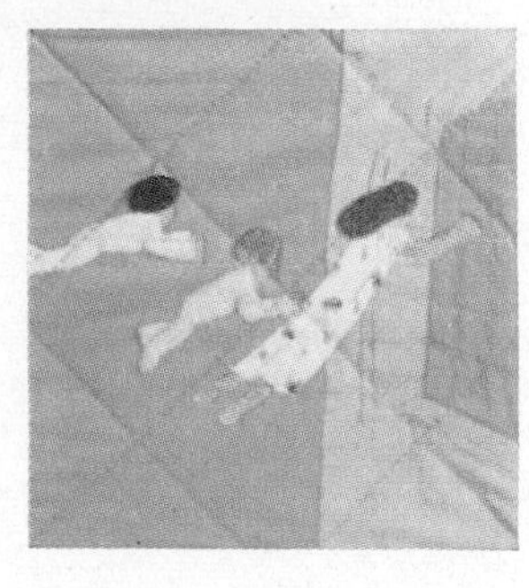

Children's Rooms

Deep are the waters we fathom in striving for health, happiness, and an agreeable disposition in our children. We know that many of the contributing factors are beyond our control, but the least suspicion that providing a pleasant place to live and play may promote these blessings spurs us to examine the possibilities and do our best to help them become a reality. The laughter of little children is all the inspiration that is needed to start anyone off to giving it a happy setting.

Many get their first lessons in long-range planning in dreams for a new baby. The medical books on the subject of decoration deal with ventilation, sanitation, isolation, and regulation. Dreams go beyond that to wanting health and happiness, and also a darling nursery or corner, at once charming and practical for the newcomer into this world. Everyone reminds us that the baby will be out of the bassinet and into a crib, out of the crib into a bed, and away at college before we know it. This may be true, but in the meantime we would like the child to have a pretty room to start in and, eventually, happy memories of childhood.

Whether you are deliberately giving yourself and your child something pleasant to remember, or working out an efficient and practical place for the baby, it can be pretty and planned to grow and change with each new development. Nurseries, like baby's clothes, are no longer limited to pink, blue, and white. All the pastel tints and even some deeper shades are popular. Yellow with pale green, peach with Alice blue, and lavender with yellow make good nursery colors. For a baby everything must be washable, antiseptically clean. Hence walls that can be wiped down, draperies or curtains that are easily and frequently washed, furniture that can be scrubbed go without compromise. Decorating in the baby's room and for small children is not concerned with these musts, but rather with a choice of patterns that will not grow tiresome and an effort to

This double-decker bed is a real space saver.

LADIES' HOME JOURNAL'S MORE HOUSE FOR THE MONEY PORTFOLIO NO. 1

The bureau-desk arrangement has a hinged top on the center compartment that swings up, rests against the wall, and then presto, turns into a mirror.

LADIES' HOME JOURNAL'S MORE HOUSE FOR THE MONEY PORTFOLIO NO. 1

avoid wallpapers, fabrics, and furniture of no artistic merit. There are many famous children's designs taken from the original illustrations for stories like Peter Rabbit, drawings by Kate Greenaway, and more recently Walt Disney's Bambi, as well as good modern ones. If your aspirations in art education for children are even greater, even a little child will love Dürer's squirrels or his drawing of a rabbit.

Small children play mostly on the floor, but a few pieces of furniture scaled to their size are very convenient. A small table and chairs for mealtimes can be as simple or elaborate as you want to make them. Really tiny furniture is of little use, as it is outgrown before a child is big enough to use it. A very comfortable low chair can be made by simply sawing off the legs of a wooden side chair. A small

Good general lighting is a necessity in a child's room. The ceiling fixture in the room, below left, takes care of this.

Removable sides on a youth's bed and general style of decoration give the room, below right, a better-than-average span of years for a child's use.

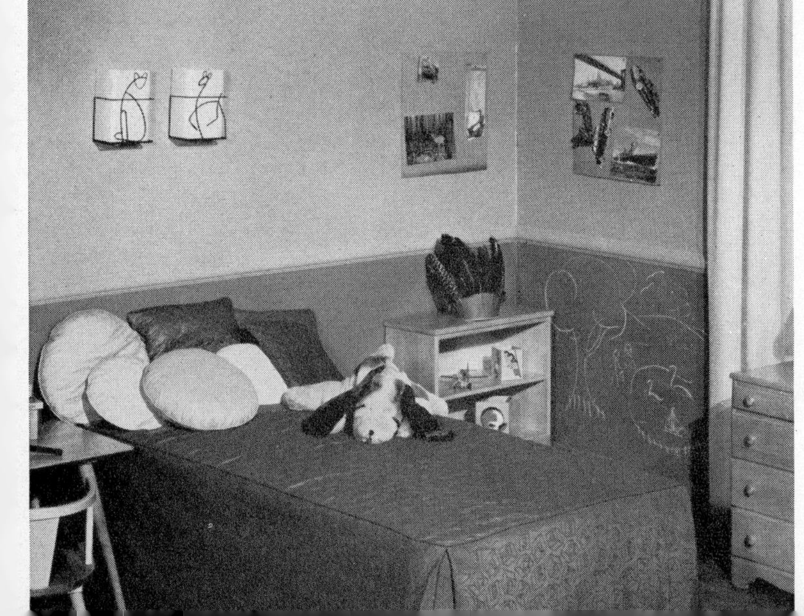

Another ingenious arrangement is followed in the room at left. Lower part of the wall is intended to be used to write on with chalk. It is painted with a special paint that stands up remarkably well under the ministrations of active young hands.

CLEANLINESS BUREAU

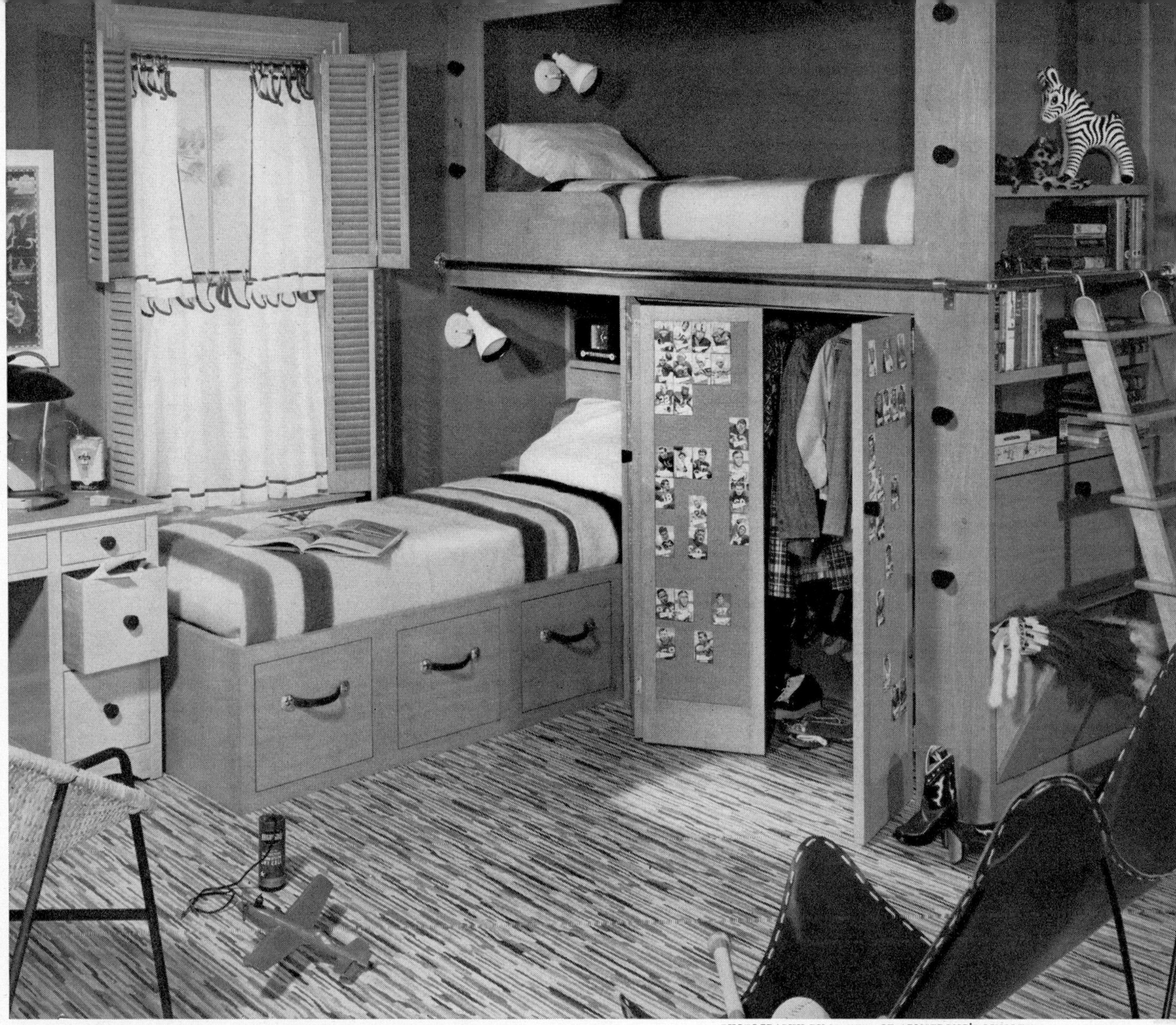

PHOTOGRAPHY BY MAKERS OF ARMSTRONG'S LINOLEUM

The small child's room, above left, can be practical, washable, and interesting.

Two young scholars would find the room above with bunk arrangement interesting and very nearly indestructible.

coffee table serves as the table. Both of these pieces can be used in their rooms for different purposes even when they are grown up.

Every child's room should have at least one, if not two full-size chairs, a rocker or an easy chair, if possible. This is for parents and visitors for storytelling and reading time and to make a child feel that grownups will sit down and stay awhile or play a game instead of standing around or moving along quickly.

HAROLD FOWLER

Just-for-Fun Rooms

When it comes to what is fun and where to pursue it at home, all would agree that everyone is entitled to a time and place for it. Hence the rumpus room with all the name implies, the well-equipped workshop, or the quiet hobby corner. In fun rooms, the practical arrangements for use come first, and good planning is paramount. A color scheme is secondary, but a good one certainly will add much to whatever noisy or quiet fun you may happen to prefer.

Furnishings in this room will take considerable wear and tear—furniture and fabrics are sturdy, rug is reversible. And a quiet corner, below, lends itself to study, reading, or just relaxing.

HAROLD FOWLER

Clear, brilliant colors and hardy materials combine to make an inviting entertainment room in the basement.

For family and friends, the room opposite has a cozy, inviting air. Sofas, by a flick of the wrist, become comfortable beds.

Attic or cellar, over the garage, or just a corner to work on your stamp collection, it is fun to have a place apart from everything else for recreation. If your particular fun happens to be woodworking or dressmaking, you will certainly try for a place where things can be left out in process of making and that will not have to be straightened out between worktimes.

If your fun is informal parties, country dancing, games of all sorts, it is wonderful to have a room set up for that purpose. Since the coal furnace and laundry have moved out of the cellar in most houses, this has become an excellent place for this purpose. Gaiety, color, welcome are the keynotes whether against whitewashed walls or paneling, homemade built-in or special furniture. In cellar or attic the room cannot be formal or dressed up, but preserves a casual atmosphere with cottons, textures, plastics, and leather. The floor is covered with linoleum or one of the tiles, the walls are a plain color, and the fabrics, plain or figured, are bright. Travel posters make splashy wall decorations. Provide plenty of seats and tie the whole thing together with a pleasing color scheme. For a hobby corner, try something different, depending upon the hobby. For working on stamps, wood carving, designing, you need good lighting. For music, records, jewelry making, etching, you need good light and storage space. Whatever your hobby, it's fun to test your ingenuity in planning for it.

HAROLD FOWLER

LADIES' HOME JOURNAL'S MORE HOUSE FOR THE MONEY PORTFOLIO NO. 3

HAROLD FOWLER

Rooms with Books

"The vacant stare bespeaks the absent mind" might as easily apply to the use of books in decoration.

A house without books is unthinkable and even a room nowadays whether it is the living room, library, bedroom, or even the kitchen will tend to speak of something missing. The decorator hails this idea with enthusiasm because it lends variety to available accessories, a spot of color where needed, or even a whole wall like a gay length of chintz in an otherwise somber or formal room. The use of books also provides endless variety in treatment. Solid phalanxes of books in their brightly colored jackets give one effect. A broken arrangement with spaces left for bric-a-brac, a favorite statuette, or vase is both practical and decorative.

Bibliophiles may scoff at buying books or using books solely for decorative effect, but what is actually happening is that books are being lifted from the dusty shelves of the old den and made much more a part of everyday living. The scholarship and entertainment between the covers remains the same or better. Some of the rooms illustrated will suggest the charm of books and demonstrate how much personality may be added by their use in decoration. Incidentally, or perhaps by design, having books everywhere and ready to hand promotes good reading habits in a family whose members do not have to seek out a quiet afternoon or evening to "catch up" on their reading, but

Books make an attractive addition to the somewhat formal room, left.

Playroom at top of the page opposite has provided generous room for books.

A wall of books seems to set off this room at the bottom of the page opposite. Art books next to the phonograph are covered in white so as not to conflict with the others in the room.

HAROLD FOWLER

A modest book collection is attractively featured in this room and strategically placed behind a generous and comfortable sofa—a lure and boon to the recumbent reader.

who are constantly subjected to the temptation of finding out what is in the books right at hand.

Books are a part of everyday living—a shelf in the kitchen for the many cookbooks we need—a selection for every taste in the guest room—ample space for books in the nursery—and all kinds of books in the living room. Whatever kind of house or room you plan, remember that you will want a place for books.

HAROLD FOWLER

The hanging bookshelves in the room, above right, balance very nicely the picture arrangement on the wall above the sofa.

RICHARD WHEATLAND

Built-in bookcases in the room, right, add considerably to the décor and contribute a colorful note to the window arrangement.

Beauty is in the eye of the beholder. For you it may be a highly decorated period interior or a dining area in a modern ranch home.

FROM THE NICHOLS-WANTON-HUNTER HOUSE IN NEWPORT. PHOTOGRAPH BY EZRA STOLLER

Glossary

This list is comprised of words used constantly in connection with interior decoration. Most of the words are drawn from the text of the book and repeated here as a vocabulary guide. Others are included for ready reference to describe terms in common usage in the field. Words which are fully explained in the text are omitted.

Abstract art Any artistic form which avoids the representation of realities and ordinary conventional designs.

Acajou Hard tropical wood of the mahogany family.

Acanthus Classical ornamental design of sharp-toothed leaf, used on Corinthian capital, later on furniture.

Aniline dye Any dye made with aniline, an oily poisonous liquid which is colorless when pure. Main ingredient nitrobenzene.

Antique Any building, piece of furniture, or object of art made before the birth of any living person. Officially, "produced prior to 1830" in United States Customs regulations.

Arabesque Elaborate fanciful interlacing design of flowers, leaves, fruit, and sometimes figures of men and animals.

Bachelor chest Small chest of drawers with a folding top or pull-out shelf for writing.

Balustrade Railing formed by a range of small balusters supporting a handrail.

Baroque Elaborate heavy ornamentation with bold scrolls and irregular curves.

Batt Wadded raw cotton used for filling mattresses and for upholstering.

Bergère Upholstered armchair with wood of frame exposed.

Bevel Sloping outside edges of any flat surface such as tabletop or mirror glass.

Bibelot Small decorative article, curio.

Bolster Long narrow pillow or case which extends the width of a bed or sofa.

Bouclé Fabric with an irregular looped and knotted pile.

Breakfront Large triple bookcase or china closet with center unit deeper than side units. Usually has glass doors above and wooden doors or drawers below.

Brocade Rich woven fabric with raised design, usually in various colors.

Brocatelle Heavy upholstery fabric woven in designs using both silk and linen.

Broken pediment A pediment which is interrupted at the crest or peak.

Buckram Coarse fabric stiffened with sizing.

Bullion Heavy long fringe such as that used to form skirt of a chair or sofa. Originally made only of gold thread.

Burl Veneer wood cut from abnormal knot or growth of a tree.

Burnish Lustrous finish on wood or metal achieved by polishing and rubbing.

Butler's desk Chest of drawers with hinged top drawer letting down for a writing surface.

Cabriole A curved tapering leg frequently ending in the form of an animal's paw.

Cartouche Enclosed scroll-like design of leaves, garlands, or scrolls around a center motif.

Casement Window that opens on upright hinges.

Caster A small wheel in a swivel frame, used in sets on legs of furniture to increase the mobility.

Chesterfield Overstuffed sofa with high ends or sides.

Chrome Bright tubular steel plated with nickel alloy called chromium plate. Also used with "yellow" to denote a pigment.

Cloisonné Colored enamels applied in a design to a metal base and separated by tiny partitions of metal.

Cobalt Silver-white metal related to iron and nickel. Also a shade of blue.

Console Bracket supporting a shelf or table. Also any table designed to be used against a wall, or pair of tables to be used together to make or form the ends of another table.

Convolute bedspring One in which coils are rolled together, one part upon another, as petals in a bud.

Corinthian Greek order of architecture characterized by bell-shaped capital enveloped with acanthus leaves, and fluted columns.

Cornice Usually a horizontal molding or moldings as the top finish of a wall or building. Also board used over a window as a valance.

Credenza Sideboard cabinet, usually with metal-grilled doors.

Crotch wood Veneer cut from limb crotch of a tree, giving grain the appearance of a flame.

Dado Portion of wall below chair rail.

Damask Silk or linen fabric with satin weave of a lustrous design on a dull background. Also the color, red.

Davenport Large upholstered sofa, often convertible to a bed. Also a type of small desk.

Dentil Small rectangular block resembling a tooth, used in a series to decorate a cornice.

Diapering Design formed by the continuous repetition of a small simple design, usually diamond-shaped.

Doric Simplest order of Greek architecture, distinguished by low proportions, columns without bases, and saucer-shaped capitals.

Dormer Vertical window built into a sloping roof.

Ell Addition to a house built at right angles to main structure.

Escritoire Writing table, usually with drawers only in the apron.

Escutcheon Shield-shaped ornament used over keyholes.

Etagère Ornamental stand with shelves for ornaments.

Festoon Garland, wreath of decoration or of fabric which hangs in a curve.

Finial Terminating ornament or motif, usually in form of a knob, urn, or foliage.

Firedogs Andirons, pair of supports for wood in a fireplace.

Fluting Long lines of carving incised into pillars or furniture legs.

French-seam Method of joining two pieces of fabric by turning over first stitching to the reverse side and making a second stitching to encase rough edges.

Fretwork Open continuous design used along straight edges or in bas-relief.

Frieze Band of decoration on wall or piece of furniture. Also a heavy fabric with looped pile.

Fustian Formerly a stout cloth of cotton and flax; now synonymous with corduroy and velveteen.

Gallery Raised rim of metal or wood fretwork on back edge of sideboards and around tabletops.

Galloon Ribbonlike binding or trimming of rich material usually woven with a design.

Gilt Finish applied to any object not of gold to simulate appearance of gold.

Gimp Narrow woven tape used to cover tacks at juncture of wood frame and fabric on upholstered furniture.

Girandole Circular mirror with or without branching candlesticks.

Governor Winthrop desk Any desk with slanting drop-leaf front and series of drawers below writing surface.

Gros point Coarse cross-stitching on canvas or net. Also a type of carpeting.

Headboard Vertical portion of bed frame.

Helical Coil of wire used in bedsprings.

Highboy Chest of drawers set on legs.

Inlay Insertion of cut forms of one material into similar-shaped holes cut in another.

Ionic Greek order of architecture characterized by capitals with spiral-shaped volutes or scrolls on each side.

Kapok Vegetable fiber of silky appearance used in inexpensive bedding and pillows.

Lacquer Shiny finish made by applying a solution of shellac in alcohol—the liquid used for this purpose.

Lambrequin Straight or shaped ornamental piece of cloth, or any flexible material hanging at top of window, doorway, or edge of mantelpiece. Term used in pottery for design with solid color above and scalloped or ragged design below.

Lampblack Black pigment consisting of finely divided carbon particles, usually obtained by burning oil in an insufficient supply of air.

Lowboy Small table with drawers and unfinished back, often matches a highboy.

Luster Cut-glass pendant hung on chandeliers and candlesticks to reflect light.

Madder Turkey-red color obtained from roots of the tropical plant madder, or from alizarin.

Marquetry Inlaid work in which rare woods or other materials are inserted flush with a wood surface to form a decoration.

Matelassé Plain or figured woven fabric which resembles flat quilting.

Mortise Hole into which tenon fits in joining two pieces of wood.

Mullion Slim vertical or horizontal partition between panes of glass in a window.

Newel Upright post at the head or foot of a stair, supporting a handrail.

Ormolu Bronze finished with gold for furniture mounts, French clocks, and candlesticks.

Ottoman Low, cushioned backless seat or foot rest.

Overhang Projection of roof or upper story of a building beyond lower part.

Overmantel Ornamental cabinetwork on wall over mantelpiece.

Paduasoy Rich heavy corded silk fabric.

Palampore Printed cotton cloth panel from India.

Palladian Revival of the Renaissance period of architecture executed in the manner of Andrea Palladio (1518-80).

Papier-mâché Wet paper molded into decorative forms or used as the basic material for trays, chairs, etc.

Patina Soft glow produced on wood or silver surface by age and repeated rubbing.

Pediment Triangular space crowning roofline of exterior ends of a Greek temple, adapted for use on highboys, secretary desks, and other large pieces of furniture.

Petit point Fine cross-stitching on canvas or net used for chair seat covers.

Pewter Alloy of tin and lead used to make tableware and ornaments. It was originally intended as substitute for silver.

Pier glass Large high mirror against projecting portion of wall or between two windows.

Pile Upright ends or loops of yarn forming the surface of a fabric or carpet.

Poudreux Powdering or dressing table, usually with disappearing mirror.

Ratiné Loose-textured fabric with rough surface containing small knots and nubs.

Reeding Series of tiny convex scallops or moldings carved vertically on chair legs and tables.

Refectory table Long narrow dining table with stretcher at base.

Rococo Mid-eighteenth century style of decoration developed in France, and characterized by delicacy of line and structure, asymmetry, extravagant use of foliage, pierced shellwork, curves, and scroll forms. Overuse of detail and crowded decoration have given it the connotation of extreme ornateness.

Rosette Circle, ellipse, or square ornament of leaves or petals arranged around a central point.

Rosewood Cabinet wood from Honduras, East India and Brazil, of a dark red or purplish color streaked with black.

Rush Grasslike hollow stems of plants woven together to form chair seats.

Sarcenet Soft silk fabric in plain or twill weave, used especially as a lining.

Satinwood Light orange-colored wood of West Indies used to make furniture and for inlay.

Sconce Bracket candlestick or group of candlesticks attached to a wall.

Scrim Light coarse cotton or linen fabric used for glass curtains.

Secretary Large desk with shelves above the writing level and drawers or doors below; top may have glass or wooden doors.

Selvage The woven edge of fabric formed to prevent raveling.

Serpentine Applied to double curved (with center convex) front of sideboard, table, or chest.

Sheathing Structural covering, usually board, plywood or wallboard, placed over exterior and interior studding or rafters of a house.

Sienna An earth pigment of brownish-yellow color when raw; orange-red or red-brown color when burnt. Used largely in mixing paints to tone down a bright color without making it muddy.

Sisal Vegetable fiber used in summer rugs and box-spring stuffing.

Splat Plain, shaped, or carved vertical piece of wood which forms center of a chair back—a style dating from the Queen Anne period.

Still life Any artistic representation of inanimate objects.

Stretcher Brace or support connecting legs of a piece of furniture horizontally.

Swag Fabric draped in a looped garland, or forming the ends or tails of a festoon.

Tambour Sliding flexible panels of wood used as closing or cover on certain types of desks and cabinets.

Tenon Projection at end of piece of wood which fits into mortise to make a joining.

Tester Canopy for bed with four tall posts.

Tole Painted tinwork used for lamps, lamp shades, trays, wastebaskets, canisters, etc.

Tree of Life Pattern Design resembling tree or vine with exotic flowers and fruits; usually one design covers large panel of cloth.

Turkey work Handmade textile made in imitation of oriental pile rugs.

Varnish A paint solution of resin boiled in oil, producing a hard, glossy surface when dry.

Veneer Thin sheet of finishing wood applied in one or more layers to solid wood core.

Verdigris Green rust formed on copper. Also denotes a green pigment.

Volute Spiral or scroll-like design.

Wainscot Wood paneling used on interior walls.

Wainscot chair 17th-century wood chair executed in the manner of paneling.

Warp Threads which run lengthwise in a fabric.

Webbing Base for springs of upholstered furniture, made of jute strips interwoven closely and attached to frame.

Weft or woof Threads which run crosswise of fabric and are woven in and out of warp threads by means of a shuttle or bobbin.

Welting Covered cording stitched between the seams and around the edges of upholstered furniture to form a finish.

This charming paneled dining room is from the Tate House in Portland. Note the black-banded cornice.

Index

This charming back door ends the illustrations but begins your adventures in decorating.